West German Filmmakers on Film: Visions and Voices

Edited by ERIC RENTSCHLER

HM

HOLMES & MEIER
New York / London

Holmes & Meier Publishers, Inc.
30 Irving Place
New York, NY 10003

Great Britain:
Holmes & Meier Publishers, Ltd.
One Hallswelle Parade
London NW11 ODL
England

The paper used in this publication meets the requirements
of the American National Standard for Permanence of Paper
for Printed Library Materials, Z39.48-1984.

Library of Congress Cataloging-in-Publication Data
West German filmmakers on film: visions and voices.

 Bibliography: p.
 Includes index.
 1. Moving-pictures—Germany (West)—History.
I. Rentschler, Eric.
PN1993.5.G3W44   1988   791.43′0943   87-14856
ISBN 0-8419-0984-9 (alk. paper)
ISBN 0-8419-0985-7 (pbk.) (alk. paper)

Manufactured in the United States of America

To *Film, Filmartikel, Filme, Filmkritik, Filmreport, Filmstudio, Jahrbuch Film*, to the memory of Wilfried Berghahn, Lotte Eisner, Joe Hembus, and Dietmar Schmidt, to their visions of a possible German film culture and these important voices of the past—and to those few others who, *trotz alledem*, endure in the present.

Contents

III   Popular Approaches: Generic Models and Utopian Designs

IV   Different Ways of Seeing

Contents

Acknowledgments

This book was conceived late in 1983. Since that time I have benefited immensely from numerous discussions with my friend and colleague, Hans Helmut Prinzler. He looked over an initial disposition and provided crucial suggestions regarding the shape and content of this collection. Likewise, he generously took care of obtaining permissions from most of the filmmakers. The anthology is unthinkable without his help and the many conversations over the years in his Charlottenburg apartment, a veritable stronghold of film culture.

I am indebted to the filmmakers who allowed their articles to be reprinted here. Further, I would like to thank several individuals who granted permission to include English translations that have appeared elsewhere. And I also am grateful to Antje Masten and David Ward for rendering several articles, as I am to Anke Gleber for checking bibliographical references and to Lisa Fluor for assisting me in putting the manuscript together. The Alexander von Humboldt–Stiftung, a generous and indulgent institution, supported this project with a research fellowship that made possible a sojourn in West Berlin during the summer of 1986. I also was aided substantially by an Irvine Faculty Research Fellowship for 1985–86 and by various stipends from the Research and Travel Committee of the UCI School of Humanities.

Introduction: The Writing Out of West German Film History

The New German Film is dead. Those who created it in a collective of individuals will have to work from now on on their own. They will have it hard enough; Zimmermann will make sure of this. . . . The New German Film has had its day. It is time to say goodbye to it.
    —Peter Buchka, writing in 1983

The strength of German film is its variety.
    —The Hamburg Declaration, 1979

The taxpayer does not want to be provoked, he wants to be entertained.
    —West German Minister of the Interior, Friedrich Zimmermann, in an interview with *Der Spiegel*, July 1983

The State of Things: Calm Prevails over the Country. Everyone for Himself and God against All.
    —Wolfram Schütte, assessing West German film at the Berlin Festival, February 1985

So far as the West German film is concerned, there really is life after Fassbinder.
    —J. Hoberman, discussing the MOMA series, "Recent Films from West Germany," early 1985

I

For years mythologies circulated about the origins of New German Film: tales of a gathering of angry young men, about their strident optimism and patricidal zeal, their overwhelming desire to provoke, outrage, and enlighten. This narrative has been codified in a number of popular and scholarly accounts. In the mideighties, one no longer talks about the ascent of New German Film, however. The fashionable topic is the demise of this national cinema. Even in the United States, where observers tend to lag behind developments abroad, we have seen the first wave of necrologies. In the fall of 1985, for instance, specialists gathered at the Midwest Modern Language Association Meeting to discuss the "Commercialization of the New German Cinema." Recently I received word about a forthcoming special issue of *Germanic Review* with the title, "The 'Fall' of the New German Cinema?" These swan songs, more sorrowful than *schadenfroh* (unlike the obituaries abroad), would seem to mark the end to an epoch of excitement, enthusiasm, and discovery, at least for American friends of the New German Cinema.

Living in West Berlin during the summer of 1986, I take careful note of the current climate. In a city with a remarkable network of alternative cinemas (so-called "*Programmkinos*"), I find very few German films: in the Graffiti, Lienhard Wawrzyn's *German Dreams;* in the Kant Kino, Peter Timm's *Meier;* in the Kurbel, Niki List's *Müllers Büro (Müller's Office);* in the Lupe, Margarethe von Trotta's *Rosa Luxemburg;* and all over town, Doris Dörrie's *Männer (Men)* and Johannes Schaaf's *Momo.* The well-stocked video rental outlets carry next to no New German films in their inventories. Evening television programs, otherwise offering one feature film after another, screen hardly any German titles of recent vintage. (What a ghostly feeling it is to watch Peter Schamoni's *Schonzeit für Füchse/Closed Season on Fox Hunting* late at night on TV during the early part of a muggy August: the smoldering energies and discontent which would give rise shortly to the student movement and a new sensibility are there, quite clearly: just as striking, though, is the resemblance between the cynicism and passive aggression of the film's protagonist and the diffidence of young people in contemporary West Germany.) Doris Dörrie is interviewed on network television at the Munich Film Festival in late June. I am confounded by her automatically defensive posture (she is, after all, the country's most well-regarded director at the moment), the way even she feels the need to preface her comments with the stock phrase, "The New German Film is much better than its reputation." At the same festival, where there is apparently much more activity in the lounge areas than in the sparsely attended cinemas, a representative from the Munich Academy for Television and Film, Wolfgang Längsfeld, repeats a sentence one has heard with unvarying consistency in a number of contexts over the last two decades: "German filmmakers have to win back the confidence of their audiences." On frequent occasion I sit over coffee or beer with film journalists and insiders; attempts to broach a conversation about West German film more often than not are answered by a smirk or a shrug—or simply silence.

Combing the film sections of bookstores, Margarethe Schoeller's *Buchhandlung* in the Knesebeckstrasse, the *Bücherbogen* down the street and around the corner, the *Autorenbuchhandlung* a few steps away across the Savignyplatz, I come across no new critical works on German film of any note, outside of a volume published in Ullstein Verlag by Hans-Joachim Neumann, *Der deutsche Film heute*. This indeed is the apposite work for today on New German Film. Neumann's jeremiad reads something like an eighties version of Joe Hembus's famous squib of 1961, *Der deutsche Film kann nicht besser sein*. Hembus's work attacked the excesses and inanities of West German film during the postwar reconstruction era, inveighing against a national cinema that knew little of the nation's realities. The analysis influenced the signatories of the Oberhausen Manifesto considerably and catalyzed a renaissance of German film. Whereas Hembus was motivated by a regard for the manifold possibilities of the film medium, Neumann remains much more circumscribed in his interests, considerably less flexible in his notion of cinema. His book is a 200-page inquiry into the dead-end state of New German Film; it contains virtually every objection one has heard over the years, objections uttered by members of SPIO, film critics in *Die Welt*, the *Frankfurter Allgemeine Zeitung*, *Filmecho/Filmwoche*, various members of subsidy committees, and, more recently, by adherents of Minister of the Interior Friedrich Zimmermann and supporters of a new direction (*Wende*) in film politics. Hans-Joachim Neumann espouses a popular definition of film; he is conversant with the healthy common sense of the people, *das gesunde Volksempfinden*, a persuasion Zimmermann (as others before him) is fond of invoking:

> The true history of cinema knows no division into art and commercial films: it knows only good and bad films and all the possibilities lying between the two. A criterion for evaluation in this regard should not be to make comparisons with the established arts, but rather to consider the functional capacity of a given film within the aesthetic, technical, and economic standards of cinema. (P. 23)

A colleague described Neumann's book to me as a "*Machwerk,*" a caustic and clumsy bit of hack work. It is valuable, nonetheless, for it essentializes a certain fashionable disdain for West German filmmaking, a hostility that has endured since the Oberhausen Manifesto and only subsided intermittently after successes abroad and at festivals. Zimmermann's disinclination toward radical auteurs and personal visions and an attendant will to clean house have now found popular acceptance.

Neumann functions like a court scribe for the Minister of the Interior. He scorns every hope of the New German Film. His is, however, any-thing but a minority opinion at this time.

II

Dr. Hans Borgelt, speaking at the ceremonies for the 1984 West German Film Prizes, an event sponsored by the Minister of the Interior, summed up the previous year's productions:

> Ladies and Gentlemen, the German film critics generally viewed last year's film harvest as disappointing. It could not have been otherwise, for it was so in comparison with the quality demonstrated abroad; skepsis and pessimism were the bywords. Our jury members, on the other hand, have to be optimists: we have to be continually on the lookout for quality; our guiding principle is hope. Critics, nevertheless, are impressed by a German film that somehow succeeds in awakening interest abroad. Fortunately, these have been quite a few over the past few years. If the recently issued publication by the Berlin Film and Television Academy is any indication, then it's indeed most astonishing to see how far advanced American universities alone have become in the area of research on New German Cinema.

Borgelt was referring to an inventory of American scholarship devoted to German film studies which had appeared in the 1984 installment of *Film in Forschung und Lehre,* a catalogue of over two hundred items put together by Hans-Bernhard Moeller of the University of Texas. The gesture is a curious one. On the one hand, Zimmermann and his supporter Borgelt argue that the German film should seek more popular appeal and find better scripts. The German film would best avoid nega-tivity and outspokenness; above all, it needs to maintain high quality standards and to secure a position on the international market. For that reason, this foreign regard, the intense interest generated by German films on American campuses, is a source of official pride. On the other hand, Borgelt conveniently leaves out a crucial insight. When one looks more carefully at the ongoing discussion about New German Film in the United States, it becomes clear that precisely the personal and critical films threatened by Zimmermann's new policies and attacked by his minions have historically been the ones most often scrutinized and lingered over by American friends. The difficult and subversive auteurs have engaged this attention; without its rough edges, there would have been no New German Cinema. If it had not been for the liberal policies of Goethe Institutes, their pluralistic openness to even the most critical voices and problematic depictions of the German past, New German Film would not have found the American acclaim so ebulliently valorized by the Minister of the Interior's spokesman. It is the obstinacy of this national cinema, its stubbornness and intransigence, its endeavor to cut against the grain of official history, which made it an object of continuing scholarly work abroad.

To be sure, this literature on New German Film halts at the early eighties, as if the death of Fassbinder, the rise of the new CDU/CSU/FDP coalition, and the presentiment of commercial television and the new media—some standard criteria offered in obituaries on New German Film—really had meant the end. Timothy Corrigan's *New German Film: The Displaced Image* uses the fall of 1977 as its final station; John Sandford's *The New German Cinema*, James Franklin's *New German Cinema*, and Klaus Phillips's anthology, *New German Filmmakers*, all leave off at 1979 or thereabouts; my study, *West German Film in the Course of Time*, likewise, was finished in 1982 and contains mention of Fassbinder's passing on its final pages. The question would seem to be, after all of these books, given the seemingly desolate state of New German Film: is it—to play on a phrase quoted by Hellmuth Costard in a film of 1978—possible to write a book about West German film in the eighties? (Neumann has, to be sure, provided us with one answer.) Is there in fact any reason to reassess this past and to discuss events of more recent years?

My earlier book was an attempt to fathom the variety of West German film, to work against a clichéd notion of the country's cinema culture, and to elicit its multiple strategies and subcultures. I called the book at the time "a work in progress." This present collection is both a supplement and a continuation. In my introduction, I spoke of the many different sectors of activity in West German film culture, regretting my numerous exclusions, the omission of documentary filmmakers, experimental and avant-garde work, and feminist approaches, among other things. (With great sadness, I recall a conversation with Wolfram Schütte in which he told me that Rudolf Thome, having looked through my book, expressed his chagrin at having been all but left out of yet another history of West German film.) Over the years I became increasingly aware of my account's limitations, how I simply had not managed to convey adequately the interaction between filmmakers themselves and their cultural context, even if I had to some degree escaped the widespread tendency to champion German directors as self-sufficient auteurs. How to recapture the dialogues, alliances, and enmities that extended in so many different directions, the ongoing sense of process and collective mission which have endured over the last two decades and a half? What was called for was a new taking of stock, a different kind of film historiography.

III

With great eagerness I rushed out to purchase Alexander Kluge's collection, *Bestandsaufnahme: Utopie Film*, when it appeared in 2001-outlets during late June of 1983. This was the stocktaking Kluge had been promising for years, a collage of essays, surveys, interviews, quotations, theses, diagrams, photographs, illustrations, maps, and advertisements, the result of a cooperative effort. A postscript to the book read: "This book is the condensed reproduction of an investigation on which fifty-two participants have worked since 1980. Responsibility for the realization of the project was taken by the Ulm Institute for Film Design on behalf of the Working Cooperative of New German Producers *(Arbeitsgemeinschaft Neuer Deutscher Spielfilmproduzenten)*; likewise there was a mandate from the Film Subsidy Board Berlin. No one who reads this book is likely to have any doubts that a taking of stock is necessary now, twenty years after the beginning of the New German Film" (p. 591). A list of the many contributors spans producers, directors, distributors, politicians, and critics of both sexes. The *Bestandsaufnahme* provides a mixture of temperaments, a cooperative enterprise meant as a sort of self-defense.

The *Bestandsaufnahme* was undertaken with the intent to supply something approaching a representative cross section *(Querschnitt)* of the West German film scene. As in other collective ventures with which Kluge has been associated, his voice remains the controlling sensibility. This is mirrored in the book's creative combinations, its associative montages, tersely witty and poignant captions, as well as the volume's polemical urgency. Throughout the anthology one comes across declarations of emergency calling for immediate action. The central focus of New German Film's politics over the years, claims Kluge, was "to keep the access to film open" (p. 92), to combat delimiting forces, historical amnesia, fixation, repression, the potential threat of "a technical or administrative control over fantasy wares" (p. 454). Repeatedly, Kluge dwells on the predicament of independent image making in the age of electronic reproduction, devoting much attention to the "new media." Under the guise of offering a seeming richness of possibility and choice, the new media in fact pose a threat to our internal ecology. The media give viewers less and less of the riches of the world in a constant recourse to patterned meaning, regular programming, and serial production. More in this case means less: a vitiated fantasy life, a shrinking public sphere, a denigration of experience, and a closing off of dialogue.

Kluge extols a number of counterforces: authenticity, an open confrontation of one's present and history, a sense of sharing with spectators, generosity and plenitude, usefulness (*Brauchbarkeit*) as opposed to the simply pragmatic or instrumental. "The politics of this book: life is not centrally connected" (p. 263). The more I read, the more disappointed I became, however. For all its pluralism and heterogeneity, Kluge's book unwittingly replicated the same exclusionary practice it meant to question. When Kluge once said that "the critical measure of production is what is left out," he drew attention to a certain dialectic between possibility and reality, wherein unproduced films criticize the produced ones. In so doing, he spoke as a realist. But when he left out extended consideration of many marginalized, obscured, and indeed crucial forces in his *Bestandsaufnahme*, he excluded, to use his own words, "broad aspects of the experience of reality" to be found in West German film culture.

This was a disarming experience, to find the most passionate and persuasive spokesman for West German film, the champion of the deviant and the defiant, passing over so many voices. Kluge had repeatedly stressed the importance of the subterranean reaches of New German Film, but these side paths, so often pointed to, are rarely explored in the *Bestandsaufnahme*. My expectations had been high; my disappointment was correspondingly large. I missed a lot here; among other things, the following:

—Self-depictions and chronicles by documentary filmmakers working in the Federal Republic. Despite numerous references to the power of authenticity, continual insistence that feature films have much to learn from documentaries, and a lengthy critique of the form's vitiation in television formats (pp. 161–66), there was no more than passing consideration of the important contributions made by figures working today in the FRG to record the everyday, to investigate continuities in the German past and present, to explore the margins of social existence, to scout the provinces.

—Signs of life from filmmaking centers outside of Munich. There is a central connection in this volume, a decided bias—and that is Munich, and, as the list of collaborators betrays, a certain circle of friends, associates, and co-workers. One misses: voices from West Berlin (low-budget directors, feminists, reflections on the work of the Berlin Film and Television Academy), the Hamburg avant-garde, recollections of a once flourishing network of underground and experimental filmmakers during the late 1960s, and mention of the considerable activity in North Rhine–Westphalia and Hesse in a number of spheres.

—Certain names at decisive points. Why does an inventory of films marked by a "silent Bonapartism" (p. 228), i.e., a conscious desire to play a leading role on the international art film circuit, lack the most prominent and obvious example of the tendency, namely *Die Blechtrommel (The Tin Drum)*, a film by Kluge's friend and associate, Volker Schlöndorff? Other curious significant absences: Jean-Marie Straub and Danièle Huillet, Vlado Kristl, Werner Schroeter, Peter Nestler, individuals referred to in passing, but influential shaping impulses in Young German Film all but left out of the *Bestandsaufnahme*.

—More expansive discussion of the rougher edges of New German Film, precisely those elements Kluge is theoretically so eager to champion. The strength of German film may be its variety, but some strengths are clearly more conspicuously present than others. What about the importance of the West German avant-garde for the overall development of New German Film? (One recalls the jubilation at the 1979 *Filmfest* in Hamburg and yet easily forgets how in the midst of the rejoicing, feature filmmakers who arrived on a chartered train from Munich pushed the resident local experimental and underground figures into the background.) Where, beyond the discussion between Christel Buschmann and Margarethe von Trotta, and a less than conclusive—and later heavily attacked—description of women filmmakers by Ellen Wietstock, is the lively, articulate, and many-faceted feminist film culture? One wonders what Helke Sander, Jutta Brückner, Ulrike Ottinger, Helma Sanders-Brahms, and others, would have added.

—A regard for the riches at hand. At the center of the book is Claudia Lenssen's catalogue of what the German film lacks. If one believes the *2001 Merkheft* blurb advertising the volume, this catalogue is particularly "schön": "Alone from these pages German film could live another twenty years." The piece ("Liste des Unverfilmten," pp. 240–56) is a strange blend of inspiration and cynicism, optimism and derision. It is meant to leave an ultimate impression of just how dire the lacks are in West German film. The Kluge-like exercise (one recalls his phrase: "The critical measure of production is what is left out") reiterates the central emphasis behind the *Bestandsaufnahme*: collecting. But does the worth of a collection derive from valuing what one has or anguishing over what one does not? Does a collector seek to salvage fragments from a difficult present (lest they become lost for all time) or does one reject what is at hand for the sake of imagined treasures? In taking stock, does one work like a materialist and concern oneself with what is there or does one limit one's attentions to utopian designs? Looking more carefully at Lenssen's contribution, I was confounded by how the author claimed to find gaps and deficits where I glimpsed riches and plenitude. Does New German Film, as Lenssen maintained, lack landscapes? Does it sport no strong secondary figures, clouds, weather, rain fronts, heavies, crooks?—all of which Lenssen itemized as particular insufficiencies. At one point she provides outlines for films that in her mind have not yet been made; in fact, they read in many cases like paraphrases of recent releases. Oddly, produced titles criticized Lenssen's notions of the unproduced. In the same way, the large amount of elisions in Kluge's *Bestandsaufnahme* detracted, for me, from the otherwise important utopian impulse at work in the volume. "Collectors are often poets or scientists. We need an adventurous detective-like type of collector" (p. 427), Kluge says at one juncture. This is the inquisitive—and acquisitive—spirit one wishes might have been more evident in the *Bestandsaufnahme,* a collection which for all its scintillating findings leaves out a number of crucial traces quite central to the shape of West German film over the years.

IV

The present volume addresses two problems, then: (1) How to find an approach to the history of West German film that is more dynamic, inclusive, and process-oriented than the many previous studies in a host of languages? (2) How to counter almost universal claims that the New German Film is at the end of its tether, creatively and economically, to challenge arguments mouthed not only by the film culture's adversaries and assailants? This collection of writings by West German directors, spanning the years 1962 to 1986, provides a different account of this national cinema and constitutes a film history from the perspective of filmmakers, the most subjective sort of historiography imaginable. In no way, though, does this study mean to enshrine single creators and stimulate further acts of hagiography. If anything, the assortment of statements here aims to foster an awareness of diversity and collectivity, of individual wills and cooperative efforts, of the remarkable interactions between creators. The contributions in these pages combine certain persistent ways of seeing: insight, foresight, oversight, tunnel vision, blindness. The book is a blend of filmmakers' auto-criticism, retrospection, lobbyism, and self-aggrandizement.

The subtitle, "Visions and Voices," intimates the multiple motivations at work in West German film culture—special interests with, however, some inhering commonalities. Assembled in this fashion, these reflections allow us to glimpse collectivity where others have heralded— or derided—monadic and selfish endeavor. The ordering of these documents from the last two decades and a half enables us to see the *recurrence* of certain crises, the same problems again and again, permitting the observer to speak of *continuing* exigencies where others all too readily want to call in the coroner. New German Film has, without a doubt, shown a remarkable staying power over the years, a decided resilience, despite its repeated death notices, the first of which it received already in the midsixties. This is a film culture that has endured for twenty-five years now, obstinately and defiantly.

No other national cinema has produced such a dynamic and many-sided body of writing about its own films as West German filmmakers have over the past quarter of a century. And I am not talking about ghostwritten hype, interviews for the press, or published screenplays alone. I mean critical articles, polemical essays, theoretical statements, documents marked by care, opportunism, and prejudice, pamphlets articulating topical and historical concerns. One encounters here filmmakers speaking in a number of voices: eloquent, angry, show-offish, passionate, frantic, clumsy, pedantic. This is, to my knowledge, the first extended attempt to present the history of a national cinema in the words of its creators, statements that afford us both sweeping perspectives and close-up views.

V

My presentation, however, is not innocent. As a collector I am moved by interests both antiquarian and topical. I wish to conserve and I want to intervene. The directors speak for themselves in these articles, but I direct their discussion. The selection is my own; I made choices from hundreds of documents published in a wide array of venues: daily newspapers, film journals, television brochures, festival catalogs, yearbooks, anthologies, press booklets, and various other sources from the last twenty-five years. Clearly, my collection privileges certain voices and emphasizes particular concerns. The editing is anything but straightforward and transparent. Indeed the book is a *construction,* my construction, an assemblage of materials put together in a shape of my determination. Nonetheless, not everyone will read these pieces with, depending on the article, the same indulgence or impatience as I have. Some people will be less amused or taken in by filmmakers' tales of woe and not so eager to share their tribulations. Many will surely not rejoice in the subversive and radical sensibilities at work here. A few individuals might argue that the book has not let the more progressive voices express themselves sufficiently—or in fact that any downfall of West German film has resulted precisely from the stifling of such tendencies. I have framed this study with certain recurring patterns and motifs in mind and I hope they will be appreciated, but I also hope that the book allows for freedom of response on the part of the reader, a chance to form one's own image of this national cinema, in keeping with a consonant generosity toward audiences so often at work in West German films. The suggestions for further reading, likewise, aim to stimulate debate and encourage reflection.

This is not a theoretical book per se, even if it is the result of my grappling with certain issues prominent in recent debates about the writing of film history and the nature of national cinema. Some of the questions to which this study is addressed:

— What constitutes the corpus we call New German Film?
— Where do the statements of filmmakers and their written reflections fit in?
— What does making films have to do with writing about films?
— Why the particular value attached to the written word by directors in West Germany, individuals otherwise so hostile to forces that privilege the word, to the scripts demanded by subsidy committees and television editors, to films overly reliant on literary sources, to film criticism in general?
— How do these writings function within the multiple productions that often ensue in the wake of—or run parallel to—film projects, undertakings catalyzing such a proliferation of texts that it is hard at times to say what is the main show?

Hardly a film appears nowadays without a book (or more) accompanying the production, no rarity in the case of commercial productions, but a curiosity in the case of independent filmmakers with smaller budgets and audiences. Virtually every major German filmmaker (and many lesser-known ones) has published a collection (or more) of writings about film.

Reading the essays that have appeared since Oberhausen, I am struck by the urgency and poignancy of these pieces, the tendency of their authors to overstate the case, to argue in a fulsome and occasionally frenzied manner. It is as if one had to pull out all the stops for fear of not being taken seriously, an understandable reflex in a cultural scene where film plays such a marginal role. These are makeshift polemics staged in a context where there is no real forum for ongoing discussion about film. Instead one encounters at best ephemeral controversies and scandals. The voices collected here are stubborn ones demanding that their achievements be recognized and insisting that a nation's film culture need not simply be a narrowly defined site of distraction and escape. West German filmmakers act as vigilant souls confronting powers wishing to diminish memory and to reduce experience to stick-figure representations. That West German film culture is in the midst of a crisis cannot be denied—but this is a steady state, not an exceptional one, the state of things which has given rise to a beleaguered sensibility and a defensive stance typical of this obstinate national cinema since its inception.

Section III of this essay appeared previously in a lengthier discussion of Kluge's Bestandsaufnahme, "Kluge, Film History, and Eigensinn: A Taking of Stock from the Distance," New German Critique, no. 31 (Winter 1984): 109–24.

Regarding the Texts

The following translations are my own, unless otherwise noted in the listing of sources. Contributions appearing in this volume with a title different from the original text are marked by an asterisk. When it was necessary to edit or abridge an essay, an appropriate note has been made. Footnotes are included only when they actually were a part of the original publication. Annotations do not intend to explain each and every name and reference, but to aid the English-language reader in grasping a foreign film culture and its workings. Rather than indulge in what Kluge has spoken of as a "conceptual imperialism" that wishes to elucidate everything, the commentaries and annotations seek to be suggestive rather than exhaustive.

The following terms appear frequently in the essays; I list them here for the sake of orientation.

Arbeitsgemeinschaft Neuer Deutscher Spielfilmproduzenten: "Working Cooperative of New German Feature Film Producers," a group of West German filmmakers organized to counter the influence of the old guard

ARD: The First German Television Network

Autorenfilm/Autorenkino: A cinema of the film authors, granting priority to the creative director

DEFA: Deutsche Film Aktiengesellschaft, founded in May 1946, the centralized film production force in the German Democratic Republic

FBW: Filmbewertungsstelle Wiesbaden, the Film Rating Board in Wiesbaden, an institution responsible for awarding films predicates ("noteworthy" or "particularly noteworthy") as a recognition of quality

FFA: Filmförderungsanstalt, the Film Subsidy Board, located in West Berlin

FFG: Filmförderungsgesetz, the Film Subsidy Law, in existence since 1967

FSK: Freiwillige Selbstkontrolle, Independent Board of Control, responsible for determining the appropriate age groups for films; at times, the FSK has also acted as an agency that ferrets out "negative influences" in films

Filmverlag der Autoren: a self-help cooperative established by New German filmmakers in 1971 and later taken over by Rudolf Augstein, editor of *Der Spiegel*

Gruppe 47: Group 47, the literary circle including West Germany's most influential writers of the postwar era

Kleines Fernsehspiel: The Little Television Play, a series of new films and video works financed by the Second German Television Network (ZDF)

Kuratorium Junger Deutscher Film: Curators of Young German Film, brought about by the Federal Minister of the Interior in 1964

Paragraph 218: a German Federal law restricting abortion

SPIO: Spitzenorganisation der Filmindustrie, Head Organization of the German Film Industry, the group representing the interests of the older generations in the German film economy

WDR: Westdeutscher Rundfunk, the regional television network centered in Cologne which serves the state of North-Rhine Westphalia

ZDF: The Second German Television Network

For a comprehensive explanation of the politics and economics of West German Film, consult Hans Günther Pflaum and Hans Helmut Prinzler, *Cinema in the Federal Republic of Germany,* trans. Timothy Nevill (Bonn: Inter Nationes, 1983).

I

Manifestos and Declarations

Cooperation, collectivity, and group euphoria: this is the first impression that public statements like the Oberhausen Manifesto and the Hamburg Declaration convey. A gathering of filmmakers issues a dramatic announcement, confrontational in its tone, energetic in its impetus, ambitious in its resolve. When one looks more closely, however, this veneer of utopian idealism and common understanding quickly gives way to a less than harmonious backdrop. Filmmakers may fantasize about a new German film, but not everyone dreams the same dream, something that was clear even at the time the Oberhausen Manifesto was drafted one January evening in the back room of the Chinese restaurant "Hongkong" in Munich's Tengstrasse. One might declare the old order dead, but just because one did so it did not follow that entrenched interests would suddenly stand aside or fall over. The urgency behind the Munich Declaration makes it painfully clear how certain dynamics persisted more than two decades after some brash youths had foreseen the end of "Papa's Cinema." These documents represent an attempt to break out of a particularly fatal history and to confront the persistence of a traumatic past. Aiming to counter the official control of fantasy production, a commercial hegemony over the flow of images and representations, the filmmakers embrace a more encompassing notion of the medium film, at least on the surface. The Manifesto of Women Film Workers makes it apparent that the dream of a new German film had in the main been governed by male fantasies; in this regard, the high-spirited Hamburg Film Festival of the Filmmakers had, in its own way, been an act of exclusion. (Among the twenty-six signatories of the Oberhausen document there is not one woman.) For all their ostensible collective impact, these public communiqués never let us forget the particular interests circumscribing them; for all their highflown hopefulness, they also evoke the state of emergency which gave rise to these moments.

1. The Oberhausen Manifesto (1962)

The collapse of the conventional German film finally removes the economic basis for a mode of filmmaking whose attitude and practice we reject. With it the new film has a chance to come to life.

German short films by young authors, directors, and producers have in recent years received a large number of prizes at international festivals and gained the recognition of international critics. These works and these successes show that the future of the German film lies in the hands of those who have proven that they speak a new film language.

Just as in other countries, the short film has become in Germany a school and experimental basis for the feature film.

We declare our intention to create the new German feature film.

This new film needs new freedoms. Freedom from the conventions of the established industry. Freedom from the outside influence of commercial partners. Freedom from the control of special interest groups.

We have concrete intellectual, formal, and economic conceptions about the production of the new German film. We are as a collective prepared to take economic risks.

The old film is dead. We believe in the new one.

Oberhausen, February 28, 1962

Bodo Blüthner	Walter Krüttner	Detten Schleiermacher
Boris v. Borresholm	Dieter Lemmel	Fritz Schwennicke
Christian Doermer	Hans Loeper	Haro Senft
Bernhard Dörries	Ronald Martini	Franz-Josef Spieker
Heinz Furchner	Hansjürgen Pohland	Hans Rolf Strobel
Rob Houwer	Raimond Ruehl	Heinz Tichawsky
Ferdinand Khittl	Edgar Reitz	Wolfgang Urchs
Alexander Kluge	Peter Schamoni	Herbert Vesely
Pitt Koch		Wolf Wirth

2. The Mannheim Declaration (1967)

Six years have passed since the Oberhausen Declaration. The renewal of German film has not yet taken place. The initial intentional successes have suggested new directions. Before one can move in these directions they are already being blocked off again.

The undersigned repeat the Oberhausen demand for the renewal of German film. They wish to intervene in the international duping of the public and declare:

1. A film industry even in business matters cannot do without imagination. For that reason there is no such thing as strictly business matters.
2. The future of an industry is only as good as its younger generation.
3. An industry dare not be only a closed club for the established few.

The Oberhausen Declaration proclaimed:

The collapse of the conventional German film finally removes the economic basis for a mode of filmmaking whose attitude and practice we reject.

Those who signed the document were not wrong. But the attitude they rejected at that time once again is becoming prominent. By gaining influence over the legislative powers this attitude seeks to gain a new economic basis.

The planned Film Subsidy Law one-sidedly demands large distributors and large-scale productions.

It discriminates against the typical economic patterns of film culture and young directors ("small budgets").

We reject the law in its present form.

Signed:
Josef von Sternberg, Jury-President
Ulm Institute for Film Design: Alexander Kluge
Association of German Film Clubs: Jacob Heidbüchel, Reiner Keller, Fee Vaillant, Herbert Pötgens
Fiag—Film and Television Working Communities at German Universities: K. F. Göltz
Walter Talmon-Gros, Artistic Director of the International Film Week, Mannheim
Edgar Reitz, Jury Member
Hans Rolf Strobel, Jury Member

Norbert Kückelmann, Working Head of the Directors of the
   Kuratorium Junger Deutscher Film
Michael Lentz, Editor
Kurt Habernoll, Journalist
Heinrich Tichawsky, Producer and Director
Peter M. Ladiges, Film Journalist

The FFG, passed in 1967, amounted to a victory of the established old guard over the young filmmakers. The law institutionalized a support model for film subsidy based solely on economic and not artistic criteria.

3. The Hamburg Declaration (1979)

On the occasion of the Hamburg Film Festival, we German film-makers have come together. Seventeen years after Oberhausen we have taken stock.

The strength of German film is its variety. In three months the eighties will begin.

Imagination does not allow itself to be administered. Committee heads cannot decide what the productive film should do. The German film of the eighties can no longer be governed by outside forces like committees, institutions, and interest groups as it has in the past.

Above all:

We will not allow ourselves to be divided

—the feature film from the documentary film,

—experienced filmmakers from newcomers,

—films that reflect on the medium (in a practical way as experiments) from the narrative and commercial film.

We have proven our professionalism. That does not mean we have to see ourselves as a guild. We have learned that our only allies can be the spectators:

That means the people who work, who have wishes, dreams, and desires, that means the people who go to the movies and who do not, and that also means people who can imagine a totally different kind of film.

We must get on the ball:

Hamburg, September 9, 1979

4. The Manifesto of Women Film Workers (1979)

Press Release:

In recent weeks the "Association of Women Film Workers" was established in Berlin.

On the occasion of the "Film Festival of the Filmmakers" in Hamburg, many women once again realized that alone in the name of women they cannot make any demands. For that reason an initial spontaneous reaction of the women film workers was the

"MANIFESTO OF THE WOMEN FILM WORKERS"

The Association of Women Film Workers takes the liberty of expanding the "Hamburg Declaration of German Filmmakers" to include the demands of women filmmakers. We demand:

1. 50% of all film funding, production sites, and documentation projects;
2. 50% of jobs and training positions;
3. 50% of all committee seats;
4. support for the distribution, rental, and exhibition of films by women.

Over eighty women film workers from the Federal Republic and West Berlin signed the manifesto.

From the charter of the Association:

1.1 Women film workers are all women who are active or are becoming active in the film branch or the audiovisual media;
2.2 Goal of the organization is to support, encourage, and publicize all films made by women which are indebted to feminist, emancipatory, and nonsexist content and intent;
—to list, catalogue, and collect old and new films made by women;
—to collaborate with and to support persons publishing information on women film workers and women in film;
—to support with advice and the ongoing exchange of information women's film projects and applications for subsidies;
—to cooperate with domestic and foreign institutions and groups pursuing related goals.

These goals will be concretely implemented through organization and realization as well as participation in education and training, likewise in every possible support of all activities connected with film production and exhibition. The Association will be selflessly active in the advising, support, and representation of its members, helping them to carry through the preparation and realization of their productions in the realm of film and the audiovisual media.

The Association actively pursues sexual parity in all sectors of film and the audiovisual media. It sees the demands of the women film workers of 3 October 1979 appended to the "Hamburg Declaration of German Filmmakers" as its central goal and works for their immediate realization. To the declaration of the women film workers of 3 October 1979 the charter has been appended and constitutes its essential component.

The women film workers meet once a month in Berlin, and beyond that, are starting to form project groups. A nationwide meeting of women film workers is being planned for the Berlin Film Festival.

December 1979, the Association of Women Film Workers.

Cynthia Beatt, Heide Breitel, Jutta Brückner, Beate Büker, Clara Burckner, Christa Donner, Sabine Eckhard, Margit Eschenbach, Ingrid Fischer, Monika Funke, Marianne Gassner, Katharina Geinitz, Erika Gregor, Renée Gundelach, Petra Haffter, Eva Hammel, Ulrike Herdin, Claudia Holldack, Ebba Jahn, Riki Kalbe, Christiane Kaltenbach, Barbara Kasper, Angelika Kettelhack, Brigitta Lange, Birgit Lelek, Henriette Loch, Christine Löbbert, Ursula Ludwig, Jeanine Meerapfel, Elfi Mikesch, Renate Merck, Karin Mumm, Anke Oehme, Ingrid Oppermann, Ulrike Ottinger, Reinhild Paul, Cristina Perincioli, Ulrike Pohl, Margret Raspé, Sigrid Reichert-Purrath, Gudrun Ruzickova, Hille Sagel, Helke Sander, Helma Sanders, Claudia Schillinski, Monika Schmid, Valeska Schöttle, Claudia Schröder, Barbara Stanek, Chris Sternickel, Ula Stöckl, Anneli Wagner, Hildegard Westbeld, Krista Zeissig.

5. The Munich Declaration (1983)

The political evaluation of art has a tradition in our country, it touches the darkest chapters of our history.

This declaration is directed against everyone who with a selfish ruthlessness will stop at nothing to gain control over us, our minds, and our films.

One is mistaken, though, in thinking one can pull us apart, we have a common self-consciousness, 20 years of New German Film.

An attack on it is an attack on imagination and creativity. We will

find means and ways to protect art from its hangmen. If politicians come what may want to fight it out with us, they will find us ready.
Munich, June 21, 1983

For a collection of materials documenting filmmakers' reactions to potential changes in government policy regarding film subsidy, see "Zur Auseinandersetzung um Herbert Achternbuschs Das Gespenst und um Bundesinnenminister Zimmermanns Förderungskonzept," Film-Korrespondenz, 5 July 1983, pp. i–viii. This declaration issued as response to Zimmermann's eschewal of Autorenfilme, especially his vendetta against Achternbusch's Das Gespenst (The Ghost). Zimmermann, outraged by the acerbic portrayal of Christ returning to the modern world, refused to pay Achternbusch a final installment due the director from a State Film Prize of 1982. This was perceived as an unheard-of governmental intervention in film subsidy, as an act of censorship, and in many corners as a preview of coming shifts in governmental policies regarding film subvention and television coproductions.

II

The Price of Survival: Institutional Challenges

Declarations of independence and ebullient outpourings were one thing; the everyday reality of making films in West Germany was another. From the start the plucky tyros entertained a vision of crafting personal images, of a mode of production free from the constraints that had fettered previous generations in Germany. The *Autorenfilm* meant a film uncompromised by commercial dictates and established interests, at least in theory. In actual practice, though, this ideal of autonomous creation was challenged at every conceivable juncture by a host of forces. The fledgling young directors would soon come face-to-face with a very stern reality principle, one involving a series of hurdles each new production would have to cross: subsidy applications demanding appropriate language and criteria, frequently tenuous arrangements with coproducers and television editors, anxious moments as control and rating boards, TV partners, and critics scrutinized finished works, the often frantic and sometimes futile search for a distributor, the equally difficult task of finding exhibitors willing to screen eccentric and outspoken films, and the less than cordial relationship filmmakers enjoyed with film journalists. To be sure, mistakes were made. Numerous individuals flourished in the rich network of support systems while others languished in obscurity and resented colleagues who had succeeded. Many filmmakers took recourse to an almost obligatory (and sometimes tedious) narrative of martyrdom when describing their experiences. With the eighties came a further host of vicissitudes: the challenge of the work of film art in the age of electronic reproduction, the diminished status of personal films in an industry unceasingly dominated by high-tech American products, a country where most films unspool in "cinema centers" that resemble video arcades, a place where one finds the few remaining sources of solace amidst commercial insanity (such as the *Filmverlag der Autoren*, the

idealistic creation of a directorial collective in the early seventies) becoming every bit as unsympathetic as one's traditional adversaries. The
history of West German film since the sixties is one of continuing and
never-ceasing confrontation with a complex of institutional powers.
There is no doubt that the Federal Republic harbored—and still possesses—a large spectrum of cinematic possibility, that over the last
twenty-five years it has been the site of what one might describe as an
unparalleled profusion of images, a remarkably heterogeneous and to a
great extent oppositional national film culture. Freeing the flow of fantasy
in one's creations, however, would not be enough; one still needed a
public sphere in which these fantasies could flow.

6. Alexander Kluge
What Do the "Oberhauseners" Want? (1962)

West German Film is in a crisis: its intellectual content was never
more lacking, but today its economic status is equally threatened. This is
happening at a time when in France and Italy, in Poland and Czechoslo-
vakia, but also in many other countries, film has assumed a new artistic
and political importance. Films like Italy's *Salvatore Giullano,* which was
just shown in Berlin, or *Ashes and Diamonds* from Poland, indicate that
film has been able to interact with literary and other art forms as well as
with political consciousness. We have had numerous conversations with
members of Group 47 and have seen that there exists a quite extraordinary interest in film among people working in other sectors. It therefore
is crucial that we

1. free film from its intellectual isolation in the Federal Republic,
2. militate against the dictates of a strictly commercial orientation
   operative in the film industry today,
3. allow for conditions which make film aware of its public responsibility and, consequently, in keeping with this responsibility, to
   seek appropriate themes: film should embrace social documentation, political questions, educational concerns, and filmic inno-
   vations, matters all but impossible under the conditions that have
   governed film production.

For an Intellectual Transformation

In the film industry today there are two main groups: the producers
associated with the Head Organization of the German Film Industry

(SPIO) and their affiliated distributors; the young directors organized around the Oberhausen group, who also have their own distributors (e.g., Atlas-Film, but also to a degree Gloria-Film). The Oberhausen group in the meanwhile is not only limited to the signatories of the Oberhausen Manifesto this last February, but also includes all those forces who want not only a reorganization of previous practice in German film, but also a structural change in film production and an intellectual transformation in film activity. This group has among its members directors, producers, and authors. The group seeks close working relations with Group 47, with the so-called "Cologne School" (Stockhausen), and with other intellectual forces outside of the film industry. We are also seeking close contacts with [Wolfgang] Staudte, [Bernard] Wicki, [Helmut] Käutner, and [Hans] Abich, because we think that the failures these outstanding filmmakers have had recently are not due to personal shortcomings, but rather are a result of the faulty system governing the film industry.

The program called for by the Oberhausen group can in the long run finance itself. In the early phase, where new types of film will have to be developed in a comparatively short time (in France and Italy one took the last six years to do so, in the Eastern Bloc countries the state pays for this development work anyway), the program will at least in part have to rely on public subsidies. That means we will have to maintain a definite *noncommercial* position within the framework of a free-market economy. For these reasons the Cultural Minister Conference has recommended the support of culturally significant films in the discussions about the 1963 budget.

Three Goals

The Oberhausen group has pursued three tasks since this spring:

1. The founding of a public foundation for "Young German Film." This foundation should enable each new generation of German film-makers to complete their first feature film, granted that the filmmaker in question has proved himself in the short film realm and finished a short film. A jury will monitor the quality of the projects submitted. This foundation has in the meanwhile been established. It needs, though, further public monies. On the other hand, it is clear that no one will make money from this foundation, particularly because the profits of each film subsidized must be passed on back to the foundation in keeping with the amount of support granted. We have calculated that three successful films out of every ten subsidized will suffice to maintain a constant fund for upcoming young German filmmakers.

2. Subsidization of independent short films. The independent short film is the natural experimental field of film, just as the private school is the carrier of independent impulses and reformist endeavor in the field of education, an institution which cannot be governed by the large state school apparatus. This independent short film is seriously threatened today, particularly since the abolishment of the entertainment tax. Due to the loss of the entertainment tax in several states, the predicates no longer mean so much to distributors. The box-office returns for "particularly noteworthy" short films in this way have sunk well below the production costs. It is important that we not lose this short-film basis, even when we go on someday to make feature films. In this way the Conference of Cultural Ministers and the responsible social powers cannot make it any clearer how potentially dangerous the diminishing importance of the Film Rating Board (FBW) is. The Film Rating Board is in any case the single institution in the film branch which is not strictly commercial in its orientation.

3. To create an intellectual center for film, in which new generations can be trained and in which theoretical work and developmental work have their place, things that are necessary for every industry, even the film industry. This institution has been established as of October 1 and it consists of twelve instructors, i.e., two film scholars and ten directors, and to all appearances, it is off to a good start. This Department for Film Design in connection with the Scholl-Siblings Foundation (in keeping with the *Bauhaus* conception) links new filmic models with instruction in film design. This department likewise, as of December 1, will have an experimental studio based in Munich, in which the practical experimental work and further training of Ulm students with two years of previous course work will be carried out. The film department and the experimental studio fit into the overall framework of the film and television academy which will be established with branches in Munich, Berlin, and Ulm.

The idea of founding a film and television academy initially caused us a lot of misgivings. The problem lies in a potential academization of the already wretched film situation we have in Germany, and it's exactly that which we cannot want. Along with this came the competition between the cities Berlin and Munich, which each with a certain ambition sought an advantage in the academy question, so that discussion on this level is not free from certain prestige considerations. This was one of the reasons why we particularly concentrated on the educational model linked to the Institute for Film Design (although right now we are very much involved in film productions of our own), because it seemed necessary to us, from the very beginning, to maintain our own and independent model of creative education in a more modest form above and beyond any likely large academy apparatus. From the cooperation between the academy and the film department in Ulm a positive influence can be generated toward film. This cooperation will be made easier insofar as the *Bundestag* representative Dr. Martin has intervened continually, working on a national basis to support and encourage independent endeavors.

Hans Abich was a (for the time) progressive and enterprising film producer during the postwar era.

7. Hans Rolf Strobel and Heinrich Tichawsky
We Have Work to Do (1965)

The decree regarding the awarding of feature film subsidies by the Federal Minister of the Interior, dated November 30, 1964, means that after almost three years of lobbying by young directors the idea of support for debut films has been realized. As we come to the end of 1964 the economic foundation for a renaissance of German film has finally been created. The economic difficulties hindering the production of new German films by new directors have been removed.

The procedures for the examination and support by the *Kuratorium Junger Deutscher Film* are in place; it is now able to function.

Now it is a question whether the responsible parties can make a viable instrument out of this conception and the subsidy funds.

Now it is above all a question of what the others who now may have access to this instrument have to say and how they will express this.

There has been too much talking. We don't have anything more to say right now. We have work to do.

Strobel, according to several important sources, was a central figure in the drafting of the "Oberhausen Manifesto." Besides making a number of children's films on his own, he collaborated with Tichawsky on a series of short films and documentaries. Cf. Strobel's essay, "Kein fröhlicher Rückblick—kein trauriger Ausblick: 20 Jahre nach dem 'Oberhausener Manifest': Anmerkungen eines Mitunterzeichners," Medium, January 1982, pp. 3–5.

8. Vlado Kristl

Application for Film Subsidy* (1970)

Very esteemed Mr. President of the Federal Supreme Court, I cannot free myself from the suspicion that I am a foreigner.

Formal Application for Film Subsidy

1. A plot summary and declaration are attached in fifteen copies.

2. I declare myself willing to regard and follow all of the guidelines of the Film Subsidy Board.

3. Herewith I also declare that in relation to all of my associates I possess in the same measure and totally independently the copyrights to the material, script, idea, title, as well as all existing or future, i.e., not yet existing, rights to use.

4. A budget is, put vaguely, attached in three copies.

5. I have not put together a plan for financing the film; and I myself do not have any capital; I likewise did not intend to produce a film that is of interest to the usual and existing film distribution (or the existing and usual film industry); in this regard every possible way of finding financial backing is nipped in the bud.

6. As far as the crew goes, it can be assembled according to place and time very provisionally; besides myself, who will run the camera and take care of all the technical stuff, there is no steady employee or permanent co-worker. . . .

7. A written list of my previous activities in film and elsewhere is attached in fifteen copies.

8. There is no need to inquire about the accord between director and producer, insofar as the applicant is at once the producer, author, director, cameraman, editor, etc.

9. I acknowledge that the mere application does not entitle me to any rights as long as I have not been granted rights by a subsidy agreement.

10. I am prepared to assume the processing fee for my application; it is of course the case that when we show our films we have to pay; I do not find this unjust, because, as I stated above, these films were not made to make deals, to earn money.

11. There is not any communism at all; we have to get by with anarchy.

You see, my very esteemed gentlemen, the content of the film which I have simulated is not the content. I must admit that it is only the plot of the film. And nothing more. But this was in no way a premeditated act of duplicity. The intention to mislead you. On the contrary. I am moved to clarify this act and to explain it.

The single and true content is the film I made, one devoid of all the preparations that elsewhere lead to results that make a film look conventional. I decided to use a method of shooting which preferred bad compositions, which made the development of common or well-known techniques seem unnecessary to me, which helped me to avoid things that seemed quite easy to do or ran counter to my taste and judgment, the method that automatically imparted to me the capacity to avoid all of the conventional wisdoms I and others had internalized . . . and [which] lurk within us.

With these premises everything becomes changed; even now with the best of intentions I cannot come up with a plot summary. . . .

In short, this undertaking is a grab bag for film comedies, and the film I am showing is not meant to be used for any nonfilmic purposes. This is also a considerable part of the content, because there we disagree decidedly, this question causes breakdowns in communication. This is how it was in Knokke and this is how it has remained. While some claim that film is a medium meant to realize a political program, we maintain that the creation and vitalization of the medium can be the most authentic political program, i.e., using film, one can see which program is realistic.

In the hope and conviction that you, my ladies and gentlemen, will countenance my screening with good will, I remain respectfully yours: the producer.

I am making a film against the celluloid film industry.

You're right. This film rescues the industry; even more, it is the first film that has been made to rescue the corrupt and moribund film industry, because it is the first that has been made with this resolve.

And not only the industry rejects it, but also the filmgoers who would otherwise go to war for the old cinema.

There is something striking about all this. A film, insofar as it would be a commercial success, which therefore would be recognized by this rotten industry as its own and part of its conceptual world, would not rescue this industry. Only the film made against it can rescue it.

Unfortunately. The necessity stems from false conditions.

So, that's how it is.

16

But, when you make a film, you help this industry. It doesn't matter what your content or intention is. You rescue it even if you don't want to.

You are not exaggerating a bit in this regard.

Yes, in this sense, if you look at things this way, it is sad how the industry rejects this film and refuses to show it anywhere.

It's hard to understand, I grant that. Such blunders rarely happen. That an entire world fails to see the facts, i.e., fails in this way, is probably a distinct sign of our time and age.

To work against something, to proceed consciously against something, today means consciously to work for it.

Nevertheless I would like to know, why is this so, how come? Even if I am not aware of being presumptuous when I say that I know the concepts all by heart.

My dear spectators, now take a look at that for yourselves. . . .

These observations are taken from Kristl's book Sekundenfilme *(Second-Long Films), a collection described in these terms by the volume's editor, Wolf Wondratschek: "These are materials about his film work, films, written films, written utterances in the form of scripts or exposés which he no longer is willing to write."—Knokke was the site of an annual gathering of avant-garde and experimental filmmakers.—Kristl's most important films include* Der Brief *(The Letter, 1966) and* Film oder Macht *(Film or Power, 1970).*

9. Jean-Marie Straub

Letter to the Export-Union (1975)

July 28, 1975

You Fascists, you Ignoramuses, you Hypocrites,

Richard Roud sent me a copy of your letter from July 9, 1975 (Dr. G/ E1). I wouldn't think of accepting a penny from you pimps (Roud had written you without my permission), but I want you to know that I am registered as a *German* film director in the West *German* Office of Employment, and will—with your letter in hand—make every possible publicity against you.

With hate,
Jean-Marie Straub

Dr. R. F. Goldschmidt, Delegate of the Board of the Export-Union of the German Film Industry, had written Richard Roud, Director of the New York Film Festival, on 9 July, in English:

"Thank you for your letter of June 30, 1975, regarding the German participation at the New York Film Festival.

"We are sorry to tell you that we are in no position to help you with airfares for Danièle Huillet and J. M. Straub to come to your festival as both are French nationals and therefore the German authorities will not give any funds for such a trip.

"The airfare for Werner Herzog will be paid so that there is no problem that he will be present at your festival."

10. Hans Jürgen Syberberg
We Live in a Dead Country (1977)

The reaction to my film book which came out six months ago, and the recent events involving German film journalists, when parts of the *Hitler* film were presented, have led me to decide to withdraw the intended presentation of new excerpts from the film at Berlin during the festival, and to refuse permission for the film to be shown in Germany at all. I no longer have anything in common with it. Why, and for whose benefit and pleasure? We are living in a dead country. I appeal to the editors of our great newspapers with regular film coverage and beg them not simply and irresponsibly to make a parade of solidarity with those whom I intend to describe, if I come to such conclusions as these.

I appeal to you, publicly and in this country, because it concerns everybody who reads your newspapers, and not them alone. Because cinema and film, as I understand them, are facets of freedom, a new freedom, evidence of it or a chance for all of us. Of necessity, these have to be very personal words. Please do not regard that as an immediate disadvantage, as those I am accusing would. Therein, perhaps, resides the very value of these words. In all events my commitment is a large one, and this is the last time I shall say so. It now depends on you, on how seriously you regard your responsibility and work. It ought really not to matter to me at all. But Germany is my native country. . . .

German cinema is finished in its present structure and the rats are leaving the sinking ship. This country is not only dead, it is not even a country any longer. Centerless. Without a spiritual identity, with a disturbing film center once a year in the neon-lit ghetto of a pin table bar in Cannes. A country deserted by the Jewish intellectuals of film and nevertheless with such a large mafia? In my book I speak of a mafia of the subconscious. Our filmbuffs [sic] are grotesque in their refutation of the efforts of the anti-Semites. The Jews left, the mafia remained. But on what level? If proof were still needed to show how wrong Hitler went in this respect too, in spite of the statistics, our filmbuffs [sic], the inheritors, are the sad confirmation of it, of error and dissolution. The dialectical elite is dried out, without the spice of public responsibility. It is really a miracle that films are still being made. When *Ludwig* came out in London there was opposition too, and they are there to be read, the points at issue, but I was never made the spittoon for the brain scabs of an ideologized filmbuff [sic]. Isn't that strange? The way things are at the moment you can't expect care and patience, or even attention, dutiful curiosity for Syberberg films from any of the so-called opinion-making newspapers and their satellites. They don't turn up, don't report the facts. In some cases they haven't for years. Now right across the board. What else can you call it other than the deadly silence of the intellectually frozen desert? Has the thought never occurred to them that they were failing in their duty, the fear of being wrong, a single doubt, a single intellectual temptation to look at it all from the opposite point of view, to listen, perhaps just once to pose themselves the troubling question whether all those at the Cannes showing of the *Hitler* excerpts from London to Tel Aviv, from Rome to Paris or Madrid were really more stupid than they? Are we so much more in possession of the truth than, for example, the twelve London colleagues who placed the last two Syberberg films, *Karl May* in first and *Winifred Wagner* in second place, out of the eighty films from the current year shown at the London Festival? Has anyone in Germany ever heard about this? In many of the newspapers, neither of those films was even honored with a mention in the list of those selected from Germany. Are these English critics, like the French ones, thirty years behind the times? Were they all bribed? Germanophiles? Then why not Wenders, Herzog, and Fassbinder, who were all there to be chosen? And came lower down the list? Was it vanity that pushed one to the front?

Helene Vager, the French coproducer of the Hitler film, is now on the Berlin jury. Derek Malcolm of the *Guardian*, one of the loyal interpreters of my films in England, is also on the Berlin jury. John Simon, the discoverer of *Karl May* in New York, is in Berlin as a guest of the festival. All of them, as has been said, unimportant. All of them incompetent, dishonorable guests, nincompoops? Dunderheads? Dismissed because they're not from Germany, their opinions worthless? Therefore finally my decision to withdraw the film here. The only logical decision, the way things are today. In so doing, I am bowing to the will of the lack of interest openly paraded by the German cinema, its distributors and critics at Cannes. English and French distributors came up after the performance to show their interest. That's the way it normally operates.

None of our people were there—who would have come for whom? But I also realize that this expressed a rejection of the general public interest. They neither represent nor respect the cinema anymore. And in the absence of these instruments of public consciousness, freedom, too, cannot survive. Is it still worth it? The critics of the large, national, opinion-making newspapers are either not interested, not competent, or fearful. The film industry, i.e. distributors and cinemas, have other interests and problems. ("The interests of the commercially oriented film industry cannot be the interests of film art.")

There is no money to spare for promotion and individual initiatives. A hopeless situation. For, as I have said, whom else is this film made for, with all its references and traditions, its guilt and suffering, if not for Germany? And what is more, anyone tackling this theme has to break all the conventions. As filmmaker or audience. It cannot be expected to be a usual kind of film—and that here in Germany, in the commercial context, in the situation I have described? Where, frankly, none of our films has really worked. No one gets his investment back. Let's be honest, the fringe markets are all that are left to us. No one makes a profit. Does he have to? In the commercial market he does. As a state opera he doesn't. Everyone knows it and nobody says anything. A massive taboo. Film isn't culture. No wonder when criticism, the bridge to a potential comprehension, has gone the way it has.

If the German film critics do not put their shoulders to the wheel in representing us to the public, we shall be a long time on our road to recognition as culture and to our liberation from a minority existence. And so anyone who wants to see the Hitler film will have to travel to London or Paris. No reader of our newspapers will be able to find out anything about this film or its background as long as the German film critics have anything to do with it. Since they have already failed with *Ludwig* and *Hirneis* and *Karl May*, what, I wonder, can be expected from these people when it comes to a film by Syberberg about Hitler? Two of them made the first attempt after Cannes. Neither of them had seen the showing. And were neither sacked nor called to account for practicing deception on their readers. "Pompous bombast," "montage of associations," "scenes back to front"—without having seen the film.

I'm afraid there no longer is any point in even speaking out. Not even that. A year and a half ago, I wrote in these pages one last time about the death of the old film sector, and said that it would be the last I would say about it. For fear of losing the little places on the various boards, which had just been won, it wasn't printed and went round from hand to hand like a piece of hot goods or a samisdat, because nobody had the courage to speak the truth out loud. Today I am writing for these

pages once again, perhaps the only ones who would dare to make such words public, semipublic, because if the people I am accusing want it that way, not even reactions to what I am saying will be discussed, whatever they are. I now herewith declare to those who pride themselves so much on their youth and their cinemas, that this is the last time I shall speak to my own generation, in whose power it lies whether a film shall be seen and how it shall be seen. From now on there will be no more books, no more articles, no more letters, only a diary with precise names and deeds. Only solicitors and courts if things get really bad and the lives of my films are threatened. Finish. The end. That's that. Joy, victory, satisfaction? Something to be ashamed about. Your most passionate critic is silent. From the lack of a critical environment. I'd say that was a defeat for everybody, and no doubt about it. A land without public responsibility. No, there'll be nothing more. The way things are. . . .
20 June 1977

The book Syberberg speaks of appeared as Syberbergs Filmbuch *(Munich: Nymphenburger, 1976).—The complete titles of Syberberg's films mentioned in the essay are:* Ludwig—Requiem für einen jungfräulichen König *(Ludwig—Requiem for a Virgin King, 1972),* Theodor Hirneis oder: Wie man ehem. Hofkoch wird *(Ludwig's Cook, 1972),* Winifred Wagner und die Geschichte des Hauses Wahnfried von 1914–1975 *(The Confessions of Winifred Wagner, 1975).—Syberberg's essay responds to the lukewarm response which the screening of passages from the Hitler film received at the Cannes Film Festival, especially by West German film critics.—For a different version of the same events, see Wolf Donner, "Hitler nach Deutschland!"* Die Zeit, *30 December 1977. See also Syberberg's response to Donner, "Hitler— noch nicht für Deutschland,"* Die Zeit, *13 January 1978.*

11. Hans W. Geissendörfer

Dependent Working Conditions: About Directing and Producing (1979)

Most of my colleagues have in recent years founded their own production companies or have from the start produced their films. The justification for this was that one has more freedom, retains more of the rights of the films and remains free of others' greed, and above all can hold onto the bonuses, prizes, and subsidies, putting them into one's own productions and thus providing a financial basis for the next film.

Nevertheless: I have thus far preferred to be a slave, to sell myself and to work for a steady salary or percentage, as a director to be the employee of a company on account, as an author to be the merchant of my ideas and rights. Friends for this reason smile at me, sometimes even curse me, because I have been (and still am) entirely willing to accept money from other people to make a film, people with whom I have nothing or very little in common.

The following is an attempt to describe the advantages and short-comings of so-called dependent working conditions.

1

I don't have to worry about money, I have no or little responsibility in such matters. Even if I do believe that part of a director's job involves making ends meet with a full or limited budget, nonetheless as a salaried director I always fight for the film, demanding everything I need to make the film a success, everything that is at all possible. The agreement with the producer not to exceed a certain sum limits me, but in the euphoria of production, the hectic atmosphere of decision making, it sometimes falls back onto the lap of the producer. The director needs this and that and he has to convince the producer. If he succeeds, he has won; the producer's risk grows, but likewise the chance that the film will be better. On the other hand: if I were to produce my films, then only with unlimited means. The pleasure in my work and the daily demand for quality, for a visualization of what is in my head, all call for an adversary, who tempers any extravagance, who curbs momentary whims, who prevents starvation and bankruptcy. I have no desire to play the role of my own adversary. I would constantly lose to myself and end up in chaos. . . .

Therefore: depending on others to produce films makes one free in matters of finances. What do I offer, or what do I try to offer in return? Results. I play along with the system absolutely. If I think highly of my results, if I have the feeling after three or four weeks on the set that something is taking shape which I like and the people around me like, then I up the ante and stand steady. If I were my own producer this game would be boring and somehow I would know my limits from the start. A producer, a stranger, smoking a cigarette, with or without manners, remains a partner, whom one can confront if the film justifies it. I always hope that such confrontations involve a common cause. I always repress previous experiences with others when I sit across from a new producer to talk about a new film. I have absolutely no intention of shitting on him and dearly hope that he will not shit on me (me = the film)—and hope I will go home satisfied. I begin my work and am stunned like a child

when after submitting my first list of requisitions red lines whiz over
paper. Then the game starts and it's the director's responsibility not to
lose at the poker table. . . .

. . . The "dependent" producer knows only one rule of thumb: the
film in his head (the knife in the head) and nothing else. The struggle
over money can just as easily be a comedy as a drama. Why is one a
director after all.

2

One constantly hears the phrase: if you are your own producer no
one will interfere. Besides the fact that the producer-director controls the
money, I think it's safe to say that given the production dynamics today
even the dependent director has just about all the autonomy he needs.
The producer gets a large part of the subsidy money due to the director's
or author's reputation and he is therefore careful not to cramp this
director's style too much. If a producer knows his business any director
would have to be happy to be spared mistakes because of his producer's
know-how. Of course, though: who among the producers today working
with dependent directors really knows his business? There are few. In my
own work so far with seven different producers no one limited my (so-
called) freedom so much as the eighth, and that was me (working
through the *Filmverlag der Autoren*).

3

If direction is a craft, and it is considered as such by the Office of
Finance and most filmmakers, then part of this craft involves dealing
with the providers of capital. If I myself have to raise the capital then I
have less time to consider how I will best be able to spend this capital. I
think that a person who is producer-author-director at once takes on
more risk than someone who lets others worry about all the financing and
administration of money. Of course, that's his job. Because this person
carries a minimal risk—namely the risk of exceeding the budget—he is
entitled to the chance of making a profit, at least as long as our
productions, even independent ones, accord to the laws of capitalism. . . . Because the subsidy laws do not bind the monies in such a
way that they have to be used again by the same producer with the same
director, one should agree before shooting starts in the director's or
author's contract that the producer does not receive one hundred percent
of all bonuses, prizes, etc., but rather shares them with the director. This
amounts to a coproduction and this is for me the only just chance to
continue working together with producers. Coproduction: the one sup-
plies the ideas and the craft and the artistic part of the film and the other

watches over everything. Even the risk of going over budget is shared, things are exactly that simple and it works too. The director will think more about the expenses and will submit more readily to an economic discipline and the so-called producer does that which he already does anyway in our country: he orders, he takes care of the finances, and he keeps the books. Everyone does what he is best at.

4

When things go like I've just described them one has gotten rid of the most imposing liability that one has as a free-lance director. One can decide together with the "administrative official," alias the producer, what to do with the finished film. . . .

If you produce your own films, then you usually need another six to ten months after finishing a film to bring this child into the light of day. What nonsense; unless, of course, one really likes to deal all the time with things that leave one cold. I don't know any one who actually likes to do this. Many still do nonetheless; I cannot and do not want to, it's not my job. The right to influence decisions and to veto things if necessary, that's enough for me. These two rights are absolutely possible in working with producers, you only have to be on your guard when it counts and let your wishes be known and be a tough negotiator.

5

If you look closely, you see that in fact the difference between the self-producing director and the freelance director is of necessity becoming smaller and smaller due to the development of the German film productions to a large degree backed by subsidies and public television. The classical producer is dead. The classically employed director likewise. No producer nowadays takes on both intellectual and financial risks. The author-director as a rule carries the intellectual risk himself, he does what he can to keep the financial ones within limits and in fact is the one who makes things possible, for he is the one who brings a large part of the available monies to the producer. The pure director-artisan who is hired to film a certain book is less and less to be found here. For such an individual the producer still remains his bread and butter, for the majority of German authors and directors, "artists" and "producers" pass the bread and butter back and forth. For that reason there must and will be a just and inevitable development leading to a situation where the two function as partners and share the fruits of their labor. Many have come to this insight already. Those others who have not yet will in the long run be left out in the cold.

12. Herbert Achternbusch
Something about Nature and Censorship (1979)

Those are terrible hours when I don't remember that there is art, then I do and it's like redemption. So long, you cerebral autumn evening reveries with their fading warmth which I conjure up with falling leaves, sunsets, the last of summer and the loss of art. Conjure up? I once made the mistake of studying an art form intensively, namely painting. But when something becomes academic it becomes bourgeois. The bourgeois world has always tried to push me back with its fingertips into the abyss, so that I "by myself" lapse into a state of impotence. The bourgeois world has soaked every inch of our soil with blood and tears from all over the globe. Nature, this last bit of nature, expires out of a sense of guilt, because it is a product of this bourgeoisie. With a hot feeling of shame it tries to undo this fall from grace. All the leaves in our trees shiver because of these murders. And if they aren't shivering then they have become petrified out of fear. Nature wanted to become human and sees itself petrified in the shape of the bourgeois, the true enemy of man and nature. It satisfies its desire for more with flowerpots. It fetters things and strangles the desire for everything. The writers of the bourgeoisie describe this bourgeois disaster with millimeter-long sticks, i.e., letters, thus keeping this disaster millimeters away from us, and this kind of writing and its results are called realistic. I can't listen to these windy write-offs about the decline of bourgeois life anymore. It is no longer a question of pointing out the criminal nature of the bourgeois but rather one of saying things shamelessly. Literature should invent. Literature should bite down. It should not give in, not whine about the world around us. Experience should spring, spring into invention. Down with the miserable facts of life, long live liberating invention! Ernst Jandl should rise higher, [Günter] Grass should continue to decline . . .

"On my desk lies a small roll." For days now this sentence reasons its way through my ears. The sentence comes from TV and has to do with my latest film, Der Komantsche (The Comanche). The sentence has to do with a sentence of mine, which according to the selfish insights of the diwrecktors one cannot impose on TV audiences. In the film someone says in a dream (he is dreaming): Hitler wanted to console God with six million Jews, but that was a mistake. Next to the dreamer his wife fills out a survey in Playboy, responding to the question whether she would be willing to die for Germany, that there probably is no one around who would be willing to die for this loveless Germany. There is no love in Germany any more. "On my desk lies a small roll." This refers to "the" roll, i.e., the purged sentence from my film about Hitler and the Jews.

(Hitler wanted to console God with six million Jews, but that was a mistake.) Wasn't it a mistake? Didn't God remain silent like a needy person who needed this sacrifice? Didn't he remain silent because he was ashamed of being in need of such consolation? Or perhaps God does not exist? Or was this the work of men, the inexplicable? Once again it was the bourgeoisie that rallied around God and even once Hitler. Now it has democracy. "And that works damn well," the TV diwrecktor consoles me, and in reality the diwrecktor means that he has made my film better. In the following sentences I refer to myself as "one." One received money from television, because one went along with the censor's act, because one otherwise would not have received any money. One has also promised to remain silent about this. But I cannot remain silent, because if I were to do so, I would no longer be a writer. "On my desk lies a small roll." How expressive is this nonreproducible invented sentence of mine! It has to give way to a sentence which only refers to a single act of censorship. And what large danger lies in hindering this thought, this one sentence, namely, that my thoughts only revolve around the missing sentence instead of taking wing. On my desk lies a small line. Every act of censorship is an act of castration. One feels exposed by this state confiscation. They put underpants on you and make you feel as if you had been standing there naked. On my table lies a little penis. Yesyes, I feel castrated. How should I explain myself to a woman? What about the little finger that wants me to lapse into impotence? On my desk lies a little portion of democracy. I mean now my own table. And elsewhere? Yes elsewhere! Childish? If I admit that I start censoring myself. Fight back! In the eighties a pig's head will be upon us that would like to decorate himself with our balls. Fight back! The first fascist kick was always in the balls. The democratic grab for the balls is already happening. Defend yourselves!

12 October 1979

Achternbusch's The Comanche *was coproduced by the Second Channel (ZDF).*

13. Helke Sander

Men Are Responsible That Women Become Their Enemies: Tales of Rejection (1980)

The list of titles below includes projects submitted to television or various film subsidy committees, all of which were rejected. Among them are finished scripts, detailed exposés as well as treatments. I'm not sure about the exact dates because I didn't keep thorough records at the time. I submitted most of the projects only once, in the case of TV stations at the most twice. I did so because (a) I had no money to make additional copies and to send out the scripts, much less travel money to make personal appearances, and (b) I also gave up. I couldn't cope with this constant working behind the scenes and I didn't really have any idea where to begin. I knew next to nothing about the infrastructure of these stations or committees and had no time to find out and those people who might have been able to help me here didn't. I've often wondered why not because I didn't assume anyone had bad intentions. I simply think a lot of things I didn't know were obvious to these other people. Besides I wasn't used to this humiliating begging and that was important to me here at the start. Because my work for Finnish theater and television was taken seriously without my having to give it a second thought. I assumed that this was natural. . . .

What made things more difficult in my case was the fact that, since 1969, since finishing my training at the Berlin Film Academy, I submitted unabashed feminist projects which no one wanted. The women's movement was just getting going, I spent a lot of time and energy helping things along, that is to say, I split my interest between my job and the women's movement, occasionally spending more time on the latter, so that I could do the kinds of things I wanted to in my films correctly. Another crucial point is my bad sense of timing. I could have easily made many of the films I submitted if I had acted more strategically. If someone told me in '69 that there was no more money, I would have to wait two years, I thought: I can't wait two years to do something I just wrote *now*, by then I'll be much further along for sure. My sense of integrity prevented me from taking advantage of opportunities. Of course I should have jumped at the chance and then done something else two years later.

If I received any response at all to the rejected projects listed here, one usually claimed that my projects were "unpolitical." This was justi-fied with quotations from Marx. If this didn't bother me so much I'd call the whole thing a farce. Even today cultural editors and department heads deny having *failed* to respond to exposés and screenplays which are submitted. That's simply a lie, but it would take too much energy, time, and money as well to prove that in detail. In the meanwhile I have taken on the status of a well-known unemployed director from the film branch.

1. 1969, a suggestion to NDR [North German Televison] about a film devoted to the burgeoning German women's movement. Rejection with the justification that a woman couldn't be objective about these things. G. Bott went on to make a film about it. Review in *Frauen und Film???*

2. Exposé (1970): *Die Zeit der Mütter (The Age of Mothers).* That was conceived as a film series in numerous parts. The first part would deal with theories about prehistoric times, about the "natural" division of labor, about the remnants of matriarchal forms in contemporary societies and their use value in explanations of prehistoric developments. "From amoeba to *homo sapiens,*" I had studied all of this for quite a long time—sort of a hobby for me—but I had never had the time to put to paper or on film the results of these studies. I hoped that support for such a film would also support my research activity.

The second part of the film was concerned with the age of the witch hunts.

The third part concerned itself with the beginnings of the women's movement in America, how it arose out of the endeavors by women to liberate the blacks. The fourth part was supposed to deal with French women who were killed during the French Revolution. The fifth part looked at the beginnings of a German women's movement around 1840–1860. The sixth part was supposed to deal with the conflicts between the so-called proletarian and feminist women's movements around the end of the last century and the start of this one and to analyze the conflicts which brought about the great differences between the two movements. This was to be demonstrated using the lives of Clara Zetkin and Lily Braun, and here I wanted to present a few theses meant to explain why the socialist movement wanted to split up the women's movement, that is to say, to bring these matters out into the open. In the seventh part I hoped to use documentary footage and wanted also to find a few women still living who could share their memories about the battles of women in various political camps in the Weimar Republic, their attempts to join together different parties in a union against fascism, and their failure. The last part was supposed to deal with the new German women's movement and especially the campaigns against Paragraph 218. In no way did I want to do all of these films by myself, how could I have anyway, because they involve such a large amount of material and such a huge period of time, but nonetheless I at least thought the TV stations might be interested. Simply in terms of concerns linked to political education or, put in another way, pluralism. Because none of these subjects had been dealt with *at all.* I thought there would at least be enough interest to finance initially one or two scripts. But the response was close to nonexistent. I didn't even have a lengthier discussion with anyone nor did I receive any kind of hint in what sort of *form* such a project proposal would have to be submitted if it were to have a chance. Because that was an additional problem: I had no idea how one writes scripts and presents them appropriately. That still remains a problem at the film academies today, that most students only become aware of these things when they are this far along and their instructors do not pay much attention to these matters at all. In the film academies one supports certain methods meant to produced a finished film without taking a detour along the path of a closely conceived screenplay. And I think that's good. But without an appropriate screenplay next to no institution will give you a penny. This is a dilemma I ran into a number of times before it became clear to me exactly how serious it was. I can't work like this. In favor of my way of doing things, one can say in any case that I have never made a film that was a flop. Perhaps not each and every film I made was always really exciting—there were too many things working against me—but I never made anything I have to be ashamed of. My films never bombed in cinemas, either. In the case of my *Pillen* film (*Does the Pill Liberate?*, 1972), for instance, we received many letters repeatedly expressing the wish that the film be shown on the First Channel. It all but disappeared, nonetheless. These are all experiences one has as an individual, it takes a few years before one discovers something like a system behind all this. For me it was additionally hard because not only was I not taken seriously by the TV editors, I didn't have any support from my leftist colleagues with whom I worked. Their support ceased in that instant when I became a feminist and started to hear them tell me my films would split the working class. One can laugh about all of this today but of course this involved time and work. And the few women making films at the time either had the same problems, about which we didn't need to know anything because we didn't know each other, or they thought that they would be able to do everything for themselves quite well in the end. That all of this was a mistake has only become apparent in recent times.

3. *Rote Tage* (*Red Days*, 1972): This was supposed to be a film about everything known about menstruation, facts, myths, dreams, conventions, and customs. (It embraced the kind of materials found for instance in the special issue of *Courage* on menstruation.) I tried to do this project alone initially. Later I worked with Edna Politi in an attempt to find an appropriate TV partner. The project never went anywhere. After a short and mildly nauseated audience we were referred to the health feature department, ten minutes. All of the exposés represented weeks, in some cases months, of work.

4. *Gevierteilt oder im Stück* (*Quartered or in Pieces*, 1973?): a detailed exposé. Film with three main points. A blend of documentation and fiction. The first part dealt with the physical mutilation of women, insofar as known, for instance the cutting of clitorises, in known and less known cultures. The attempt in this way to say something about the identity of women. The mutilations from head to toe. Using pictures, photographs, sketches, stories, I wanted to depict in the second part of

the film the story of Malwida von Meysenburg, a German writer living around 1850, telling about the first train trips she took alone. Her stories moved me greatly because they describe exactly how women learn things that men take for granted. The third part was supposed to draw conclusions appropriate for the contemporary situation. I conceived it as a documentary part with women from the women's movement. Cost estimate: 200,000 marks.

5. A project submitted to WDR (1973): interviews with the few women still alive from the first German women's movement, questions about their experiences, the attempt to preserve a bit of history. A year later a series very reminiscent of my own appeared on the same channel.

6. 1973 or 1974: a crime thriller about Paragraph 218. An expanded script. "One can't make a crime thriller with this kind of subject matter." The argument would be repeated in the case of *Overkill.*

7. *Lysistrata* (1975): expanded script. About love among the jetset. Production costs at the time: about 700,000 marks. About questions of identity: older woman—younger man, social stereotypes, sexual self-consciousness. Also: the influence of modern means of transportation on matters of the heart, what do distances mean, how are they overcome, what do they depend on (e.g., power shortages, strikes)? How does one deal with these things?

8. Film and video material shot from time to time at various gatherings of the women's movement. Still no money to edit or process it. Too many occasions that might have been important where I had no money to rent equipment or people who could have helped me. For a long time there were no camerawomen, no women to do sound, and on many occasions men weren't admitted. This caused additional problems, not the least of which was the quality of the material shot when one had to work with nonprofessionals.

9. *Overkill:* script written with Edward Zoch. First version submitted to numerous TV stations and other institutions. Each rejection contained a different argument: from "excellent literature" to the sentence, "Aren't you aware that the federal elections are being held next year?" or "How can one dare to combine emancipatory thematics with such a highly controversial political subject matter?"

10. *Der subjektive Faktor (The Subjective Factor).* Not rejected, in fact actually accepted, but with reservations. Instead of the production contract previously agreed on, I am supposed to sign a script contract with the hitch that I will automatically be giving up all of the rights to the script. The TV money alone is not enough to make the film. It is supposed to be a feature film to be shown in cinemas. The script would seem to fit the stipulations for Berlin subsidy money. *Das kleine Fern-*

sehpiel no longer is willing to support films that one insists on showing in the cinema before they are screened on television. Berlin money, FFA money, BMI (Federal Ministry of the Interior), *Kuratorium*, etc., are all affected. Production costs: 500,000 marks.

In *tip* (no. 5, 1980), I read an interview with Thomas Brasch about his "undramatic change of country." Just like many other women who for a long time have suffered or still suffer from an unspoken professional proscription, I am fascinated by dissidents from the GDR. Not only because they all find support quickly—which they deserve. The whole climate surrounding the way many men from the GDR change countries throws a telling light on "male justice." The woman at their side is always thrown out as well—sometimes even more than one, in the case of [Rudolf] Bahro, but never the reverse in the case of female dissidents. No matter, Thomas Brasch says in the interview, so naturally, a naturalness that fascinates many women, "It was simply the case that the things I wrote in the GDR weren't published or performed—for reasons which I in part could comprehend."

The question that poses itself is which country we could emigrate to. Only a rhetorical question, of course.

Courage was a feminist monthly that was published in West Berlin.—Brasch was a dissident writer who, together with his companion, the actress Katharina Thalbach, left the GDR. He later become a filmmaker, director of Engel aus Eisen (Angels of Iron) *and* Domino.*—Rudolf Bahro is another prominent dissident who moved to the West. He is the author of* Die Alternative: Zur Kritik des real existierenden Sozialismus (*Cologne: Europäische Verlags-anstalt, 1977*), trans. David Fernbach as* The Alternative in Eastern Europe (*London: New Left Books, 1978*).

14. Alexander Kluge

Theses about the New Media (1983)

1. All films are survival pictures.
2. Film = movie = the *medium of feelings* (not of distribution figures, nor of Beta-Film, not of producers, also not of authors).
3. All feelings believe in a happy end.
4. One cannot choose the future. Not even alternatives.
5. In the near future films will be produced for five main markets with accompanying submarkets (cinema, television, video, satellite, local).

6. A film that tries to fit into all of these markets cannot be interesting for any one of them. A film that is specifically designed for one of the five markets will almost always be interesting for the other markets.

7. Films that are lethal to the survival chance of German films are ones that do not fit into any of the five markets and are not art either. Anything that is not at all radical cannot survive.

8. After twenty years of trying out possibilities and of the widest development in New German Film, one can expect decisiveness in the dangerous situation confronting us. One cannot eternally remain *particularly mediocre.*

9. The decisions lie in one's position. Here there is no freedom: either a film takes a position or it does not, someone has contact or has none. *One cannot not take a position.* Formation or nonformation, avenues of distribution, form content of films, answering, remaining silent—the freedom to do all this ends at the one border: one cannot not take a position.

10. "The conclusion is that whenever possible the public must be informed" (A. Hitchcock).

11. Information is a matter of context. The plot action in German films can be shorter.

12. The renewal of the feature film from the spirit of documentation. Feature films can take more facticity: more efficient forms of information are needed. Most feature film projects stretch an idea worth ten minutes into a laborious ninety minutes in order to look like a full-length project.

13. Each of the five markets of the future poses a challenge to films. In keeping with these challenges art works as well as new kinds of utilitarian wares are conceivable for each of the markets. Attempts to circumvent this challenge in the form of watered-down, fivefold amphibian products, be they art works or utilitarian wares, are *out of the question.*

14. As long as video cassettes look like books, film can relate to this medium as a friendly relative.

15. Video cassettes demand films that can be shown repeatedly. Just like a record. No one buys records if you know their "plot" after one listening. The enigmatic receives a new opportunity.

16. Intimacy and the public sphere are separated in our culture. None of the new media (and certainly not public television) can bring intimacy and the public sphere together again. It must be noted that the division of the future into five markets amounts to an external division, one that relates only to the means and routes of distribution. There is an internal division, according to the positions: whether someone eternally

accepts the exclusion of the most important and intimately verifiable questions from the public sphere or not. The feature film can step over every border.

17. Particularly because films do not duplicate reality, as the Lumière Brothers still assumed, that which is real (authenticity) about film must be right. Particularly because film is fiction, it dare not fudge in its elements. That is the central core of the position that seeks to survive.

18. Cinema dare not be balanced in any way.

Beta-Film, headed by the controversial figure Leo Kirch, the object of much scrutiny in Der Spiegel and Stern, is a company that purchases the rights to films and sells them to media concerns.—The Hitchcock quotation is from François Truffaut, Hitchcock (New York: Simon and Schuster, 1967), p. 52.

15. Volker Schlöndorff
Zimmermann's Execution Directives (1983)

In a Paris suburb, in the soundproof room of a studio, a member of the French nobility parleys in front of a microphone. Background conversation for the salon of the Duchess of Guermantes. Two telephone calls interrupt my work: from Munich news of agitation about film subsidy matters, from London comes Hans-Werner Henze's request for a couple of lines for the soprano voice of Odette de Crécy, who deludes the jealous Swann with her lies.

During the afternoon I read the text of Minister Zimmermann's latest film decree and wonder whether Ornella Muti might not dub her voice in the German version. Her childhood is well behind her, but German was her mother tongue, because her mother is unmistakably from Riga. The question remains: can Proust's Odette de Crécy speak with a Baltic accent?

I wish Mr. Zimmermann could answer my question. Instead of this he hatches new decrees, ones meant to hinder projects like my Proust adaptation in the future. He'd rather have Heino instead of Henze and Purzer instead of Proust. How gladly I'd like to follow his challenge to make only good entertaining films. I've tried. The titles are long forgotten: *Die Moral der Ruth Halbfass (The Morals of Ruth Halbfass)*, for instance, and *Übernachtung in Tirol (Overnight Stay in the Tyrol)*. Popular literature is not my line. The more difficult the textual source, the greater the challenge. But that isn't a recipe either.

I try to explain to my French friends, the blue-blooded ones and the sans-culottes, what is at issue: in Germany we have two sorts of film subsidy (oh, lala), an economic one and a cultural one.

Someone asks: *où est la différence?* I declare that here as well there is a small difference. It is for us no small matter of controversy (even if statistics support this) that quality and success are related. At this point several people shake their heads: one does not discuss matters of taste. Who nowadays pretends to know what quality is? I object: we make a clear distinction; the Ministry of the Interior is responsible for the economic aspect of film. "Film is art," someone counters.—"We don't have (thank God) a ministry for that, culture is regulated by the individual states," I answer.—"Aha, then that means that the Federal film prizes are awarded by the states?"—"Wrong, by the Minister of the Interior."—"He's responsible for the police and foreigners."—"Right. But in his free time he plays patron of film art."—"Better to have a patron with bad taste than none at all. Yours is after all a rich country . . ."—"A miserly one: there's only five million a year."

I'll spare you the rest of the conversation. It is clear that from [Hermann] Höcherl to [Gerhart] Baum to Zimmermann the quality of German films has been recognized by the Minister of the Interior. Due to a lack of interest in these matters or to avoid sliding on the slippery ice of the art world, the ministers of the interior have left their decisions to a group of artists, writers, journalists, and church leaders, with the unquestioned conviction that among colleagues one distinguishes equally relentlessly between the inferior and superior, that is to say also rewards the mediocre. Exotic sorts are tolerated for their local color and seen as otherwise inoffensive.

Do I have to be the one to respond to Zimmermann? He doesn't listen to me anyway. Don't the conservatives and the liberals have just as many decent people as other groups for whom art is not a luxury but rather a necessity of life? They shouldn't put up with a minister who like others before him appeals to the healthy common sense of the people and instead of art demands entertainment for the masses. Weren't the conservatives always the ones who defended art against the masses? They should be the ones who feel more challenged by these film execution decrees than I do.

The fact is that everything that previously fostered quality is being done away with. The committee of writers and artists (in the Federal Ministry of the Interior) previously responsible for scripts and film projects is being robbed of its powers. A committee of lawyers, church and television functionaries (on the Film Subsidy Board) is taking over control and deciding what is worthy of support and what isn't. At stake is a total of five million marks (what a disgrace, our culture nation), but nonetheless petty criticism is raised to the power of an unreasonable bureaucracy: a twelve-member committee of lawyers (Film Subsidy Board) determines in the future along with another twenty-five-member committee (of the Ministry of Interior) whose hands Mr. Minister will shake when he awards "the Golden Cup." The first committee (FFA) has an eye out for potential commercial successes, the second committee scrutinizes the artistic merit; Mr. Minister, with his new and highly personal standards of cleanliness control, recognizes finished films.

Doesn't this procedure defer to Moscow? I wonder whether the Ministry of the Interior has been infiltrated.

What luck that I as an author, director, and producer am a free businessman and don't have to check with anyone to make decisions. Given this model I would have been finished, artistically and economically, long ago. A modicum of free market economy would do the Ministry of the Interior and the Film Subsidy Board good. Instead of seeing to the editing of my film, I sit here and formulate these angry words: your decrees are suffocating the German film, Mr. Minister, and your directives, Mrs. Film Subsidy Board. I realize (unhappily) that as a German filmmaker I have to weather the American competition without any protection, but I won't put up with the chicaneries of an arrogant clique of bureaucrats any longer! I'm not asking for the thanks of the fatherland, but a helping hand now and again would help me more than a kick in the pants.

Mr. Zimmermann, are you really afraid of culture? That would be understandable in the case of a Minister of the Interior. After all art lives from conflict, it expresses conflict and occasionally brings things to a head. This can be most disquieting for a minister otherwise responsible for the police. If the cultural subsidy of film—and this is your bailiwick alone—is such a burden for you, why don't you pass it on to the minister presidents of the states? There are still lovers of the muses, in fact even among those who voted for you.

I want to stop here. I don't want to curse and scream bloody murder, I'm trying to understand why the Minister of the Interior is interested in film at all. For all my love of my profession I am cognizant of our relative insignificance. Certainly writers, musicians, painters, and sculptors shape our culture more crucially than filmmakers. Why has a minister (and an entire government) singled us out? The answer is simple and tempers one's feelings of vanity: because film alone is governed by a federal law. Once again it's a vicarious war: if we filmmakers are to be silenced, others are meant as well. When F. J. Strauss, during a television visit to the editorial offices of *Die Zeit*, railed against "Günther Schlöndorff," it was clear that this slip of tongue was directed not only against Heinrich Kluge and Herbert Herzog, but also Alexander Böll and Werner Grass.

A decree that wreaks vengeance and desires censorship needs a protective, and, if possible, Christian, shield. The Press Speaker has found it: Mr. Minister wants to save the German film. This is his last chance. No doubt, German film has smaller audiences. Wouldn't it be nice if we could win them back by decree. (Germans buy German wares?)

No one knows exactly why we Germans, in contrast to the Italians and French, not to mention the Americans, would rather see other people on the screen, anyone but ourselves. It's clear nonetheless that if there is an audience for the German film at all, at home and abroad, we will need a German film of good quality to find it.

At this point the Minister speaks up and with him an entire lobby: what's lacking is entertainment. One longs for the weepies of the fifties. From now on we're only going to demand films for the readers of *Bunte*, declares the Minister. And means of course to bless commercial successes. What a laugh, the readers of the *Bunte* don't go to the movies, they sit in front of the tube.

OK, the Minister might say, film belongs on television anyway. Cinema is (for the police as well) an opaque business, it plays in the dark; all sorts of elements hide out there, communicate and laugh and cry together and dream about all kinds of things in a way we can't oversee. Who knows what's brewing there? People should stay at home and watch the old Ufa films, *Heimatfilme* from the fifties, and when we've run out of those we will make certain to subsidize new films along these lines for television.

This is where the logical circle of the decree closes. It's not a matter of a few filmmakers, it's also not a matter of preserving German film (the nation can also do without it), it's a matter of entertainment for everyone, it's a matter of valium. Television, the new media, cable, and the satellites rest firmly in the hands of the new government.

It's only a matter now of what will be programmed. A few artists resist stubbornly, refer to their talents, and even find some favor among audiences. Yes, I repeat: well-crafted films find a following. The best German films were also the most successful ones. The list is well-known, less well-known (only Mr. Purzer knows for sure) is the list of flops that pretended to please the mass market. *E.T.* was seen as an outsider and was rejected by the large distributors. Spielberg took a chance and produced the film himself. Foolproof projects bombed. All producers would agree that one cannot foresee a film's possible success. Only bureaucrats seem to think they know better.

There is only a single formula that will win the German film an audience, enrich our lives, and give wings to our hopes: quality.

Art and commerce are not mutually exclusive. Entertaining serial productions from the U.S.A. are less expensive for us because they've already made a profit at home. Culture is Europe's strength, it is the last of our natural resources, and it is up to us to see that it still flourishes at a time when the last bits of coal and oil are being drained from the earth. But I think it's shabby to have to defend art in terms of its commercial potential.

I realize that most distributors and exhibitors are in the market for successful entertainment films; I realize, that many politicians yearn for soporific *Heimatfilme;* I realize, that a certain Minister President yearns for the primeval which he deems healthy; but I do not understand why a Minister of the Interior, a conservative one at that, forgoes his opportunity to foster quality, giving up our national identity for a few dollars more, and wanting to take leave of European cultural history. If I had voted for him, I would have him impeached.

Heino is a pop singer well known in Germany.—Manfred Purzer is an old guard film director and an influential conservative film politician.—Bunte Illustrierte is a glossy weekly magazine published by the large Burda concern.—The Minister President referred to in the final paragraph is Bavaria's Franz Josef Strauss.—The essay as a whole describes Schlöndorff's work on the film Eine Liebe von Swann (Swann in Love, 1983), *an adaptation of portions from Marcel Proust's* A la Recherche du temps perdu.

16. Wim Wenders
The *Filmverlag* against the Authors* (1985)

"Finally in the cinema" was the sales pitch of the distributor, and seeing that many people will probably have thought that the battle about *Paris, Texas* was finally over and done with. And many may well have thought that the great to-do was only a clever advertising ploy. But it wasn't, God knows it wasn't.

What was behind it all will become clear in the case that is beginning on February 21, 1985 in the Berlin State Court, proceedings I've been awaiting impatiently for months now. "Finally in the cinema" was how things seemed from the perspective of the distributor, the so-called *Filmverlag* "of the authors," who had succeeded in a number of summary hearings, with preliminary injunctions, to protect its interests in a merciless and groundless power struggle.

For my part, I say: "Finally in court." Finally a hope that there might be light in this shadowy matter and that one can calmly depict what this was all about. Finally then a chance for truth and with that perhaps even in the end justice. What was it all about?

It was about a battle between a production company and a distributor. The object was a film, *Paris, Texas.* There are enough crooked deals in film business, people are lied to and cheated, many a person gets taken to the cleaners, and many wake up one morning and find themselves betrayed and sold out. That happens. That's also how things went in this case, but they need not have been the reason for all the brouhaha. At least not a reason for yanking the matter into the public arena. I'd hold my tongue and start my next film if it were only a "private feud" at issue here. But something else is at stake here. Why we're litigating, even though *Paris, Texas* has for a long time now been "finally in the cinema": not only a film and a small independent production company were lied to and cheated here, betrayed and sold out, but an idea, an entire concept.

This concept is the *"Autorenfilm,"* or whatever you want to call that which once was the "New German Film." This "New German Film" was for a decade the strongest bastion in the world protecting the idea that cinema is not only a business, but also a form of expression, and therefore not only a question of cash, but also one of art. Nowhere else than in the FRG was there such an open space for the idea of the "independent film." And this idea for a long time had a homeland created by the filmmakers themselves, in the institution, the *Filmverlag der Autoren.*

That this institution in the meanwhile has become perverted into its opposite and no longer serves "the authors," but rather exploits or ruins them, that's what this present case is all about, and for that reason we can't let things slide. This story between the *Filmverlag der Autoren* and *Paris, Texas* will make it clear that independent producing is no longer possible in Germany as long as the apparatus that distributes films increases its powers to the point that it actually becomes more powerful than the people who create these films and produce them while taking on the entire risk and sole responsibility.

And when this power also pairs itself with stupidity and cynicism, then things get really sinister.

In the hopes of bringing a little light into this darkness, we're going to persist, in court.

For an account of the Filmverlag der Autoren in the mideighties, see two articles by Helmut H. Diederichs: "Der ungeliebte Mäzen: Der 'Filmverlag der Autoren' seit der Übernahme durch Rudolf Augstein," epd Film, September 1985, pp. 22–26; and " 'Futura Filmverlag'—Augstein hat verkauft," epd Film, October 1985, p. 9.

III

Popular Approaches: Generic Models and Utopian Designs

What shape was the "new German feature film" going to take? Clearly, the young filmmakers could hardly start from zero, even if myths of new beginnings had had—and still maintained—a decisive appeal for cultural producers in postwar Germany. From its very inception, the Young German Film vacillated between *Kunst und Kommerz*, between an essayistic-deconstructive-artbound cinema and a more accessible film cast along lines of the classical narrative. The largest successes of New German Film in the seventies would come of a singular blend of radical discursiveness and conventional appeal. It is hardly the case, though, as adversaries have been saying repeatedly since the midsixties, that West German filmmakers gave no thought to their audiences and instead cultivated a rarified and onanistic *Autorenkino*, of interest only to a small circle of friends and cineastes—and death at the box office. (For many years the quip circulated, "Life is too short to waste time watching Young German films.") Shortly after the Oberhausen Manifesto appeared, it was apparent that anything but unanimity existed regarding the often invoked new German feature film. It was equally clear that not every *Jungfilmer* wanted to challenge the conventional realistic narrative. Over the years, the confrontation with the seamless, straightforward, and entertaining mode of presentation one knew well from Hollywood productions and domestic variations prompted different reactions. The responses ranged widely: some opportunistic spirits, who, after all, had grown up surrounded by the culture of Allied occupiers, fully embraced American cinema, its patterns of recognition, its stars, its flair. There were others who, having learned much from French auteurists, saw subversion, originality, and invention where most people only viewed the same old commercial fare. On occasion their paeans to American film take on an epiphanous quality, without a doubt. Still others approached the realist narrative with a mind to refurbish it, to transform it in their critical exercises. And, to be sure, a large number of West German filmmakers, students of Horkheimer and Adorno and ardent enemies of the "culture industry," would reject mainstream cinema as a vehicle of manipulation, a means of social domination. As a new wave of genre films made by young directors flood West German cinemas in the mid-eighties, comedies like Niki List's *Müllers Büro (Müller's Office)* and Peter Timm's *Meier*, Spielbergesque effusions such as Roland Emmerich's *Joey*, gripping dramas in the vein of Peter F. Bringmann's *Der Schneemann (The Snow Man)* and Carl Schenkel's *Abwärts (Out of Order)*, to say nothing of the resounding commercial successes by Xaver Schwarzenberger/Otto Waalkes, *Otto—der Film (Otto—the Film)* and Doris Dörrie, *Männer (Men)*, it is important to remember that they did not come out of the blue and do not necessarily signal the "selling out" of New German Film and sound the death knell of *Autorenkino*. From its beginnings, New German Film has not lacked voices in favor of more popular strategies, individuals smitten by cinematic convention, directors hardly averse to the prospect of commercial success.

17. Eckhart Schmidt

". . . Preferably Naked Girls" (1968)

Jet-Generation wasn't supposed to be my first, but rather my third feature film. But *Nach Amerika (To America)*, my first script, soured at Houwer Productions (Marran Gosov will direct it soon) and *Der kalte Kuss (The Cold Kiss)*, written for Roxy-Film, fell through due to financial reasons.

To America and *The Cold Kiss* were relatively light subjects with few characters and a dominant, somewhat crime- and action-oriented plot; they probably would have been ideal debut films. Today I am nevertheless—for commercial as well as artistic reasons—very happy that these projects were not produced.

Jet-Generation is, in terms of handiwork, a complex and difficult film: five main characters throughout the entire action, fourteen other figures with a precise function, and more than sixty locations are, I think, a challenge not to be underestimated in a debut film.

There were two production possibilities for *Jet-Generation*: I decided to work with Roger Fritz, because he, a former photographer for large periodicals, knows the world that my film seeks to present better than any other producer and I therefore could count on his understanding for all sorts of necessities. At the time it still was not clear that Fritz would play the lead role. We looked together for a suitable actor for the role of Raoul (necessary qualifications: attractive appearance, natural vitality, international appeal), but we had to give up: this kind of character apparently does not exist in Germany and the foreign actors I considered (e.g., Tomas Milian from *Kill Django!*) were not available. Fritz fit the role almost exactly and so I decided to use him, although I had my misgivings about having the producer stand in front of the camera in the lead role. We had, to be sure, some difficulties. But they did not escalate, except in the case of two scenes (above all the scene in the fashion boutique), so much so that the film might have suffered. Roger Fritz will no doubt make his mark as an actor now after *Jet-Generation*. It was more difficult to find a female lead—a young American woman in the film—who is present in almost every scene of the film. Necessary qualifications for the role were: attractive appearance, international appeal, and a face reflecting a certain innocence and at the same time a certain worldliness. And talent. Jane Fonda or Carol Lynley came closest to my conception, although I at no moment fancied I might be able to get either of them. We started looking in Germany (we looked at fifty girls or more), then in Paris (we combed through all the model agencies and actress agencies, interviewed the girls we found interesting and had them do screen tests), and finally in London. After hundreds of photos and composites and roughly thirty screen tests we narrowed things down to a handful of candidates. We chose Chrissie Shrimpton, Jean's sister. After less than a week of shooting, things didn't work out with her anymore: we stopped the production. It wasn't that Chrissie lacked talent, but rather she was not up to the emotional and physical demands of the role in a foreign surrounding. The search began again. The film as well: this time with Dgin Moeller in the lead role, a topnotch model from Paris used to hard and demanding work.

Jet-Generation is not an improvisational film, but rather a film whose plot and dialogue were exactly laid down in the script. A question of potential interest is whether what I intended as I wrote the script has become a film. Anyone who has read the script and then sees the film will, I hope, answer in the affirmative. I kept to the script as closely as humanly possible. Nonetheless: I did not close off new ideas and accents. In this way, for instance, the second male lead, Jürgen Draeger, whom I absolutely wanted to have, was given more lines than had been foreseen in the original script. I also wrote two love scenes for him: a love scene with Isi ter Jung and a scene between Fritz and Draeger. Working with Jürgen Draeger was fun. We only clashed once: whether he should stop on the stairs one step earlier or later. Today we laugh about it.

Further scenes I added: fashion photographer Khan with whom we shot part of the interiors, was the impetus for a scene in which Raoul takes a photograph from his bed with a monitor. From another photographer for magazines came the idea to use the naked mannequins on Lake Starnberg. Finally, I also cut several photo-taking scenes into actual events like for instance the Munich Week of Fashion or the opening of a boutique.

This debut film did not provide any noteworthy surprises. This of course does not mean that my satisfaction with *Jet-Generation* will be the same as that of my former film critic colleagues. From the start I didn't intend to make a film for cineastes (of course I would be happy if they liked the film as well), but rather for the widest audience possible. Even as a critic I was always more interested in the so-called commercial films than the so-called art films.

What I like: a solid, linear story and characters who are distinguished more by what they do than by what they say (in this regard *Jet-Generation* is anything but an action film—it is a romantic film). I like: attractive and interesting faces, costumes and visual effects in front of the camera, and a camera (Gernot Roll) that serves the action and doesn't rape it with filters. I prefer filming a naked girl rather than chattering about problems. That sounds profane. I can't help it: I think everyone should make the kind of films he likes.

Eckhart Schmidt represented Young German Film's more commercially oriented sector during the late sixties. He ceased making films throughout the entire seventies, devoting himself to film criticism (including numerous attacks on the New German Film) and occasional scripts. Schmidt made a comeback as a director in 1982 with a violent portrayal of adulation that turns into fanaticism, Der Fan (The Fan, 1982). *His subsequent work includes* Die Story (The Story, 1984), Loft (1985), Alphacity (1985), *and* Das Wunder (The Miracle, 1985).

18. Wim Wenders

Emotion Pictures (Slowly Rockin' On) (1970)

Sergeant Rutledge, The Man Who Shot Liberty Valance, The Last Hurrah, The Horse Soldiers, The Searchers, She Wore a Yellow Ribbon,

Wagonmaster, Three Godfathers, Fort Apache, My Darling Clementine, Stagecoach.

These Westerns by John Ford and perhaps several more were shown in Munich during the last few months. Only for one or two days, often just in the late shows. In bad copies, often poorly dubbed, that hurts, but what's worse is having to put up with this audience that constantly reacts ever more impatiently, which makes it clear that the horrible Z-films have taken over the future, images that obstruct your vision and sounds that hit you over the head.

To what other films does one want to go these days outside of a few exceptions? Seeing there becomes a question of pure missing: I miss the friendliness, the care, the thoroughness, the sureness, the earnestness, the calm, the humaneness of John Ford's films, I miss the faces which are never forced to do anything, the landscapes which are never only back-grounds, the emotions which are never importunate nor comic, the stories, which even when they are funny, never make fun of things, the actors who constantly and intensely offer variations of themselves, I miss the blustering likes of John Wayne, the hardbitten Henry Fonda, the upright Constance Towers, shy Vera Miles, humble John Qualen, Irish Victor McLaglen, maternal Jane Darwell, rugged Russell Simpson, boy-ish Harry Carey Jr. The Comanches who are in *The Searchers* have the names: Away Luna, Billy Yellow, Bob Many Mules, Exactly Sonnie Betsuie, Feather Hat Jr., Harry Black Horse, Jack Tin Horn, Many Mules Son, Percy Shooting Star!, Pete Grey Eyes, Pipe Line Begishe, Smile White Sheep.

John Ford has stopped making films.

The new American films are hopeless, like the new unusable iron pinball machinery from Chicago which makes it impossible to have any fun playing pinball again.

American music is more and more making up for the sensuality which is being lost in films: out of the merging of Blues and Rock and Country Music something has come about which cannot only be experi-enced aurally, but also visually, in images, as space and time.

This music is above all the music of the American West, whose conquering was the subject of John Ford's films, and whose second conquering is the subject of this music, which instead of on the "Euro-pean" East Coast has developed between Nashville and the West Coast of the United States. In San Francisco and Los Angeles the American cinema has its roots. But motion pictures have in the meanwhile become synonymous with music.

In *Easy Rider* the film images are already superfluous, because they only really illustrate the music, not the other way around, and are only vestiges of a clarity which has developed much more markedly in the music than in the images which are vitiated and cold and only remind one of films which had a beauty, a nostalgia, a pathos of their own, one they filled out and carried themselves.

"Born To Be Wild" by Steppenwolf or the song "Wasn't Born to Follow" by the Byrds are in reality the film about the search for America, not the images of Peter Fonda.

> I used to walk on the city streets,
> Now I wandered for a while,
> And I never found my happiness,
> Till I moved to the countryside.
> Now follow me all quietly,
> I am riding on the trail
> Away from smog and traffic flog
> Where all the pigs have tails.
> Oh dear shady groves,
> It's shady grove, my honey,
> Shady grove, my true love,
> I am bound for shady grove.

"Shady Grove" by the Quicksilver Messenger Service (Capitol Records, SKAO-391): images of emotions, the likes of which you only find at few moments in the cinema, no blurred or sentimental images, but ones marked by a clear and self-conscious pathos.

As a live recording the double album, "Live Dead" by the Grateful Dead (Warner Brothers, WD 1830 distributed by Decca) is perhaps the clearest and best example by a West Coast group. Quite slow and calm and effusive and melancholy movements and images.

Long shots of California, in color and cinemascope.

"Retrospective: The Best of Buffalo Springfield" (Atco SD 33-283).

"3614 Jackson Highway." By Cher (Atco SD-298).

"Spiritual Guidance": Sonny Bono. You remember Sonny and Cher, singing "The Beat Goes On," 1965. "The Ballad of Easy Rider," by the Byrds (CBS, 63795).

> If you'd been watching the city streets,
> You can't see them get much greener,
> And I'd know, where we're going to
> Our heads are feelin' much cleaner
> Oh, shady grove. . .

The best record by the Rolling Stones is their only American one: "LIVEr Than You'll Ever Be," and the title is as good as the music, it's a pirated copy of cuts from the American tour of the Stones last year. More lively and powerfully and metallically and aggressively they've never sung on a record. "All right, here we go, slowly rockin' on," Mick Jagger says at one point, one has never been able to hear such long guitar solos by Keith Richards. The numbers are: "Carol," "Gimme Shelter," "Sympathy for the Devil," "I'm Free," "Live with Me," "Love in Vain," "Midnight Rambler," "Little Queenie," "Honky Tonk Woman," "Street Fighting Man." With some luck you can get the record even in Germany, likewise the already legendary "Great White Wonder" by Bob Dylan, where one can hear thirteen numbers from around the time "John Wesley Harding" came out, numbers which Columbia would never have released, among others "Tears of Rage," "Mighty Quinn," "I Shall Be Released," and "Wheels on Fire."

There are still no "pirated copies" of Ford's films, but one perhaps should start making some.

Wenders reviewed Dennis Hopper's Easy Rider *at some length in another context. See his notice, "Easy Rider. Ein Film wie sein Titel," Filmkritik, November 1969, pp. 673–78.*

19. Christian Ziewer
The Aesthetics of the 'Worker Film' * (1972)

Two ideas were the starting point for *Liebe Mutter, mir geht es gut* (*Dear Mother, I'm Doing Fine*, 1972):

1. It had become very clear to my colleague Klaus Wiese and myself, when investigating the situation in factories during the recession of 1966–67, how great the difficulties were for most of the workers hit by layoffs, short-time work or cuts in wages if they wanted to get beyond the experience of their individual fates in order to acquire more extensive knowledge of the politics of the running of their factories, of the economic aspect of the total social framework and of the possibilities for the employees of changing their situation.

2. In the English and Italian films which we valued and even the few German television productions which analyze similar problems, there has not been sufficient concern either with individual fate or with social problems over and above the personal.

In addition to this came the experiences which I had had in my work with target groups in the Brandenburg area. There it had become clear how receptive, almost zealous, the people we were addressing were when films confronted their concrete situation, their direct needs. For needs did not just arise out of passive consumer attitudes but also from self-awareness and knowledge—that is, if the viewers had their situation presented as being open to change, as a situation to which they do not have to succumb. Then the workers gained access to sophisticated points of view, to principles of analysis, to abstractions. The saying that "They cannot think beyond their four walls" was no longer valid.

Guidelines for the script were as follows:

—Extreme accuracy in the description of everyday life.

—Analytical deductions about the different interests which are clearly defined and thus determine social conflict.

I tried to take both these aspects into account in the first drafts of the script by taking up the dialogue with those who had initially assisted me with reports of their work situation after I had made lengthy investigations: organized and unorganized workers, shop stewards, shop committees. The final form of the shooting script gradually emerged through a process of proposals and counterproposals and revisions being made after much criticism and deliberation. In this way a range of scenes changed and developed.

The longer we looked for ideas for scenes where the dialectic of production and worker existence (which is generally viewed as "something personal and individual") could be posed, the more we were compelled to give up the dramatic technique of story as continuous action. We had to introduce the "epic I," which took up a position outside the events (commentaries, titles, self-portrayals). Where connections were not made openly transparent in the human relationships, montage and editing produced new forms of narrative. In this phase of work, places in the filming became significant, where, during the *mise-en-scène,* the action was protracted and had to be brought to a standstill. Breaks should encourage the viewer to take up a position and by referring to his own experience, he should reach a greater understanding at these moments.

It was surprising to see how ready the workers were to forgo a well-formed "dramatic plot" once they were motivated to use creatively their own fantasy. This concern with taking control of one's own destiny led to the form of an "epic film."

At the same time as trying to provide the viewer with the appropriate stimulus, I was also trying to achieve a similar image of change in the filming of material which embraces elements, some of which are spontaneously authentic and some of which are constructed and static. Each of the four sections in the film contains some of the naturalism and obsession with detail of other television plays. Yet the realism does not arise as a result of pure imitation. The inclusion of information which was beyond the immediate experience of the viewers provides a context for each of the everyday events so that these may be sifted, appraised, and revised. A multi-layered complex of signs mediates each piece of information. Its clearly constructed nature makes the author very evident. He is not supposed to persuade but rather to encourage greater perception.

For a comprehensive exploration of Ziewer's career and the "Worker Film" in general, see Richard Collins and Vincent Porter's monograph, WDR and the Arbeiterfilm: Fassbinder, Ziewer and others *(London: British Film Institute, 1981).*

20. Robert Van Ackeren
Relationships, Reality, and Realism* (1977)

Many films really only tell a superficial story, and because one also needs people, one of necessity creates some in one's head. In the case of these film people one notices that they only carry the plot and are uninteresting as people, lacking any intensity. *Das andere Lächeln (The Other Smile, 1978)* is above all a film about people. The narrative action stems from their behavior, their wishes and desires alone, and because they are exciting people, I think their story, the story of the film, is very exciting. And that's how the film was made: I filmed people and I tell a story with them, and not the other way around.

The most important thing about the figures—and the story as well—is their high degree of dynamism. All of the figures are going through a process, one grounded in their persons, one they cannot avoid. The nature of this process interests me, the almost compulsive changes, especially the metamorphosis of women: how a woman dives into the identity of her girlfriend, occupying it with such precise acrobatics that not even a shadow remains behind. Her exploratory venture, from the fingernails to her sex: everyday vampirism, but not viewed metaphysically as in most genre films, but rather seen as being bound up in concrete social conditions. That's the one side, the other is: a woman calls upon her girlfriend and in a certain way dresses her up as a double. Like someone setting traps, she brings her successor into the house and increasingly pushes this person into her own role. This symbiosis fascinates me. For all of the horror about it, it has a strange harmony to it. This relationship between the women is for me the actual love story of the film, not the love story with the man.

In the relation of the women to the man, I try to tell something about the interchangeability of such love relationships, ones that are actually only subjugation relationships. Neither of the two women can develop her own personality around the man, each is constrained, because in keeping with the way things are, they only submit to his premises and do not develop any of their own.

Most romantic relationships irritate me because they are interchangeable: someone loves someone, the relationship breaks up, and in the end one simply loves someone else, with the same persistence and stubbornness and the same illusions and misconceptions. In this story one also finds the same signal values which the persons develop for each other: the signal value of the attributes which one carries into a love, which in fact even make it possible for someone else to fall in love with them and to move from falling in love to being in love. Bourgeois behavior, bourgeois values, the points of orientation for the figures in this film, all of their rituals—everything which is considered normal and commonplace—have for me a very oppressive and strange aspect: something frightening. It's therefore all the more crucial that one does not reduce this frightening element down to something extraordinary, but rather shows that it is something quite commonplace.

There are a lot of things going on around me which move me. They have an effect on me and I try to understand them. These are my experiences with reality and with people. Then one goes on to communicate these experiences, one's views and critical insights. In doing so the intensity of one's perception is most crucial. That's how scripts come about, that's how films come about. I only make films about things with which I have an intense relationship, a relationship in the widest sense. Women often stand in the foreground of my films. I am more able to comprehend the ways in which women act than the specifically sexist mannerisms of men. I find most women more imaginative and creative than men.

I think all films out to imitate reality are hopeless, ones striving for authenticity by imitating: the well-known confusion of realism with naturalism. Realism has something to do with truth and one does not attain this by depicting surfaces. Every E.T.A. Hoffmann novella is more realistic than a newspaper.

See also Van Ackeren's essays on Ernst Lubitsch's Angel and That Uncertain Feeling, in Lubitsch, ed. Hans Helmut Prinzler and Enno Patalas (Munich/

Lucerne: Bucher, 1984), pp. 179–80 and 189–90. Also, "Nutte sucht
Dressman," tip, 25 February 1983, pp. 32–36.

21. Hark Bohm
Taking Leave of the Security of Esoteric Aesthetics (1977)

Cinema is the only medium whose roots, evolution, and importance
are due to the simple people Siegfried Kracauer once embodied in the
figure of the shopgirls. No other medium is owned as decisively by these
veritable representatives of an entire nation, a medium over which they
up until now have been only—but at least they have this chance—able to
dispose by casting their ballots at the box office.

I think German cineastes are learning to make films that better
relate to these owners' needs. The owners provided cinema an operating
base because they wanted to relive their own legends and experiences in a
form both familiar and surprising. Cinema is the mirror in which they
seek themselves both as individual and collective entities and if the
mirror reflects correctly, they do indeed recognize themselves in it. That
is the pleasure cinema provides.

I see that many German filmmakers are finding the courage to take
leave of the security of esoteric aesthetics, a realm lorded over by compla-
cent critics, without succumbing to the temptation to traffic in literature
and seek the protection of the recognized luminaries among German
writers. The German shopgirls of Kracauer's age found the stories by
these writers every bit as boring as their granddaughters do today.

I witness filmmakers here responding increasingly consciously to the
demands of the owners, the demand that they make a German cinema
oriented to the reality of the owners. One reason for the success of the
Karl May films and the films based on Simmel novels was surely that they
were at least German films even if they were made with foreign actors in
Yugoslavia and only offered a very nebulous view of the German nation.

I believe German filmmakers right now have a singular opportunity
in this medium's history, the opportunity to work directly for the owners
of the medium. This is perhaps the positive side of the collapse of the
traditional film industry, whose blind tax advisers were even too stupid to
invest at the right time in future generations who might have served their
interests—which led to a situation where most German filmmakers had
to become their own producers. As such they enjoy a previously unknown
freedom to attend to the interests of filmgoers.

The recent success of films like *Stroszek* by Werner Herzog, *Das Brot des Bäckers (The Baker's Bread)* by Erwin Keusch, or *Der amerikanische Freund (The American Friend)* by Wim Wenders confirms for me a tendency I saw at work and one that will continue in 1978. I also hope that my next film, currently being made with the working title *Von Kopf bis Fuss (From Head to Toe)*, will draw the necessary consequences from the claim that cinema is owned by the masses. And that the grandchildren of Kracauer's shopgirls will enjoy my film.

The title of the Kracauer essay is "Die kleinen Ladenmädchen gehen ins Kino" (1927).—Bohm's finished film bore the title Moritz, lieber Moritz *(Moritz, Dear Moritz, 1978).*

22. Niklaus Schilling

Cinema, Melodrama, and the World of Emotion* (1977)

One can say that the special qualities of German film are its countryside, its regions, the soil, and perhaps its people in general. And likewise its myths. A "German world of feelings" if you will, which can be an almost ideal cinematic subject. In this sense, the German films of the thirties, forties, and fifties have more to do with cinema than the films of the sixties and seventies. And our surroundings have lost nothing of their mythologies at all; and these are of interest to me.

It is really quite simple: cinema should involve the senses. I think of "cinema as an experiential realm," as an experiential form, something that makes it—or should make it—different than television. Seen in this light, film is by no stretch of the imagination merely to be equated with cinema. If there is anything I bemoan it is surely the increasing impoverishment of cinema, especially in the Federal Republic of Germany, where it actually has become a form more and more like television and connected to it. Once again we find among us a particularly fatal tendency not to trust the power of the filmic medium, but rather to construct films from the most classical literary sources available so that we might escape the danger of having to work with images and in that way tell our own stories. One prefers to produce visual sentences with verbal forms, to explain and edify.

Melodrama—what a strange concept: another cubbyhole in which one places scenes with crying men, childless, rich women, passionate love-hatreds, and setting suns. It also is used as a disapproving and disdainful response to a precisely choreographed attack on the world of emotions, something a cinematic film can do if it takes itself seriously. I take it seriously and no doubt use these forms taken from the melodrama, because these forms likewise contain something that is specifically cinematic: an optical narrative structure which does not explain and edify— a way of dealing with emotions.

23. Walter Bockmayer
Come Back, Peter Kraus!* (1978)

Come back to your Gloria star-studded sky, come back to the nurturing breast of your mother dressed in her lilac-colored taffeta dress. Trust Ilse again, we don't have anyone else now, even the Constantin-sun has set and to make matters worse has had red cherry sauce poured over it, what is left is at best a big thrill for our TV-mommies, but one dare not forget: red sauce is sticky.—

Most of us haven't ever seen your films because it was beneath their dignity, and nonetheless you are something like ten years of German film culture. Don't feel bad, I'm certain that someday you'll be discovered again, even if this is long overdue. I only hope that it won't be too late when one starts scratching together the last remnants, whatever is still around, of your films in the archives. Not even the German TV stations have recognized your phenomenon, or are they so blind that they constantly mix you up with Count Bobby if only because your name is also Peter?

A Marlene Dietrich retro—OK, it's an international festival, after all, but why not in your honor a "Peter Kraus Festival," given that most of our film critics know you only by name and even they are interested in reviving the forgotten German musicals of the sixties.

One of your films has the title *Alle lieben Peter (Everyone Loves Peter)* and those of us lucky enough to see the film then will continue to love you.

Come back to our matinee program between 2 and 4 P.M., come back with "Melody and Rhythm" and your "Teenager-Melody," you German Elvis, and let us be proud about the so-called years of misery in German film.

The graphic descriptions in the first paragraph refer to the logos for the film companies Gloria Film and Constantin.—Ilse Kubaschewski was a prominent and active film producer in the postwar era; she was the founder of Gloria Film.—Graf Bobby, i.e., Count Bobby, is a role played by the popular star, Peter Alexander.—The Berlin Film Festival featured a two-part Marlene Dietrich Retrospective in 1977 and 1978.—Bockmayer would also pay tribute to Peter Kraus in his film, Flammende Herzen (Flaming Hearts). *Hans-Christoph Blumenberg, much later, would follow Bockmayer's suggestion and revive Kraus in his films,* Tausend Augen (Thousand Eyes) *and* Der Sommer des Samurai (The Summer of the Samurai).

24. Rudolf Thome

That's Utopia: The Cinema of My Dreams (1979)

Today is Thursday, June 14, 1979. The thermometer outside of my window registers sixty-eight degrees. The weather is uncertain. In front of my window in a Kreuzberg two-bedroom apartment is a gray-brown fire-proof wall without plaster. That's all I see. Sparrows chirp. From somewhere comes Turkish music. Street traffic softened by the houses comes and goes. Next year the eighties begin. I am a filmmaker and critic. What do I expect of the cinema of the eighties? What would I like to see when I go to the movies next year? . . .

The cinema of my dreams is exact, is concrete and sensual. I can't make anything of most of the films I see. They don't have anything to do with the fire-proof wall in front of my window, with the people who live behind it (whom I don't know), or anything to do with me. They tell their stories in a stiff, impersonal manner without really taking them seriously. They don't deal with details. They don't tell of the sparrows, for instance, who have a nest across the way in a hole in the wall on the second floor. They limit themselves to telling the essentials according to dramaturgical rules and leave out the unimportant. They forget—as every detective story demonstrates—that it is precisely the unimportant which is important. Going to a film should at least be as exciting as reading a crime or detective novel. One should be able to discover something of the reality around us of which we know so little, because we have to do other things to make money and because we're afraid.

The cinema of my dreams is simple. And without imagination. I learned that in Hellmuth Costard's last film, where I laughed more than I have in all of the comedies I've seen recently. Not long ago on TV I saw some old film by William Wyler (one from the forties). Despite a few unnecessary traveling shots, it was truly refreshing. For the most part the camera stood at a point where you could see everything. And that was it. When I watch such old Hollywood films, I suddenly realize what the films of today are doing to me. There I am hit from all directions by shots and jump cuts, so that after ten minutes of film I no longer know where and who I am and what is going on. Or: the person behind the camera thinks he is an artist and wants to prove it. He moves the camera and pans, films from above, films from below, films through reflecting window panes, through bottles, trees, grass, and forgets, because he is concerned with beauty, that the only thing which makes a film beautiful are the people in front of the camera. What they do, how they move. How someone lights a cigarette (Humphrey Bogart in *The Big Sleep*) or how someone drinks a glass of wine. And the others, the filmmakers, who pack their films full of ideas, want to force me, after they have translated their ideas on film, to forget that they have done so and make me think their thoughts. That makes me unhappy and angry.

The cinema of my dreams is funny, is spontaneous, is extremely subjective, and also sometimes boring. Going to the movies also should be like an exciting conversation with a stranger whom one slowly gets to know. What do I know about Schlöndorff after having watched *Die Blechtrommel (The Tin Drum)*? What do I know about Fassbinder after having watched *Die Ehe der Maria Braun (The Marriage of Maria Braun)*?

The cinema of my dreams is recalcitrant, it thinks and feels like me, it's audacious, challenges me, takes risks, is sloppy, and knows every second exactly what it wants. Above all that's most important. That I know, that I feel the other person who made this film always knows what he's doing. (I know that's a utopia, because when I make films, I move through the world like a sleepwalker). Going to a film should be like meeting an exciting woman and getting to know her. One's pulse should beat more quickly. And when you come out of the cinema, you should walk through the streets more elegantly and more self-assured than before.

The cinema of my dreams is a cinema of innocence and naïveté— and that is a utopia.

The Costard film is Der kleine Godard an das Kuratorium junger deutscher Film (The Little Godard, *1978).*

25. Alexander Kluge

Utopian Cinema (1979)

The art of the cinema is young, barely seventy years old. It does not have a feudal past. Compared to the refinement of forms which music, architecture, literature, oil painting, and sculpture cultivated over the centuries, supported by the traditional unity of culture and property, the cinema displays an amazing vigor, robustness, at least in its early days. Not obliged to follow the intricate ways of "civilization and its discontents" (S. Freud), film takes recourse to the spontaneous workings of the imaginative faculty which has existed for tens of thousands of years. Since the Ice Age approximately (or earlier), streams of images, of so-called associations, have moved through the human mind, prompted to some extent by an antirealistic attitude, by the protest against an unbearable reality. They have an order which is organized by spontaneity. Laughter, memory, and intuition, hardly the product of mere education, are based on this raw material of associations. This is the more-than-ten-thousand-year-old-cinema to which the invention of the film strip, projector, and screen only provided a technological response. This also explains the particular proximity of film to the spectator and its affinity to experience.

26. Rainer Werner Fassbinder

Michael Curtiz—Anarchist in Hollywood? Unordered Thoughts about a Seemingly Paradoxical Idea (1980)

December 80. I start reflecting about the filmmaker Michael Curtiz and his work for the time being lacking, intentionally so, information about the facts surrounding this director's life and work.

I want at the start of my reflections about Curtiz, for me right now the most brutally unrecognized film author, to deal with nothing else than the films of his I have been able to see.

Of course I know that Michael Curtiz was born in Hungary, where under his real name he probably made about fifty films before going to America to make around a hundred films, mostly B-pictures, under the name of Michael Curtiz.

But I don't know anything about his Hungarian work, nothing about why he left Hungary for America. Don't know any dates, any interviews, essays on Curtiz, any important essential articles on individual works, any of the secondary literature, anything of primary interest other than a few films.

In my present situation, which it goes without saying will change, no doubt, at this moment, at any rate, my thoughts center around thirty-five films, a wild, random, in no way at all representative selection.

Almost everyone for whom the cinema and film mean something like love, tenderness, and sensual delight has seen the Humphrey Bogart film *Casablanca* with Ingrid Bergman which has long since become a cult film. I'm convinced that only a few know that *Casablanca* was made by Michael Curtiz. And those who know it believe that Michael Curtiz only made a masterpiece here by chance. This widely held opinion among cinephiles is wrong and unjust, there are better films by Michael Curtiz, even if the dialogue of an elderly German couple wanting to emigrate to America and for this reason learning English diligently—"What's the watch?" "Ten watch." "Such much?"—is in its simplicity and beauty unforgettable, one of the most beautiful dialogues in the entire history of film. Michael Curtiz did more important things than the Humphrey Bogart film *Casablanca*.

Anarchism is a strange thing. Heliogabal, the only anarchist on the Imperial throne of the "Holy Roman Empire," was bound to fail. Within a functioning system, no matter what kind of one, only a powerful person can pursue his true desires, to be an anarchist, that is. On the other hand this sort of unrestrained behavior by an individual brings with it at least two dangers. First, those people who have not learned to do anything but conform with society will be troubled and repulsed by the wishes and actions of this individual, if indeed they don't simply declare him insane. Second, the system in which they have a function and in which they know how to behave, will be reaffirmed as the correct and true one and in that way they will be scared away from their real wishes. Their imagination is killed, they will identify dreams of the freedom of wonderful insanity with power and in that way solidify their sorry impotence, so that in the end they are ashamed of their own dreams.

It's a lot different on the other hand in the case of the anarchy we find in the work of Michael Curtiz, something I have admittedly taken up for the moment with much hope. Although I am on the one hand almost certain that Curtiz would have resisted with real conviction the thought that he was an anarchist, or would simply have found the idea ridiculous, I nonetheless dare to ask in all earnestness whether this Michael Curtiz possibly did not leave behind a body of work, one consisting more or less, naturally depending on one's personal taste, of good and controversial parts, I dare to ask whether Curtiz did not indeed make films that no matter how different they might appear at a fleeting first glance, as a whole nonetheless provide a distinct image of the world, in which each individual film, yes each individual sequence in these films, constitutes something like an integral part of Michael Curtiz's distinctive world view.

This is the beginning of what was to be a lengthy essay on the American director. It was scheduled at one point to appear as a monograph in the Hanser series, "Arbeitshefte Film."

27. Sohrab Shahid Saless

Culture as Hard Currency or: Hollywood in Germany (1983)

I made a film. Its title is *Utopia*. For five years I went in and out of the television stations. Again and again I submitted the script to state subsidy boards and again and again I was turned down. The milieu of film is a whore's milieu. But not one that does much for one's potency. I went around for a long time and stubbornly enough until things fell into place and the film was made and had to become as long as my patience!

Because I've been living in the Federal Republic for almost nine years now, I have gained an obligatory sense of how films are produced here, the films I or my colleagues are planning, in order that we might, so to speak, export our films. I have done penance with ten films "far from home." Many will say: boy, was he fortunate. But, unfortunately, that is not the case. People like us who make somber and hardly entertaining films are not fortunate. They write letters, come up with treatments, put together scripts that are never filmed and once in a while a good soul appears, gestures to them and says—just like in Kafka—: it's your turn now. You too can have a chance!

Strange things happen then. Because I am a foreigner (*"Aus"-Länder*), I am not allowed to be a producer. I have to find a producer who will grant me the honor of working with me. Fortunately the television stations are usually the ones who finance half of the budget. While I sit there with no say the production firm comes up with a calculation. Real numbers! Just wages for the collaborators!

One starts filming and suddenly notices: they're cutting corners. Less and less is spent and in the end it's the film itself that suffers. Whether a film becomes good or bad is of no consequence. Never. One figures that the somber film won't be a popular success anyway. And that the people who watch it on TV will either fall asleep or change the channel. Why is that so? It's a mystery to me!

No one complains more than producers. You as a filmmaker run your ass off, get your script accepted, find a television partner, and in the end you have to listen to how generous your producer was with you. Which unfortunately does not correspond to reality.

Of course independent producers are businessmen. They have to watch out for their interests. But at what price? It sometimes happens overnight that a second independent coproducer for whatever reason invests a small bit of money in your film. You don't even have the chance to choose your own coproducer or to turn him down. And because all of these secret games remain internal matters, it's always the producers who are the ones to suffer, who have to pay for any losses, and it's the directors who are seen as the henchmen who are unreasonable and difficult. In the course of time it's become clear to me here that some of the things which concern our profession—cinema—simply don't work right. The Hollywood illusion has wrecked a lot of things here.

The masters of expressionist films never tried to emulate Hollywood. And nonetheless there was a "classical German film."

One can't simply produce a series here like the American one *The Streets of San Francisco*. Because we fortunately haven't come so far that people here kill each other under a clear blue sky. A film like *Jaws* also cannot be remade here. Hollywood is a place which produces one piece of junk after another like a company making fly repellent.

A tradition, a culture, or an image of real American life is not to be found in these films. Because it is continually ignored.

The reality of life today in the Federal Republic of Germany is increasingly not to be found in our films. The excuse offered is that this won't make any money. It has no economic potential. Culture is culture and business is business! Didn't you know that?

It also often happens that one reaches for old literature or rescues dead geniuses from the grave and tries to reconstruct them. All those young people running around without a job and turning to drugs and alcohol. All those separated women living alone with their children. Children who instead of a father often get to know five uncles, one after the other. Aren't those worthy topics? In a democratic system like that of the Federal Republic one would think that criticism should be allowed. That one might be able to tell somber stories based on the facts. The public is always willing to listen. It's interested in learning something about the society in which it lives.

Of course there must *also* be entertainment, there must also be room for Peter Alexander. Naturally one has to think of the old people who need distraction. But why should these old people not tell their own stories? Making a film, i.e. getting a story accepted, is sometimes so strange that one is reminded of the myth of Sisyphus.

I say openly and without any fear of the possible disfavor I will fall into: in the Federal Republic there are perhaps eight producers who will protect a filmmaker so that he can make that which he originally intended. And there are very few cultural editors (*Redakteure*) who are courageous enough to fight for a project, to go to the barricades so that a realistic film can be made. Two of these cultural editors, this became clear in the production of *Utopia*, work for ZDF.

This all is meant as information for my young colleagues who are in the process of making their first films. If because of these radical notes I have to sit around in the future without work, then I will find the time to write a history of German films for the Germans and not for Hollywood.

That was everything I had to say.

Far from Home (In der Fremde) *is the title of the first film the Persian director Saless made after settling in Berlin during the midseventies, continuing to live and work there in the subsequent decade.*

IV

Different Ways of Seeing

Perhaps the major shortcoming of the term 'New German Cinema,' i.e., the appellation used for the codified and streamlined version of a very small part of West German film culture, was its exclusionary quality. It sanded off the rough edges of an extremely unwieldy phenomenon, a remarkable gathering of different possibilities, diverse approaches, and conflicting discourses. Along with the more celebrated festival successes and arthouse breakthroughs existed a multitude of other sites of activity and spheres of discussion: communal cinemas, the Arsenal, X-Screen, the *Kamerafilm*, journals like *Boa Vista* and *Filmartikel*, the annual trip at year's end to Knokke, the International Forum of the Young Film, the *Initiative-Frauen-im-Kino*, to name only a few examples of the alternative public sphere inhabited by *Das andere Kino*, the not so easily classified reaches of West German film. This less compromising fringe of the nation's film culture clearly issued from the sixties and has to be seen as the product of a time that gave rise to the student movement, happenings, anti-establishment sensibilities, and an overwhelming desire to subvert and refurbish. It is a mistake, however, to view these other voices of West German film culture as marginalia, to ghettoize them as idiosyncratic oddities, to cast them off as interesting exoticisms—for a number of reasons. The radical character fueling much of the so-called 'New German Cinema' derived from an awareness of alternative praxis. Mainstream filmmakers followed the work of less well-known, but still highly regarded, experimental and avant-garde directors, work that would leave traces in the exported successes. Fassbinder, Herzog, and Wenders would in fact alternate between films intended for an international market and other small productions of a highly personal nature, difficult films obviously of interest to a more limited public. Most importantly, though, one need not justify the gallimaufry of creative endeavor in West German film culture in terms of its use value for a popular packaged version. What makes film activity in the FRG so continuingly and consistently provocative—despite the predictable and inexorable declarations of devolution and death, cries that have reached a crescendo in the mideighties—is its remarkable nexus of different possibilities, the many-faceted quality of image making in that country, the spectrum ranging from formal experimentation to political explorations, from a hardy feminist film culture to lively groups of video artists, documentary artisans, gay activists and zanies, earnest students of early cinema. One voice can be heard no matter where one turns: the will to be generous to spectators, to leave empty spaces in one's flow of images so that viewers can find their own points of entry and have room for reflection and intervention. These are, in many cases, special films for special audiences. West German film culture remains so intriguing precisely because so many of its filmmakers refuse to countenance a narrowly popular brand of cinema.

28. Ottomar Domnick
Freeing Oneself from Old Hat (1965)

The phrase "economic and artistic crisis" seems to me a problematic one, even if it does describe the current problem exactly. It creates the illusion that the two factors are inextricably bound. But in fact just the opposite is the case. Every compromise made by art for economic reasons renders the term "art" illusory. Mass tastes (and these are essential for economic success) can never become essential for artistic decisions. Adorno, speaking about music in light of the more general thesis that art and popular taste always diverge, quotes the phrase, "the division of all art into kitsch and the avant-garde," a phrase that holds for film as well. In all branches of art, economic success (music as part of concert programs, the market value of paintings) only comes about when the art form finds public acceptance and that, according to Franz Roh, only happens fifty years later. Exceptions to the rule occur when a respective work contains factors already operative in mass consciousness, even if at first apparent only subliminally and vaguely.

Because film, in contrast to painting, music, and literature, depends for its production on economic factors, it is important to keep production costs to a minimum. This is absolutely possible, if one frees oneself from the old hat of the overinflated production staff and the common practice of trips abroad and travel allowances, etc. What is crucial for the artistic result is not financial backing but rather artistic spirit. Give young people eager to experiment a chance to get behind the cameras, people who denounce perfectionism.

Economic factors are necessary in film (as in music) for reproduction, so that works find an audience. Distributors and cinemas here should explore new possibilities: for instance as in the case of experimental theaters. The studios have failed. Today they no longer assume risks. Many films are not shown publicly. This hinders the initiative of filmmakers. For this reason city and state should support small cinemas (something already done for theater) where new films can be shown and discussed. Special screenings alone (in universities and youth clubs, etc.) are not enough. They are only attended by the initiated anyway. One needs to create forums where, on a regular basis (and not only always under special circumstances), such films are presented, so that they can sharpen one's critical eye and visual sense. Under such conditions artistic films which otherwise will never be made or never be shown might find an audience.

The film should be free of antiquated methods of production, of restrictions, censors, rating boards, entertainment taxes (where is the entertainment in the contemplation of art?), and cinemas with 2,000 seats. I would recommend we develop this "independent film" in 1965.

Domnick's experimental features, especially Jonas (1957) *and* Gino (1960), *represent exceptional examples of alternative filmmaking in the postwar era and stand as decided forerunners of the Young German Film. See Domnick's biographical account,* Hauptweg und Nebenwege: Psychiatrie, Kunst, Film in meinem Leben *(Hamburg: Hoffmann und Campe, 1977).—These comments came in response to a survey conducted by the journal* Film *asking for answers to these questions: "1. In your opinion what has been done in the year 1964, perhaps through your own initiative, to overcome the economic and artistic crisis of German film?—2. What in your estimation remains to be done in the year 1965 and what will be your part in this endeavor?"*

29. Wim Wenders
Kelek (1969)

A film by Werner Nekes and by everyone who has seen it so far.

"I sat down and waited for her to begin to speak. She stared at the wall and didn't say a word."

"The place didn't look as though something exciting had happened here recently. It was peaceful and sunny, and the parked cars had a placid look, as if they were quite at home."

"He bent forward and looked through the keyhole."

Raymond Chandler

Kelek is the first Nekes film with a story. The story of a consciousness. The consciousness has to do with nothing other than seeing. Seeing is the subject of the film.

Until now there have only been films for watching. Although the contemplative cinema, those films in one long single take, had undermined this process, there had never yet been a film so exclusively concerned with seeing. Nekes's own earlier films, such as *gurtrugs* (1967) or *Muhkuh* (Moo-Cow, 1968), or Mommartz's *Eisenbahn* (*Railway*, 1967) were still too fascinated with themselves to give any sense of where they were leading: to the identification of the filmmaker and viewer at the level of the voyeur.

There are only one or two clumsy precursors, those porno films where excitingly taboo events transpire behind a keyhole mask. And that fantastic little film by Kurt Kren, *tv* (1967), which no one knew what to make of because it persistently concealed any indication that all it showed was seeing, that there was nothing else to watch except seeing. Besides, *tv* was an experiment. *Kelek* is no experiment. *Kelek* is an event. It shows something that's excitingly allowed: seeing.

Film critics will lose their jobs. They won't need to go to the cinema anymore. All that will be left for them to do is to go for strolls in the park, look at their toes, or at manhole covers as they walk along, have it off, and when they turn into suburban streets, slowly open and shut their eyes.

That's movie.

Kelek is an evenly paced film. There's no more "and then . . ." and "at this point . . ." *Kelek* is a film that works on only one level, the level of seeing.

"All this means that films cling to the surface of things. . . . Perhaps the way today leads from, and through, the corporeal to the spiritual?" (Kracauer).

Kelek is an incredibly physical affair.

Wenders quotes the Chandler passages, contrary to his usual practice of citing in the original, in German translation.—"That's movie" appears in English in the article.—The Kracauer passage is from Theory of Film: The Redemption of Physical Reality *(London/Oxford/New York: Oxford University Press, 1960), pp. x–xi. Here as well Wenders quotes in a German translation.*

30. Klaus Wildenhahn
The Method of Direct Observation: Two Examples*
(1974)

Example 1. Farmer Petersen does not wish to burden himself with debts. But under the pressure of rising costs and his own increasing financial needs, he is constantly obliged to expand his farm. The sheds and outbuildings for his growing dairy herd and the herd of young cattle are things he can only afford little by little. He does everything himself, so as not to incur any debts. His twelve-hour working day allows him only limited time to carry out the necessary improvements to buildings and to erect new ones. The result of this is that part of his herd has to be kept in dirty old buildings. There is no alternative. Petersen would either have to erect new stalling and would thus effectively pawn his cattle, or he must slowly slave away with his wife day after day, until his farm has reached the appropriate level of equipment—that is, if he can achieve it at all.

We filmed on Petersen's farm for two months. After fifteen days of shooting we were as usual at 5 P.M. in the milking stall: the second milking. We were ready to record the daily production process. Frau Petersen, the farmer's wife, crossed the yard to an old cowshed in which the eleven six-month-old bull calves were locked. It was May, and had become quite warm. The calves had to be let out of the stall into the meadow at the back. The farmer's wife wanted to get the calves through the door. We followed her with our equipment, without thinking any more about it; it was just another working record, routine. She tempted them with fodder, but the calves did not want to come out of the enclosure. Frau Petersen went to fetch her husband. As soon as he saw us, he didn't want us to film there. We were on a part of the farm that was taboo. The cowshed looked in poor condition, it was piled up with dung and the boarding was in a rough state. It was the unkempt reverse face of the coin of farming, of the attempt to manage without borrowing money.

But where, if not in such an immediate and obvious example, were we to record the pressure under which the farmer lived; the economic pressure that manifested itself in the scanty boarding and the cow dung left lying around, and in the nervousness of the farmer himself? The calves were treated rather roughly and were finally driven outside. We filmed a number of scenes with water running off us, not because we were literally hot, but because we were aware of the farmer's feelings, that he felt himself cheated by us. For two days he did not speak a word to us, while we continued our daily filming. It was not a good situation.

Then his wife intervened; her husband was annoyed, because he did not know how we would use these scenes on television, whether we did not propose merely to exploit the sensational aspects, as one knew only too well. He was afraid of his fellow farmers and of the reactions of viewers, who would be quite incapable of understanding his situation: the dirty cowshed, the young cattle in their own dung.

We spoke with Petersen over coffee. After the two days of silence he suddenly came out with his worries. "We are trying to remain efficient in this economic system; but we can't do it without the negative aspects as well. All improvements take a long time, according to the means at our disposal and our own working strength. You know how we work. We can't do more. It's impossible for everything to look spic and span. But you can't show that on television. If people were to see that! The farmer wallowing in dirt and manure, they'd say; but they wouldn't know why. There have been enough bad things said about us. You can't do that, please, not that." We spoke to him, told him that we didn't intend to humiliate him, but had to communicate something of the reality of his life. We wanted to attempt to show a real picture of him and his situation, and thereby contribute to an understanding of it. But in order to do this, he would have to allow us to work and make our observations freely. He said he wanted to have the courage to do this. It was difficult, but if we succeeded in capturing the real Petersen, he was prepared to accept it, the negative reactions as well, if need be. But then we must show the whole thing and not just the dirt.

We all felt much relieved after the discussion. We obtained a viewing table from Hamburg and showed Petersen the critical parts after the material had been developed. That involves a great risk. Unedited material can arouse the most unexpected reactions in the person filmed. They can be frightened or they can become stiff and reserved the next day, or imagine they have to speak formal, correct German. It is one of the most difficult things in filming documentaries to persuade people to retain their own language and naturalness. They are so accustomed to the middle-class standard language they hear on television that they distort themselves almost compulsively in order to achieve a similarly lifeless style of speech. We took the risk, for we believed that only in this way was it possible to establish a critical relationship of trust. We showed Petersen and his wife the passages in question, explained and let them explain to us. There were some heated moments on the first-floor hallway of the Flensburg farmhouse where we had set up the viewing table.

As it turned out, in the course of the next few weeks, we gained additional material that quite clearly showed the pressure and ner-vousness under which the farmer stood—even more clearly than the scene in the cowshed. It was also embarrassing for the farmer himself, but he had changed his stance somewhat. He had shed a little of his distrust as a result of the discussion and viewings. Not all of it, however; he frequently remarked, "You have all done too much on television."

Much later, after putting the film together, we showed the Petersens the finished product. It was as much their film as ours. We felt we had included everything, the hard situations and the pressures, as well as the explanation for all of this. But we were anxious to know what the Petersens' reaction would be.

It must have been the same for them. "The whole way here I had a stomach ache," he said, having arrived in Hamburg from Flensburg. They had completed the first milking and still had time before the second had to be done. Thus, a year after we had begun filming, we sat together in the cutting room with the finished product before us. After the first twenty minutes, he said, "If it's all like this, it will be all right. But let's wait and see." At the end he said, "That will certainly provoke discussions among the other farmers. Without a doubt. And in the way I wanted, the way you wanted it. As we all wanted it in the beginning."

Example 2. The agricultural worker, Horst Ehmke, is constantly working with machines. During the harvest he drives a combined harvester worth 100,000 marks. That is three times as much as our film equipment is worth.

We had him explain his machinery to us, function, maintenance, frequency of repairs. We explained our equipment to him, the principle of synchronism of sound and picture, the quartz-crystal control, microphones, light sensitivity of the picture material, the wear and tear of our materials, the method of direct observation. That was no problem. More difficult was explaining to Horst Ehmke that we earned on an average some 2,000 marks more than he did with his 800 marks net. Why shouldn't he compare our earnings with his own, just as he compared his work with ours? He soon realized what it was all about, once we had told him, right at the start, that we did not want to make a sentimental film using the local background of Lauenburg, that we were not primarily interested in the gentle hills and reeded roofs. "I know," he said, "you're inquisitive." Toward the end of shooting, he began to joke with Thomas Hartwig, the cameraman. "Thomas, we'll make the next film together. I'll do the sound, and I can ask questions as well, I'm inquisitive anyway. That'll be a real film." Horst Ehmke, the agricultural laborer, had lost his respect for the aura surrounding television. We were pleased with our success—at least for the time being.

Wildenhahn made a pair of documentary films produced by the Hamburg television station NDR bearing the collective title, Die Liebe zum Land (Love of the Land, 1973–74).—*For a comprehensive statement of Wildenhahn's thoughts on documentary filmmaking and its modalities, see his book* Über synthetischen und dokumentarischen Film: Zwölf Lesestunden (Frankfurt am Main: Kommunales Kino, 1973).—*See as well Wildenhahn's forceful contribution to a debate about realism and veracity in documentary film which took place at the* Duisburger Filmwoche *during the fall of 1979, reprinted as* " 'Industrielandschaft mit Einzelhändlern': Nachtrag zu den Duisburger Debatten um den Dokumentarfilm," Filmfaust, *no. 20 (1980): 3–16.*

31. Werner Nekes
What Really Happens between the Frames* (1975)

I want to give you a general introduction to what I think cinema is. There was a short mention of the title of one of my films. It was pronounced *T WO MEN*. I pronounce it *TWOMEN*, and this pronunciation is the verbalization of the visual effort the brain has to make when it reads images in films. I have chosen this title because, with its programmatic qualities, it approaches the center of cinema. This title is programmatic because it deals with the legibility of film in a horizontal way: that is, horizontal as opposed to vertical reading. Horizontal refers to the time axis: receiving the information from frames in different time segments as they follow each other. Vertical reading happens when the viewer receives amounts of information on different pictorial levels within one time segment. This means that horizontal and vertical reading of images can happen simultaneously. Not everything that I say will be clear immediately or understood easily, but some things I have to say are quite important, it seems to me, because I have never found them in any other books, or in other thinking about film.

So you all know that film is a strip of celluloid with frame after frame transported and projected within a determined amount of time. If you think of having the strange writing of the title *T WO MEN* on three frames following each other, the T on frame one, then the WO on the next, and the MEN on the third, and you project this, then you have a small chain of filmic information. You are reading "two women" because the laziness of the retina combines the frames. You are fusing or melting frame A with frame B, but also frame B with frame C. The semantic ambiguity is the result of joining the smallest filmic information units, which I call *"kine."* What I'm saying is that if one wants to treat cinema seriously, disregarding the other media disguised by film, such as literature, vaudeville, theater, painting, etc.; if you just concentrate on the medium of film, and if you ask yourself: what is the medium? What does it do? Out of which elements is it built up? Or, what is the smallest filmic element? I came to the answer that *cinema is the difference between two frames:* the work the brain has to do to produce the fusion of the two frames. This small unit which I call *kine* is the smallest particle of a film one can think of. Though it is composed of a lot of elements, the visual components do not yet determine the filmic language. If you, for example, take this big unit, a single frame, you have a photographic information; if you take two frames, the difference between them defines the smallest unit of filmic language that is possible, one filmic information. Every film can be regarded under the principle of this difference, which is a construct of a time/space relation. The analysis of the *kine* enables us to come to conclusions about the language used, to determine the level of filmic information connected to the work the spectator has to do. Until now, most film criticism or theory, and also much of what I read of semiotics, has regarded only longer film units, such as the montage sequence.

If you take a short look back at the history of cinema from the viewpoint of information theory, you can say that film is always used for the transmittal of information. With the first films you have the camera set up and a cassette on top of the camera, and the camera ran for a time equal to the length of the film. Those were the one-reelers, at the very beginning lasting three to five minutes. If I look now at the differences between the frames, the *kines,* I find that the time/space differences are all very minimal; the frames have the same relations to each other. I call the frames a_1, a_2, a_3, a_4 until a_n, which is the end of the film, the last frame. A new time/space relation was discovered accidentally by Méliès; when he shot a traffic scene at the Place de l'Opéra in 1896, the camera stopped shooting for some seconds. The effect in the projection was that a bus drawn by horses was transformed into a funeral procession, men into women and vice versa. Among all the *kines* carrying the same time/space differences, or loads of visual information, there was one *kine* in which the difference was wider, the time was shortened, the difference was stretched.

The new quality of a *kine* was the subconscious start of the evolution of film language. When a great number of *kines* carry this time difference, we call it quick motion, or if we shorten the time differences we have high-speed shots. Naturally, in such a sequence the information level is as high in a continuous normal shot, because the predictability is very high from frame to frame in respect to the time difference. In other words: the lower the chance to anticipate the next *kine,* the higher the information level of the film. We can now deduce for cinema: *the predictability of a* kine *determines the level of filmic information.* This idea corresponds to the fact that the higher the level of filmic information, the more film realizes its own possibilities. Or, expressed negatively, film is not laden with the grammar of the other media.

Another historical step in the development of the language of film was the change of the location, or of the space. One example for the change of different shots is *The Life of an American Fireman* by Porter. He took what we would call today documentary footage of the work of firemen, which had been shot by others a while before, and combined it with other material he shot himself of a young women and a child in a burning house. The fire was extinguished by water that was sprayed maybe a year before and recorded then. Saving the woman with the child certainly is important, but I think what is more important about it is the new *kine,* the junction of different spaces or localities and also different times.

After that a lot of other steps followed, building up the narrative structures of film. Their framework mostly looks like this: scenes with low information *kines* from a_1 to a_n, and starting with b to b_n, c to c_n, etc. Not very much attention was paid to the *kines* with the higher load of information, that were included as the *kines* a_n/b_1, b_n/c_1, c_n/d_1, etc. Among the first who realized the importance of the opposition of two scenes that follow each other (a_1 till a_n opposed to b_1 till b_n, etc.) were Kuleshov, Pudovkin, and Eisenstein.

The association montage principles of Eisenstein became well known as the montage of attractions. This meant, to give an example, that Eisenstein worked on the fusion of ideas that were drawn out of shot one ($a_1 - a_n$ $b_1 - b_n$) showing an animal and shot two showing a cap-italist. The opposition of the content of the two whole scenes gave in this case the ideological fusion, the information. This question—What does this scene mean to the next scene? Or, what do they mean together?— was the basis for all montage theories that followed.

Until now film theoreticians have concentrated their efforts around the montage when they wanted to say something about the language of film. This viewpoint has been successful to some extent with narrative cinema, with overlaying literary contents. But when this content was not so obviously hiding the visual qualities, in other words, when the film itself was using its own medial possibilities, then this method of criticism failed. The critics didn't even see, or pay attention to, such unexpected films. Extraordinary films like *Ballet Mécanique* by Fernand Léger didn't fit into the known and used categories of thinking about film. Léger didn't use film as a literary medium, he invented a great number of new *kines* based on visual motion. It is typical of criticism that the one who works seriously to free the medium of its old limitations is put into an outsider position. One respected only the painter behind the work, but one didn't understand that he worked as a film artist or filmmaker. . . .

Just compare the slowly streaming information in the epic films at the beginning of film history to those we understand today, or compare the television ads made twenty or ten years ago to those we are used to today. Nowadays we are used to superimpositions, very small units of flickering frames, etc. For ads the problem is to have as much information on the product within the shortest time. In general the level of information is much higher than before. The trend you can conclude from this is "to transport *a maximum of information within a minimum of* kines." Film is a constantly transforming, living language, that we are learning, that we have to learn to perceive. The process of learning happens with film mostly subconsciously, by repetition. And so that's where we are.

What can this mean? Where is this tendency leading? That's why I think it wrong, when films are analyzed in film theory, to look only at this special point in a film, where the montage is. I say: *every change from one frame to the next is a montage.* But this statement won't make too much sense, firstly because the expression has been used too much for a different purpose, and secondly, because if film consists only of montages the expression becomes tautological, useless. So I call this small unit, the smallest element of filmic language, a *kine,* and maybe this term will be picked up. The difference between two frames determines the *kine.* . . .

In thinking of the efficiency of film to transport information, I remembered the old English optical toy invented in 1826 by Fitton and Paris: the thaumatrope, which is a small disk made out of cardboard with two different drawings on each side, that gave the illusion of a third when it was twisted quickly around between the fingers. The bird was on one side, the cage on the other, so the bird was seen sitting in the cage when they were viewed in quick succession. This thaumatropical effect is an example for me of how efficient the *kines* in a film can be. What an amount of information these two frames a/b give, compared with the a_1/a_2 which gives the illusion of movement! The perception of movement is always dependent on time segments, which can be understood very easily for film. However, it is not so easy to understand the dependency of "*Gestaltssprünge*" on segments of time. One pays attention to them normally only if they are small units. But if you think of greater time segments, you might produce *Gestaltssprünge*. The example I gave before of the Méliès films was still a relatively small one. But if you add camera movement as one step and the location of the camera at a different place as the next step, this could make a huge difference. The difference could give the illusion of "a bird in the cage."

We mustn't forget that there is still a not obvious time/space relation. I deduce: *there is always a time/space relation in a* kine. The *Gestaltssprünge* are nothing but a special form of movement, a widely stretched time/space distance. Parallel to the perception of such thaumatropical films, I recognize the demand of the French poet Guillaume Apollinaire: "Our intelligence has to accustom itself to understand in a synthetic-ideographical way, instead of in an analytical-discursive way." In this context one might also think of the possibilities of understanding that are given by Chinese ideographs. The collision of the two signs produces a third on a different level, with a new meaning. The illusion produced by the *kines* in the head of the spectator is the imaginative content of film. . . .

Nekes presented these thoughts in a lecture at the Center for Twentieth-Century Studies at the University of Wisconsin, Milwaukee, on 8 December 1975. For an earlier elucidation of Nekes's notion of the "kine," see his "Spreng-Sätze zwischen den Kadern," Hamburger Filmgespräche IV *(1972): 135–38. See also his "Theoretische Texte," in* Avantgardistischer Film 1951–1971: Theorie, *ed. Gottfried Schlemmer (Munich: Hanser, 1973), pp. 101–6.—A recent film of Nekes's, a prehistory of cinematic expression, bears the title,* Was geschah wirklich zwischen den Bildern? *(Film before Film, 1985).*

32. Rosa von Praunheim
Gay Film Culture* (1976)

My situation as a gay man has not changed much even after the appearance of my film about gays, *Nicht der Homosexuelle ist pervers, sondern die Situation in der er lebt (Not the Homosexual is Perverse, but the Situation in Which He Lives).* I hoped for solidarity, for a group with whom I could work collectively to change my situation. I felt isolated in the hostile subculture (vain bars, dark parks, and toilets). The film forced me to take a position: I could no longer hide my problems or take refuge in bitchiness and complexes. It was not until a television interview that my parents found out that their son is a homosexual. I had not dared until then to talk with them about it. Although tolerant in a bourgeois way, one did not talk about sex at home.

After the sensational premiere of the film at the Berlin Film Festival [in 1971], the film ran for a long time at the Arsenal cinema, always with a discussion afterward. We encouraged the gays in the cinema to join our organization and in this way we formed the first gay groups in Germany.

The mainly student-based groups were too theoretical for an artist like me, too unspontaneous and unimaginative. I constantly provoked contradictions and aggressions, no one wanted to respond to my blind actionism. I wanted to see more boys from the people in these groups, but they were turned off by the elite student jargon and antiseptic atmosphere. The political discussions became increasingly unbearable and it seemed to take years until the first practical work transpired (demonstrations, subculture actions, participation in political actions).

Because of my profession I was not able to participate steadily in this political work. I basked more or less in my fame at demonstrations where I was admired as a pretty piece of exotica. I was too impatient, too much the artist or journalist who saw things from a distance and criticized things rather than participating in a productive capacity. In America I was fascinated by the strength and the great organization of the gay groups, but no matter where I spoke about this, people soon lost confidence in me and I think it was right that my work was continued by many other people.

Despite my steady relationship with Peter, I was still dependent on the subculture. My strong sex drive forces me, no matter where I am, to find satisfaction. My hope of finding emancipated and intellectually compatible sex partners through the homosexual action groups soon had to be forgotten. We talked, but we didn't fuck. Soon after the television screening of my film, I felt very strange in toilets and parks, and particularly in the baths. I was afraid and felt guilty, after all I had totally damned the subculture in my film and was still the first person dependent on it. It is true that we had tried a few times in the group, for instance in the baths, to overcome the frustration, inhibitions, and narcissism of these places and to bring about a more relaxed and honest atmosphere. But the desire for oppression, repression, the fascination of well-known situations was larger, one fucked in the end anonymously, without saying a word, or in pitchdark mass fucking rooms, so that one did not have to challenge oneself. Nonetheless everyone seemed to be yearning for a solid relationship, but everyone played it cool and shy and reserved. Everyone acted as if he were above it all. Everyone wanted to be the one who was seduced, out of fear of rejection, self-hatred, or inferiority complexes, something forced on them by society for centuries. A few bars would no longer let me in after the film was shown. Radical right-wing gay organizations were formed which cursed us as communists. In the Berlin bar Trocadero I was beaten up and threatened with knives, dogs, and pistols. The group showed its solidarity and demonstrated in front of the bar the next night. Since that time the entire group is barred from entering the club.

The film is five years old now, but remains more topical and necessary than ever before. In all of these years no film has been made about gays which has an emancipatory impetus. Only commercial shit like *The Boys in the Band,* self-pitying stuff like Fassbinder's *Faustrecht der Freiheit (Fox and His Friends),* which ostensibly only coincidentally happens to take place among gays, the umpteen numbers of idiotic gay porno films, exotic underground crap à la Warhol which only views gays as funny noodles.

The group work is less apparent. In America the activities have moved from the big cities to the country, a very positive development. At home now many short-lived groups appear and old ones disappear. The heroes have gotten weary: revolution isn't fun any more (not only among us gays).

Today I wouldn't have been able to make this film for television, it would have been censored in this age of conformism.

Sometimes I think about a commercial feature film about gays: a love story between two men which describes gay kitsch but also attempts to be emancipatory. For which one must struggle if one is not to lose all courage and desire to keep going. Work in general and for others is exhausting and it's no coincidence that I have made things too easy for myself and taken refuge in my artist's world of fancy. Because I'm not the only one who suffers from an inhuman situation, anonymous sex, the difficulty of finding the right partners with whom one can fuck and talk, people one accepts both intellectually and humanly and vice versa. A dream?

The Arsenal cinema is in West Berlin and has, for the last decade and a half, offered one of the most dynamic, comprehensive, and varied film programs anywhere in the world.—Cf. Werner Schroeter's review of Sex und Karriere, *the book from which this selection is taken, "Eine Tante wie eine Arie," Der Spiegel, 15 November 1976, pp. 225–28.*

33. Klaus Wyborny

Unordered Notes on Conventional Narrative Film
(1976)

The Reality of the Fixed Gaze

The image of human beings in the cinema: people who look each other in the eyes, unrelentingly. People who observe objects, landscapes, and other people with eyes that do not move. People who return every gaze without blinking, for if they do not, they must have something to hide. A man in thought fixes his gaze on a fictive point in space without moving his eyes: this demonstrates that he is thinking.

In contrast to this the way things really are: people who rarely look each other in the eye, people whose irises constantly oscillate when they watch something carefully, people who never think of staring down others, and a type of thinking which is inextricably bound to an involuntary movement of the eyes, so much so that one might suspect this oscillation of the eyes is the activity that sorts out necessary bits of information and nerve cells from the residue of previous trains of thought, in so doing freeing the way for new thoughts.

People being interviewed move their eyes with nimble agility. If I am talking to someone and he does not move his eyes, then I am sure he is not listening. When I recite a poem, I can hold my eyes on a fixed point only as long as I have the text in mind. If I have to stop to think what comes next, I have to move my eyes.

It is no coincidence that film actors move their eyes so rarely. They have memorized their lines beforehand. When they move their eyes, they do so mechanically, fixing their gaze on objects around them: flowers, ashtrays, desk tops.

The eye movement of a person thinking, on the other hand, is not object-oriented. It is unfocussed. When I think, I cannot simultaneously focus my eyes clearly on something around me. If I stare at a fixed point in space, I lose the larger field of vision. In order to see well, I need movement. If this movement is not provided by the objects around me, it must be produced by me in my iris.

And conversely: people in movies who constantly divert their eyes are the ones with something to hide: criminals, neurotics, and the insane. Narrative cinema transforms thinking into quasi-criminal behavior.

Narrative cinema treats the interactions between people as the visible interaction of fixed bodies with a well-defined purpose, a well-defined direction, and a well-defined form. Any change in purpose, direction, or form has a well-defined reason in a well-defined interaction with another well-defined fixed body.

The main task of narrative cinema is to combine heterogeneous units of space and time into homogeneous ones. The criterion for such a homogeneous grammatical combination is the initial appearance of a harmonious time and space conjunction. This means that each part of the resultant time/space conjunction implicitly has a geographical and a temporal coordinate and that these coordinates are not contradictory. Contradictory, for instance, would be a fixed body's simultaneous presence at two different geographical coordinates.

The time/space constructions of narrative cinema are achieved almost without exception through a single principle, namely through the exchange of existents in different time/space units. These existents are usually fixed bodies, among them generally the fixed bodies we call actors. Often time/space relations are also produced by existents demonstrating a well-known invention of narrative cinema, i.e., the fixed gaze. In the context of narrative grammar this gaze causes an indivisible unity with the existent which is reduced to a fixed body and mere carrier of the action.

One does not overlook representational anomalies like extreme overlighting or manipulation of angles. In these cases, the unity of representation and the represented appears so endangered, that within narrative grammar it is commonly subsumed under the category of the psychotic and half-criminal anomaly.

An extremely dark representation, which curiously enough is given the time coordinate night, even when a thousand things speak against such a reading, has a singular significance indeed. A brownish tinting of black-and-white material is seen as a document from long ago, even though this brownish coloring was never a part of the chemical process used with film materials.

One might be tempted to say that narrative cinema and its grammar amount to a limited number of small tricks to which the spectator responds with Pavlovian predictability. But such an interpretation overlooks the fact that these representational anomalies are only border areas of narrative grammar. They have little to do with the substrata of time/space constructions which form the backbone of this grammar. Any analytical investigations that are side-tracked by this secondary issue will not succeed in grasping the narrative principle.

The systematic way in which this questionable identity of representation and the represented has been overlooked explains the singular notion of reality present in narrative films. Films that allow clearcut time/space constructions are perceived as being particularly realistic. The synthetic character of the process behind these constructions goes unnoticed. Especially those films which most successfully display such a clearcut character are by and large synthetic. And that must perforce be so. Such films demand for instance the fixed gaze.

Any society whose notion of representation confuses representations with reality, even though countless considerations militate against such a confusion, must be or will become exceedingly schizophrenic. How is one to grasp reality if one attributes reality to its systematic deformation? If one attempts to gauge reality using deformed reality as a norm. How is one to interact with others if one's notion of reality is grounded in the reality of the fixed gaze?

A complete translation of Wyborny's lengthy essay appeared in Afterimage *(London), nos. 8/9 (Spring 1981): 112–32, rendering by Philip Drummond, edited by Barrie Ellis-Jones, with additional material by Elizabeth Reddish.*

34. Helke Sander

Feminism and Film (1977)

"I like chaos, but I don't know whether chaos likes me."
(From a paper given in Graz, Austria in November 1977, on the occasion of the annual fall literature and theater festival there—the so-called "Steirischer Herbst"—on the topic, "Is There and What Is Feminine Imagery?")

After thinking about it for a long time, I have come to doubt whether this question makes any sense. But it is so frequently posed, along with its variations about the forms of feminine aesthetics and feminine creativity, that it has come to belong to the repertory of many festivals, seminars, and symposia; and the very peculiar conclusions arrived at at these conferences have also begun to work their way into professional terminology, where they tend to confuse rather than clarify concepts as well as to distract attention away from other more pressing questions.

In posing the question, people often make no distinction between *feminine* and *feminist* imagery; they use the words interchangeably, even though one word is a biological and psychological term and the other a political one.

As for feminism, the most contradictory and utterly irreconcilable definitions of the term are represented among women's groups that call themselves feminist, whose only common denominator is that they see all women oppressed by patriarchal power structures. But in defining causes, political consequences, and relations to other theories about society, opinions diverge so widely that thus far we have not been able to use an exact terminology or refer to a single predominating position which might have set definitions of these terms.

And there has not yet been a feminist art manifesto of the sort that either directly or indirectly political movements bring about, as for example the manifesto of Russian artists shortly after the revolution or of the many European artist groups in the twenties.

But perhaps the initial question also implies that through the feminist movement, certain as yet unrealized feminine qualities—that is, characteristics which have been socially smothered in men, such as sensitivity, fantasy—can be expressed with confidence first in art works by women.

The question about feminine imagery cannot even begin to be answered due to the lack of film-producing women, and it would break all rules of statistics to force a deduction about aesthetic similarities from the 100 films women have produced at different times, in different cultures and countries, about the most varied topics and most diverse genres. Such an effort might be worthwhile if there were anything approaching equal participation of the sexes in the arts, but I doubt then if this would still interest us.

In addition, we should consider that until very recently, femininity was always defined by others, and that only now have women begun to comprehend themselves as social subjects and to throw off alien interpretations of their nature and being. The organized expression of these efforts is the women's movement, which from all sides and with dissimilar results and battles is feeling out the question of what women want, more than the question of what women are.

Women have just begun to *dare* to see themselves and others, society, with their own eyes; to compare alien opinions and theories to their own experiences; to formulate first concepts with the help of which we can begin to comprehend the nature of past feminine oppression, today's social contradictions, and our expectations for a different human future.

And in every woman's behavior toward herself and in others' toward women—in laws, traditions, and work regulations—nowadays we always find both images: woman as object and as subject; therefore both—the traditional and conditioned, and the politically new—will be present in work by women, including that of contemporary women filmmakers. It is yet to be seen whether women, when first given a chance to do whatever they want, will explode in never-before-seen forms, contents, and techniques—and it will then result from entirely different social conditions.

The visual arts at least tend to answer this question about feminine imagery with "yes." Women's preferences for certain genres, materials, and forms also seem to express particularly feminine aesthetic concepts; something like this also floats around in the women's movement, though it has been adequately recognized in the meantime that women have usually painted still lifes and portraits because they were *forbidden* to make studies of nudes, to say nothing of the barriers to sculpture.

This approach in film aesthetics is by its very nature senseless because we are dealing with standardized materials and equipment. But that does not prevent similar theses from being proposed in the area of film, claiming that women prefer, out of feminist conviction, video, documentary film, and semiprofessional work in groups with other women. Every such argument has economic causes but this is totally ignored. If one wants to work with film, video becomes a cheaper compromise, documentary films are usually cheaper than features; and the fact that some women filmmakers call on their women friends to help on sound, directing, and in other capacities stems from pure need.

So if for all the above-mentioned reasons we cannot speak of feminine imagery, and the women who film or paint, etc., interest themselves less in the question of whether their products are feminine, but rather in whether their products are authentic, then the penetration of the women's movement into the arts has made it possible for the first time, systematically, to recognize patriarchal ideologies in art works, that is to say, mostly male art works. The *absence* of certain sexist stereotypes which we could find throughout film history in films by women does not yet constitute a feminine imagery, but rather at the very most leads to attention to sensitivity for image-predominant ideologies.

Until now, with a few exceptions during the silent film era, film has been purely a male domain; and as such a widely distributed and immediate means of communication, it has also shaped women's images of themselves, their roles, their ideals, and standards of beauty. Women in film were for a long time the artistic creations of those who made the images.

We can perhaps measure the meaning of this indoctrination through false images if we consider that only about two percent of the population reads literature, and literary production has always been less standardized than film production; but nearly everyone shares in film culture through movies and today through television. Although the participation of women working in these media has grown in recent years, women still make up just a fraction of the whole and are almost never involved in decision making.

The women's movement in the arts now reveals the masculinity mania in art and is freeing the image of women from a "natural feminine state" and from an assumed "natural" relation to men visually as well. A very simple example of this is that in film even more than in reality women are expected to be shorter than men; for example, no serious romances could ever occur between partners of the same height, much less between tall women and short men. If this happens, it is always only comical and means that the *man* in such a relationship is not to be taken seriously. It is new that such a relationship today can be treated with irony, as in that TV news report showing a visit to Mao by Kissinger with his wife Nancy—a head taller than Henry; Mao, giggling, pointed repeatedly at Mrs. Kissinger while looking at Kissinger, as if Mao were bringing a good joke into politics. The newscaster announced this item with a slight smile.

In recent years, many Hollywood actresses have complained that scripts are no longer being written in which women appear. We at *Frauen und Film* have suggested that this could be perhaps unconsciously a correct and honest reaction to the women's movement. If one has nothing to say, one should remain silent; it is only in keeping with principles that women's roles get eliminated altogether.

I hope I have made clear thus far that the denial of female imagery does not mean that art does not vary according to sex, any less than it varies according to class, as socialist theory has analyzed. I do not mean by this that these aspects and others—national characteristics, for example—add up to determine a work of art, but rather that they enter into the formal experience that only an artwork makes accessible.

But just as a progressive social theory has led to a dogmatic aesthetics, that is, the equation of "social realism" with a thesis about knowledge (about how we experience the forms of knowledge), feminism has also had the tendency to make certain aesthetic categories a measure of the aesthetic experience. Thus spontaneity, in women not so much oppressed but rather socially patronized, has been sharply ideologized, and the form into which this spontaneity flows has been summarily declared to be art. This phenomenon is like the fact that science's being antipathetic to women has led to women's groups showing an antipathy to theory.

In a turnabout, social deficits are simply idealized and declared artistic victories. From such tendencies within the women's movement itself, then, definitions can be arrived at which always see women and their works only partially and not in terms of our whole living condition.

But underlying those sometimes so emphatically expressed women's demands for collectivity and spontaneity is also the wish to abolish the dichotomy which makes some responsible for the production of goods and the others for the arts. At the base lies the wish that it be the fundamental right of every person to work out experiences in every direction. In the realization of this demand, with all the catastrophes and horrors it brings, lies a piece of utopia; there is only rarely, very rarely, a lucky case when the joint work of nonprofessionals results in outstanding productions.

I have already implied that women today find themselves in a situation perhaps best compared to that of Kaspar Hauser or the Wild Child. We must first learn to see with our own eyes and not through the mediation of others. And when we have just first begun to talk, we still stutter and write no poetry. This leads feminist artists to conflicts for which there are no solutions and which affect them qualitatively totally differently than male artists.

The women's movement is striving to examine our fragmented history from the point of view of women's interests. So far there has been virtually no division of labor at this, only gargantuan efforts to gather individual insights piece by piece. The questions touch everyone existentially. The forms of confronting issues require again and again that we abandon our own line of work and choose between things of immediate importance to the movement and the requirements of our own work, which is in many ways, however, also based on the entire movement's insights. We are not only building a house, but simultaneously gathering and assembling the materials for it ourselves.

Women artists have worked not only on art but on the movement's pressing problems, always in the hope of soon making their presence there rather superfluous in order to be able to concentrate again fully on developing their own talents. Almost all the women's movements' projects with which we have meanwhile become acquainted are unpaid and have arisen from this inner contradiction, such as the first women's film festival organized by women filmmakers to familiarize themselves with otherwise inaccessible knowledge; the art exhibitions; the journal *Frauen und Film*, for work on which even today no one makes a penny.

Many film projects have also arisen in order to contribute to social campaigns, for example around Paragraph 218, contraceptives, etc., all born of the desire to support the women's movement in such a way as to have an immediate effect. But this often distracts from women artists' own projects, which are more complicated and stand in a much less direct relation to the movements. The pressure of making many such works without financial support, and often with untrained people, quickly leads to unbearable conflicts with the women filmmakers' own standards of excellence; and such films are frequently used in an official context against the filmmakers when they are applying for money.

Furthermore, the art and film market will scarcely allow even a temporary absence. Artists must rigorously pursue their own interests or else be lost. It means being torn back and forth between the women's movement and its demands and its advances on the one hand, and the conditions of artistic work on the other. This contradiction leads to nearly insoluble internal and external problems, which necessarily become apparent in our work. Besides, the competition in the free-lance world is murderous. This system again turns women filmmakers themselves into competitors, because in comparison to their male colleagues they receive fewer commissions to begin with and do not yet have a lobby of any sort.

Beyond this, many of the qualities which are encouraged in and through the women's movement, such as eliminating hierarchical behavior and irrational authority, and recognizing and paying attention to underrated abilities, are in actual work situations likely to result in catastrophe. Filmmaking conditions are so intertwined with the laws of the market that humane behavior at work is often interpreted as feminine weakness. Consider too that normal professional work teams derive from labor traditions which fully accept capitalist values.

In short, wherever women land, within a very short time there is nothing but confusion, shock, excitement.

If we also consider that many women, in keeping with their principles, propose to make films on subjects which have arisen from a movement which the ruling powers ignore or fight, then we can get a pretty good idea of what happens before productions, that is, where decisions about financial means are made. Examples of this are almost all of the works which came out of the campaigns against Paragraph 218. Because the political demands of the women's movement could not, in fact, really be theoretically grounded with the public media, this resulted in the semiprofessional works which I have already mentioned, often formally quite lacking. These works born of necessity have led, as I said, in definitions about feminist film to the sort of conclusion that feminist film is presumably "primarily interested in the documentary and mistrusts the power of fantasy."

Still other aesthetic points of friction have arisen in these confrontations. Quite materialistically and simply, the women's movement has begun with itself, with the female body, thereby exposing injustices and alien definitions. Now in many of these films, nude bodies and sexual organs play a role, these being filmed not to awaken erotic feelings in men nor to be sexually neutral or medically functional, but rather to picture the female body so as to lead women into the blank regions of unexplored subjectivity.

Because a female sex organ is immediately associated with pornography and thus banned from all public media, we can imagine the collisions between themes of this kind with public broadcasting stations, for the stations follow general guidelines which clearly forbid showing anything which violates customary moral feeling or which in principle challenges marriage and family. This challenge, however, forms a basis of the entire women's movement. On the international scale, this chapter of women seeing their bodies with their own eyes is far from having been written to the end; and it will become explosive anew when contributed to by our Arab sisters, who must struggle to win not only the filmic right to their own bellies but also even the right to their own unveiled faces. Not long ago a newspaper article mentioned that the Turkish censor had forbidden showing love scenes or women in bathing suits in films.

When we perceive our own interests, we do not express that only in tearing down ruling ideologies, but really concretely in confrontations at the work place, now among women filmmakers in the arts industry. To put it in other terms: women's most authentic act today—in all areas including the arts—consists not in standardizing and harmonizing the means, but rather in destroying them. Where women are true, they break things.

With visual material, this "breakage" has been the most progressive in analyses and the most diffuse in practice. It often makes productions disjointed and inconsistent, especially with women artists who have just begun to work, those not trained in and then building on an art tradition before joining the women's movement and then consciously distancing themselves formally from this tradition.

Of course, we also should not forget that there are women filmmakers and artists who because of personal distance from the women's movement remain altogether untouched by these problems and can for this reason often work much more effectively; unburdened by politics, they can get commissions and sit on certainty instead of on chaos. In contrast, feminist artists say with Bob Dylan: I like chaos, but I don't know whether chaos likes me.

Sander was the editor of Frauen und Film, *the only feminist film journal appearing in Europe on a regular basis, from 1974 to 1981.*

35. Alexander Kluge

The Spectator as Entrepreneur* (1979)

The film and television corporations live off the money and the cooperation of the imaginative faculties (unpaid labor) which they extract from the spectator. They designate anyone a mature citizen who is willing to pay. Kant says: "Enlightenment is man's release(*Ausgang*) from his self-incurred tutelage *(selbstverschuldete Unmündigkeit)*." Leni Peickert says:

> "People are mature
> when they have their day off . . ."

In order to cheat the spectators on an entrepreneurial scale, the entrepreneurs have to designate the spectators themselves as entrepreneurs. The spectator must sit in the movie house or in front of the TV set like a commodity owner: like a miser grasping every detail and collecting surplus on everything which has any value. Value per se. So uneasy this spectator-consumer, alienated from his own life so completely like the manager of a supermarket or a department store who—even at the price of death (heart attack)—will not stop accumulating the last scraps of marketable goods in the storeroom so that they may find their buyers. How disturbed he is when people pass by his store; how nervous he gets about objects in the storeroom which do not sell immediately.

In a similarly entrepreneurial fashion the spectator—having reached the desired consumer maturity—scans films for their spectacle and exhibition values, for complete intelligibility, just as one is taught to gnaw a bone thoroughly, as the saying goes, so that the sun will shine. The sun, however, "taking its thunderous course," according to its own habits and unconcerned with human communication, does not care the least whether or not we clean our plates.

Understanding a film completely is conceptual imperialism which colonizes its objects. If I have understood everything then something has been emptied out.

We must make films that thoroughly oppose such imperialism of consciousness. I encounter something in film which still surprises me and which I can perceive without devouring it. I cannot understand a puddle on which the rain is falling—I can only see it; to say that I understand the puddle is meaningless. Relaxation means that I myself become alive for a moment, allowing my senses to run wild: for once not to be on guard with the policelike intention of letting nothing escape me.[1]

1. Fafner in (Wagner's) *Rheingold* was once a powerful giant. With his brother, he built Valhalla, a feat the gods themselves had been unable to accomplish. Then he killed his brother and is now guarding the treasure. He sits there like a dragon.

Leni Peickert, played by Hannelore Hoger, is an expert in circus reform and the protagonist of Kluge's film, Die Artisten in der Zirkuskuppel: ratlos/The Artists under the Big Top: Perplexed *(1967) and the short,* Die unbezähmbare Leni Peickert/The Indomitable Leni Peickert *(1969).*

36. Birgit Hein
Some Notes about Our Film Work (1980)

For many years I have tried to explain our own films and those of other filmmakers to the audience. Now I have come to realize that this is impossible. The explanations have become a system of their own, which has less and less to do with the films. Finally there was the situation that we tried to adjust the films to the systems.

Such a system is the "structural film," which in the meantime has become a sort of "instruction manual." At the moment I can't use its definitions any more. Therefore, I simply will make some statements about our work.

When we started making films, we were painters and all our knowledge and enthusiasm were bound up in painting, mainly the abstract painting of the twenties. We didn't know much about film. Until I was twenty, I only went to the movies once a year, and this was always after Christmas, together with the whole family.

We also never watched television. (Today of course everyone has a TV, even in Germany, and I watch a lot, too.)

How we changed from painting to filmmaking is difficult to explain. I hardly can recall the transition period. It seems as if life only started after that point, the moment when Wilhelm and I found a way to work together, something that had been impossible while painting. Definitely it had something to do with Buñuel's Mexican films. I remember the film about the jungle with the burning postcard of Paris, in black and white (as in dreams), although later I saw it again in color.

But the main thing was that we wanted to work with film as with painting: not to tell stories, not to represent reality, but to show rhythm, movement, and light. This sounds like the theories of the twenties. It is true, we had no knowledge about film history and had to invent it ourselves anew. We tried to find out how we could get hold of *Film*

Culture. It must have been a little bit later, about 1965, and [Stan] Brakhage was the greatest. His theory was wonderful: out-of-focus, dirt, paint on the filmstrip.

The first images we shot with our new secondhand camera were disgustingly trivial and realistic. So we had to cut the shots shorter and shorter and to shake the camera while shooting to achieve an "abstract" sequence. *Rohfilm* (*Raw Film*, 1968) was the first pleasing result. The explosion of image particles, paper, dirt, tobacco glued on the blank film strip, caused a physical visual experience. We had found one way to overcome reality: to reproduce the same material by refilming it several times in different ways.

—To insiders, yes, yes, I know Ken Jacobs's *Tom, Tom, the Piper's Son* . . . And this is not an "innocent" effort to say that we had already started refilming from the screen a year earlier. Today this doesn't mean anything anymore, because only the result counts, which obviously is different.

Ken Jacobs's system and didactics were totally out of keeping with our interests, but there is the same lust for film material, grain, stains, dots, and flicker (flacker would be a nicer word if there were such a phrase in English). Only eight years later with the *Materialfilme* (*Material Films*) did we really come to the presentation of the film material. They are not a repetition of an old idea *(Raw Films),* but the realization of the idea: not refilming, no artificial destruction, but the real, fragile, brittle, crumbly, friable, broken material, with its burst emulsion, in its unique visual quality.

—The *"objet trouvé"* is always also an intellectual decision, and of course it is not new. Dear Ernst Schmidt, dear Hans Scheugl, who was the first? But what counts is the result (as I said already). Those who can't see what is there on the screen will never understand our films.

The preoccupation with the process of reproduction led us naturally to give up filming reality and to start working from reproductions: photos, film sequences, in 16mm and super 8mm. The series of the *Portraits* shows this work since 1970. The compilation is arbitrary in the sense that there never was a plan we followed. Over the years there were several versions, according to the dominating interest at the time. Some *Portraits* are in *Strukturelle Studien* (*Structural Studies*, 1974) (or have been), or they were in other films. Our work as a whole is a continuous process and not an output of eternal products. Of course the "work" becomes smaller and smaller and there is so little left.

This period is over! Now we are in a very productive phase!—But really, what are the films all about: only the material, the reproduction process, a visual, sensual experience? Nothing higher or deeper, greater, like at least the four elements, or the universe, or something transcendent? Unfortunately not. But why always these repetitions! Because they are what is interesting to us: the same image that always changes, the process from the image content to the image quality, and to see both together, to see how the image quality determines the content. We don't tell stories about those who are represented (only casually), but about how they are represented, about what is there: not about them, but the image, the film strip, and about what we see or make visual when we produce a film.

Bazin talks about a certain type of montage that is unrealistic and constructed and aims at creating a meaning that is not objectively in the images but comes from the relationship of the images to each other.

The sequence of films in the *Portraits* works in a similar way. The content results from the confrontation of the different units.

—What an effort to explain this to somebody else!

And why at all?

It doesn't really help anyhow, as the essential can't be told but must be seen instead.

Birgit and Wilhelm Hein have been married since 1964 and been making films since 1967.—Hans Scheugl and Ernst Schmidt, Jr. are the authors of Eine Subgeschichte des Films: Lexikon des Avantgarde-, Experimental-und Undergroundfilms, *2 vols. (Frankfurt am Main: Suhrkamp, 1974). See the entry on the Heins in volume one, 356–61.—For further reflections by Birgit Hein on their work and its contexts, see "The Avantgarde and Politics,"* Millennium Film Journal, *vol. 1, no. 2 (Spring–Summer 1978): 23–28, and "Geduld und eiserne Nerven: Zur Situation des Experimentalfilms in der Bundesrepublik," in* Jahrbuch Film 79/80, *ed. Hans Günther Pflaum (Munich: Hanser, 1979), pp. 80–89. A comprehensive collection of documents depicts the Heins' career as a whole:* W + B Hein, Dokumente 1967– 1985: Fotos, Briefe, Texte, *ed. Christiane Habich (Frankfurt am Main: Deutsches Filmmuseum, 1985).*

37. Jutta Brückner
Women's Films Are Searches for Traces (1981)

Women are waking up as filmmakers and becoming aware of how society creates and regulates our sense of the media. In this media world, women, who have always been instrumentalized, even in most sociological investigations, because their forms of existence only assume a negative significance, are supposed to, suddenly and overnight, become active subjects. Behind the camera, pressed into modes of production bound in male modes of thinking and sensing which take apart and reassemble, they are now supposed to function as creators, to express something society has not allowed to exist ("feminist aesthetics"), neither in the historical public sphere nor in the intimacy of the private one. The transition from beloved and other-directed object to autonomous, self-directed subject occurs a little too suddenly so that it is not free of losses stemming from the frictions between employer and employee, crew and director, and films and audience. But, above all, women rub themselves raw. And the temptation is great to become daddy's sulky little girl, whose caprices are confused with autonomy, a role that we, after all, know well from our childhood reading.

I want to talk about the women who resist this temptation, however, and only these women. Even if one assumes that the time for women has come, because, among other things, the wretched lot of women still has more strength than the healthy state of men, one must say in the same breath that this society is still well enough organized and has the strength to do us in. And the instinct that defends itself against feminist radicalism remains firmly entrenched. For feminist films are not something that women could or would want to make only for themselves, they are not films for limited audiences or minorities, contrary to what one hears even well-meaning souls occasionally claim these days. Like every movement with an avant-garde impetus, women filmmakers seek to redefine history, including art history, going back all the way to the Western reflexive premise of *cogito ergo sum.* The aims of women filmmakers are expansive. This makes things difficult, but also more vital, because women, precisely due to their "lack," have not yet forgotten that there exists life which is more than the sum of functions, roles, and emotions. Capitalism as the mortal enemy of art as well as woman (Ernst Bloch) senses, with good reason, the all-out attack. The fact that women were permitted for centuries to partake of the fine arts as a recreational activity while their husbands pursued the more serious task of creating a society that denied this art any epistemological value and conceded it only an ornamental one, stems not solely from patriarchal arbitrariness but also contains an inherent logic that might now be turned against patriarchy. Namely, women may now assume an active role at the moment where an art form becomes accessible which virtually redeems their most crucial loss: prelinguistic sensory reality, the sensuality not only of the eye. Exposed to our collective conformity at the price of collective repression, we find in the cinema a space to wish for our own images, our own experience of lost speech and lacking images, because increasingly we were made into images instead of having ones of our own. We do not have this space, but we would like to have it.

This negative inventory hardly smacks of the carefree hours one supposedly now and again whiles away at the cinema if it is to survive as culture. Rather it is somewhat frightening. But the recognition of lacks is today the necessary basis for realism, and this does not exclude fantasy production. What does not exist in society should not appear in art as something real. Up to now women have refused to continue the sorry German legacy of making art into a substitute for meaningful social activity.

Women's films are searches for traces, affirmation of identity as film's theme and process, hopeful stories looking forward to a self-confident life, in which one can feel and think at the same time. Feminist aesthetics expresses how hard it is to see emotionally in an age where the eye has become the most abstract of all the sense organs and now carries objectification to hyperbolic extremes. It also expresses a process whose goal is in fact what fuels this process: feminist aesthetics. This much-discussed phenomenon is not simply there because women now have the opportunity to stand behind cameras. Damaged sensuality also reacts to a damaging reality in a damaged way. The films bear witness to things that one lives with at the price of sickness and dissatisfaction, not as the representation of feminist insights, no matter how important they might be as the replication of a certain syntax, but rather the integration of self-consciousness, a sort of seeing with one's head and stomach and knee. Perhaps there exist moments in this process where one gets a glimmer of what might be possible, if only.

When women's films here succeed in being radical, many people feel frustrated. Even the many yearning, intellectual men who love the cinema are scared away, because women insist on their desire to show things that all those people sitting in the dark of the movie theater who do not want to reconcile themselves to the reality of the functional, can only vaguely sense as a desire. Feminist films do not lend themselves to cult worship and cineastes, they are signposts on the road to a gradual liberation of individual and collective creativity and not the stimulus for cineastic celebration.

The difficulties, however, do not diminish even as we seem to become more familiar with the means and techniques of production. This is because women, whose self-confidence is only fragmentary in terms of what is acceptable in modern society, first of all have to organize themselves before they organize anything else, not their lives, but themselves: the connection of their stomach ulcer to the head busy adding up figures; the relation of the "neurotic" need to sleep to the demands of an overly organized shooting schedule; the bearing of the intimate desire to try and recover obscured notions of creativity on the exigencies of getting the product of these labors onto the market immediately, to make a profit or at least to break even. We are developing social resilience at the price of never really developing for ourselves the body of experience we are trying to document.

The path leads at once inward and outward, the gaze forward and backward, the search for traces into the past and into the future, the present as a moment of passage to that which is not yet, not real anymore. Gabi Teichert digs about in German history, we are digging about in ourselves as well and finding German history, also and even in the way we are digging.

The result is often the deadly silence that exists in the heart of a real hurricane, which does not only take place in the cinema, a very slow anger, but also an anger that painstakingly makes use of existing aesthetic forms, the anger that functions for us as an important gauge indicating that the principle of capitalistic rationalization, something we are at least in part subjected to in the filmmaking process, has not yet taken control over us from the inside. The leap from deficit to self-confident creativity has something suicidal about it. Women can tell you what kind of strength it takes to see through the schizophrenic strategy society demands of female artists. Persevering between pragmatism and utopia. The story of Münchhausen, who pulls himself out of the swamp by his own hair, is for women a political parable in which outside is inside, and inside is outside.

Women's cinema lives in and through contradiction, existing as a utopia in the never-ending process of coming nearer, constantly threatened by the social mechanisms that would like to extinguish its life, not only through active enmity, but also by passive nonacceptance. What is still at issue today is not so much the plain truth, but rather the lesser untruth. The undeveloped, whose forms we do not yet know and can only sense, is still not yet an alternative to what we know, but nonetheless not a deficit in the real, but rather in the possible.

Every step toward overcoming this situation becomes part of self-perpetuating strategies as long as they lead up the rungs of the ladder. And therefore even behind the important demand of 50 percent of all subsidy funding made by the Association of Women Film Workers lurks the danger that all these small steps up the ladder will end suddenly in a bottomless pit, that of the status quo.

It makes sense that women, who have been "behind" and "below" for so long, now also want to be "ahead" and "above." One must possess considerable autonomy to turn down an offered plate of sweets, knowing well it can only make one sick, instead insisting to one's benefactors that one has the right to eat a balanced meal as well. What strength it takes to express the truth unabashedly in the face of state television arrangements, the moral sensibilities of CSU-TV and listener organizations, also in the face of the conventions of established art, whose crisis is obvious, and—for usually this is most difficult—unabashedly to oneself as well.

Even with a new theoretical consciousness and a few lawsuits which have rattled social bastions, things have not gotten easier. The courage demanded here makes a mark on autonomous female individuals at the same time that it frees them: they are no longer lovable. The dialectic of the process—creation through destruction—does not only apply to a culture in which women will not, should not, cannot make themselves comfortable, but also to women themselves. No one is sure what the synthesis will look like.

One of its possible aspects might be allowing ourselves to get rid of our warranted inhibition about using such words as happiness and beauty—our inhibition about the words themselves and also what they signify.

Gabi Teichert is the female protagonist of Alexander Kluge's film, Die Patriotin (The Patriot). She is a schoolteacher and an inquisitive soul who searches for "the foundations of German history," trekking through a wintry landscape with a shovel over her shoulder.

38. Margarethe von Trotta
Female Film Aesthetics* (1982)

If there is such a thing at all as a female form of aesthetics in film, it lies for me in the choice of themes, in the attentiveness as well, the respect, the sensitivity, the care, with which we approach the people we're presenting as well as the actors we choose. In the case of women it is clear that we do not seek the same apparent sorts of beauty. (Even Hanna [Schygulla] will look different in my films than in her others.) The most essential thing is that we make no distinction between reason and emotion, large and small events, for we still have retained to a degree the antihierarchical beliefs of matriarchy. Under matriarchy all people were equal because they were all the children of mothers. The love of mothers is granted without conditions or limits, one does not have to earn it through some effort or accomplishment. Patriarchy introduced the notion of a favorite son, he had to earn the love of his father through his accomplishments and his obedience. That marks the beginning of hierarchical thinking. Hierarchy brought the splitting of various realms and gradually led to the opposition between public and private. In *Die verlorene Ehre der Katharina Blum (The Lost Honor of Katharina Blum)*, Böll has his prosecuting attorney cast aspersions on K.B.: "It is inconceivable to me how hard it is for many people to separate one's job from the private realm." With that he hit the nail on the head, this difference between public and private life. For that reason we stand up in public for what we think in private and are not so able and eager to make compromises. I think that is a virtue and precisely this virtue, which is to be found in our films, might lead perhaps to a new aesthetics.

39. Ulrike Ottinger

The Pressure to Make Genre Films: About the Endangered *Autorenkino* (1983)

Fridolin was a nice little mouse. He did what everyone else did and saw what everyone else saw. He had long since removed himself from the wild and dangerous life in the country and taken up lodgings in a small apartment in the city. Every day he nibbled from the overflowing feeding dish of a big fat cat, and he never went hungry. He even had gotten more or less used to the monotonous kitty chow and he had just started to enjoy the predictable routine of his daily life when all of a sudden something unexpected happened: the feeding dish was empty. But next to it stood a gigantic casserole with fish: trout in Riesling with fine herbs.

Granted: it looked tempting. But—so he asked himself—what would occur if he tasted it and let himself be seduced by such exotic delights? Enough is enough. He had a right to his habits. Who dared to make him so agitated? And in fact this irregularity upset him so much that he did not hear the big fat cat come back. She ate Fridolin first, then the trout, then she licked up the last bit of the sauce. And only in the cat's stomach did Fridolin notice with some irritation how wonderful the sauce tasted. But by then it was too late.

The continuing endeavors of the film industry to limit filmmakers and directors to the most narrow, stereotyped genre cinema possible cannot be overlooked. The more one remains limited to the things which are ostensibly common to everyone, the less one can hope to further understanding for singular, particular, or independent developments of certain individuals, groups, minorities, countries, etc. The consequence of this is an ignorant, intolerant society whose intolerance grows in accordance with its lack of information and its corresponding lack of understanding for different things.

The film industry has a vested interest in binding creativity in the most harmless and, in its eyes, most effective way to its conceptual framework. For instance, a joke writer is allowed to say unusual things within the traditional framework, because the exception only serves to prove the rule—and hence poses no threat. If one resists, on the other hand, being placed in this framework, then one quickly gains the status of a black sheep and is rejected. Here one still enjoys creative freedom, but no longer any production money.

Artistic-aesthetic arguments are in the end always countered by box-office arguments. Right now for instance the film and TV producers are gathered in unison against the *Autorenfilmer*. An example is Günther Rohrbach's speech about "The Fateful Power of Directors"—that is the exact title of his speech—in which the otherwise conservative figure, who has a preference for leftist rhetoric, attempts to show that the power of directors cannot accord to the divine plan, in this way trying to put control back in the hands of the producers.

A lively gauntlet consisting of TV editors, program directors, producers, distributors, exhibitors, film subsidy committees, all of these await the unconventional film that cannot be readily cubbyholed, which might even provoke some angry letters from viewers, these are all out there. One might argue that this has always been the case, but what is new here is the way in which forty- and fifty-year-olds demonstrate a particular zeal for using the arguments of '68 in a surprisingly perverse manner. . .

I remember how in 1968 [Pierre] Bourdieu's *L'Amour de l'art,* and its publication of statistics regarding art appreciation among all classes of society and different levels of education moved me and many of my friends to become intensely involved with the reception of art and in conjunction with the events of '68 transformed no small number of artists into unhappy producers of posters, into consciously popular and trivial comic-strip designers, social workers, or even in one particular case I can recall into a suicide candidate. In this exciting time, full of changes in our thoughts and lives, we went through experiences that allowed many of us to carry on with heightened aesthetic and artistic expectations.

The daily regimen of many hours of TV training limits the visual habits of most people so sharply to television conventions that they are effectively unable to understand any other visual and aural language. If one tries to use different possibilities—and there are any number of these, especially in film, ones not used, ones waiting to be discovered, for instance, the visual language of the silent film which is much more advanced than what we see today—to reach a general audience, one is almost bound to fail. The resistance is absolute. Thus the absurd situation comes about that film, the youngest of the arts, is already completely administered. And it almost seems to be the case: the greater the unused potential, the greater the fear among the film industry, for there is no telling what a (still) unbought film author or filmmaker might do with these untapped possibilities.

Even some of the alternative cinemas are in the meanwhile programming American B movies, adventure and entertainment films. If they were doing so because they have a weakness for these films, or simply because they think it will be more lucrative to show the well-established genres, then it wouldn't even be worth mentioning. But they justify this with public statements claiming that the independent German film is bad, boring, burdened with problems, etc.—and they mean the *Autorenkino*, the few remaining people who film freely and independently, not sure whether they are a nearly extinct breed of dinosaurs, the last adventurous souls, or heroes of our time.

New aesthetic forms, which function in accordance with our expectations, which provoke or irritate, have to be searched for and found. Example: Nowadays I wouldn't show a National Socialist in a fascist uniform nor would I show de Sade any longer in laced booties. Another possibility is seemingly to follow the clichés of a certain genre, playing up of course to the traditional expectations of the audience, in order to resolve the cliché in a novel way. An example of this is my pirate film, *Madame X—eine absolute Herrscherin (Madame X)*, which consciously works with genre expectations and nonetheless transcends the false, that is, customary, expectations.

The three apes who do not see, hear, speak: film language. Film language is not only dialogue. Most of the television films or series, or films made according to the patterns of television dramaturgy which we see nowadays, could be understood even if we closed our eyes. Maybe this might be an effective way of fully realizing just how banal the dialogue is, just how entirely devoid of imagination the entire sound track is. If we try and do without the sound and only watch, we will not—in contrast to silent film—be able to follow the action.

Visual language no longer functions. A constant coming and going, even the car door is regularly opened and closed. Poorly shaped images, no use of color schemes, images for illiterates. Wild tracking cameras, usually for no good reason. Technical effects for their own sake celebrate joyless victories. At most it's a joy for the little boy behind the camera who has in the meanwhile grown up, even if he still likes to play with his train set.

First the expectations which a large audience has of a spectacle were systematically toned down. And then reduced to the most common denominator. If one as an artist does not act in keeping with this dictate, then one is labeled "asocial, undemocratic, not comprehensible for the masses, elite" and things worse than that. The *Bild-Zeitung* has a much larger circulation that the *Frankfurter Rundschau*. This fact is seen in a positive light by the film industry and in a negative one by the film-makers.

A potential French coproducer recently recommended that I make my films technically as elaborate and also as realistic in their detail and story as a James Bond film. The audience simply is used to things being like this. It makes no sense running at windmills like Don Quixote and shutting oneself off from this fact. And with my imagination and my powers of emotion it surely would be possible for me to come up with an identification figure for a very large audience, a person who then could go on to experience all kinds of bizarre things, because it goes without saying that she didn't want to impose any further limits on me. I told her that I might be able to agree with a limitation in the final point, but in no case could I accept the other ones. The coproduction fell through.

The intention of the film industry is, as was the case long ago in Hollywood, to change directors according to financial considerations every bit as often as other crew members. One final sentence in this regard: a *Querelle* by Fassbinder is something different than one by Schlöndorff or one by Genet or by Schroeter or by von Trotta or by me.

We make the originals, other people make the wallpaper.

Rohrbach's speech was published as "Die verhängnisvolle Macht der Regisseure," in Medium, *April 1983, pp. 40–41.—The influential book discussed by Ottinger is Pierre Bourdieu and Alain Darbel's* L'Amour de l'art, les musées et leur public *(Paris: Éditions de Minuit, 1966).*

40. Alfred Behrens
New European Film and Urban Modernity* (1986)

I am an author and a director, I live in a city with a population of two, more accurately, three-and-a-half million, in the British sector of the former capital of the German Reich, Berlin. I use a Japanese typewriter, my boxer shorts are "made in France," my pants, my shirt, and my shoes come from Italy, my socks from the Federal Republic of Germany, my typing paper as well, I make my films with an Aäton from France and a Nagra from Switzerland.

What kind of films are made under these conditions?

Last year I made a half-German film with an English title, *Walkman Blues*. In West Berlin, in the northern part of the suburb Moabit. As a coproduction with Basis-Film, ZDF–*Kleines Fernsehspiel*, and Channel 4. The film stars the Austrian actor Heikko Deutschmann, a twenty-year-old musician from Hamburg who has just come to Berlin. The Canadian actress Jennifer Capraru plays a twenty-year-old photographer from London who has recently moved to Berlin. The two meet in the "Loft" on Nollendorfplatz where the group Blurt from Stroud/Gloucestershire is performing. Both actors were living in Berlin when I hired them. Ted Milton and his band come on tour at least once a year and play in the Loft. The group has a much larger following in Germany and France than it does in Great Britain.

Life in the big city—and not only there, but also in the so-called provinces as well—is no longer a life with a national specificity, a life of rustic havens. This is a different reality which the *New European Film* should depict, in color or in black-and-white. In the form of a low budget film, an *Autorenfilm*, a B movie, a film for three actors, as the kind of endeavor which makes a virtue out of the limited budget, the virtue of truth, the virtue of veracity.

What is at issue?

It has to be possible to think of a European film. To think of film in European terms. Without the consequence of a thoroughly watered-down Euro-film. The European film might once again model itself as an *Autorenfilm*. It could look to Jean Renoir for guidance: "All my life I have tried to make author's films; not out of vanity, but because God instilled in me the single desire to define my identity."

The *Autorenfilm* is no longer in fashion, both critics and popular audiences turn to trendy forms of entertainment; people who no longer have an identity, no longer need an identity, also no longer go to the movies to seek self-definition. I went to the cinema when I was sixteen, when I was eighteen, when I was twenty years old, at the time when I started to think for myself, in order to see images, to hear sounds, to partake of stories. Quite coincidentally the films of Godard, Truffaut, Resnais, the films of Sergei Eisenstein and John Ford defined me as well. Of course I still go to the movies for the same reasons, of course there still are films around that fascinate me and define who I am: *Vagabond* by Agnès Varda, *Stranger Than Paradise* by Jim Jarmusch, *Paul Chevrolet and the Ultimate Hallucination* by Pim de la Parra, *Caravaggio* by Derek Jarman, to name four examples. I would like to mention two others. Two films, both made in 1985, which intimate what a European film might look like. *Tagediebe (Hangin' Around)* by Marcel Gisler and *Schleuse 17 (Lock Number 17)* by Sebastian Lentz.

Gisler, a Swiss who has been living in Berlin since 1981, produced his film with Swiss subsidy money and the cooperation of the *Kleines Fernsehspiel*–ZDF. The film takes place in Berlin, much of it in the American sector, it features the three idlers, Max, Laurids, and Lola. Lola is played by a French woman with the German *nom de guerre* Dina Leipzig, Max and Laurids are played by Rudolf Nagler and Lutz Deisinger, neither of whom are professional actors and for that reason perhaps they bring all the more authenticity into the film. The director and players worked out the material in a long series of preliminary improvised video sessions, only after this work was a script written and a film ultimately made in black and white. In German and in part also in French. The idlers live for the moment, they wander aimlessly through the city, they too are drifters, drifters just like Sandrine Bonnaire, like John Lurie, Eszter Balint, and Richard Edson in the films by Agnès Varda and Jim Jarmusch. The idlers let themselves wander through the phase in which they live, their early twenties. They are in search of a possible life, a life style, seeking to form themselves, to formulate themselves. Completely playfully and at the same time completely seriously they try to pose the question, "How should one live/how can one live?"—and to answer it. *Hangin' Around*—a European film, an *Autorenfilm*, a low budget film. A film about life in the big city. Here, now, authentic, almost a documentary.

Lock Number 17 was Sebastian Lentz's final project at the Academy for Television and Film in Munich. A black-and-white film in the tradition of the *film noir*. The film is set in France, it has no real plot to speak of, three American gangsters take off with ten million francs. It doesn't really try to tell a story, the film isn't about a story, it's about much more. About the gangsters' cars (the casting here is perfect!), about their movements, about the confrontation of *three* languages in *one* film *without* subtitles, which nonetheless is at every moment comprehensible. There is a woman in this film who speaks German without an accent, who speaks American every bit as free of accent. She lives in the country home of a German writer near Gien. There she hides one of the gangsters who has been wounded in a shoot-out. The film was shot on location in France, the bit players speak French, the main roles alternate among the three languages. Original sound, no subtitles, no dubbing. One goes to the movies and really is in France. The film deals with the unknown in the familiar, the familiar in the unknown. The languages the film plays with are at once a constitutive dramatic element and a surplus, an aesthetic surplus value. *Lock Number 17*—a European film, a B movie, a poor film. The three languages are its wealth.

Crossing borders, going from one country to another, has become an everyday occurrence during the last twenty years. On vacation or on a

business trip. With a touch of the television remote control button. With
the cassette tape one pushes into the Walkman. While shopping in a
supermarket. In 1960 you had to go to France if you wanted to eat French
cheese, today one has France in the refrigerator. One shelf lower, Frascati
Secco or Rioja Blanco, Italy or Spain. I lived in London for four years, I
listen to English and American rock music, I leave Germany every year as
often as I can, as often as the low budget will allow, so that for a few days,
for a few weeks, I can become *un-German*. Because one life and one
nationality are not enough. Because one doesn't only want to be just one
person, but another one as well. The European Film might be defined
through the sound of its language—the Dutch voices speaking over the
English subtitles in Pim de la Parra's *Paul Chevrolet* are pure aural poetry.
"Not understanding definitely enhances one's pleasure," says Chris
Marker.

Perhaps the European film should also be defined as well by money
from the Common Market. Hamburg 1987, eight years since the Hamburg declaration of 1979, the beginning of self-administered film subsidy
in the Federal Republic, Hamburg 1987 might be the right place to
demand a self-administered film subsidy, to initiate it and to think ahead.

A subsidy system not in the hands of the Common Market bureaucracy or the big money alliance of the old producers and the new
media, but rather a cultural and economic support system for scripts,
productions, distribution, and exhibition, self-administered from below,
by directors, scriptwriters, cinematographers, editors, producers, people
who run cinemas and low-budget distributors.

*Behrens's comments were prompted by afterthoughts he had following a "Low-
Budget Film-Forum" held in Hamburg during mid-June of 1986.—He is also
the director of* Berliner Stadtbahnbilder (Images from the Berlin S-Bahn,
1981).

V

Discovering and Preserving German Film History

As international attention was focused on a collection of New German filmmakers who made a great splash during the midseventies at festivals, the resulting press accounts, with a remarkable consistency, insisted, as one commentator put it in *Horizon*, that these directors "began virtually without mentors or models. There was no tradition, nothing to follow, and, subsequently, no fear of duplication or triteness." Fassbinder was quoted in *Time* claiming, "We had nothing, and we started with nothing." Herzog, we learned in a tribute published in the *Soho Weekly News*, was like his peers: "We are all orphans, you know. We had no fathers to learn from." The disavowal of their parents' legacy remained a powerful mechanism; it was a way of clearing the ground for one's own efforts as well as absolving oneself from any links to a shame-filled past. Young people who had grown up in an environment of prevarication, obfuscation, and repression, began to confront their elders especially toward the late sixties, holding them responsible not only for being complicitous in the Third Reich, but also for seeking to eradicate and manipulate memories of that experience. The past per se—and that meant German films of the past as well—became a "bad object." In one's subsequent recollections, though, and above all in the films of New German directors, we find substantial evidence that the young filmmakers were not as apodictic in their rejection of the past as it might seem at first glance. Fassbinder's later films would make it clear how much he had learned from German films of previous epochs, just as recurring references in Wenders's work indicate his awareness of certain contours in German film history. Portions of the national film legacy could be and were recycled, even the left-for-dead *Heimatfilm*, a genre that stands as one of the most often revisited possibilities in West German film culture of the seventies and eighties. And, to be sure, in retrospect certain directors regretted missed opportunities, moments where the angry youngsters might have gained considerably if only they had been willing to listen to well-meaning elders. Lotte Eisner became something of a patron saint for New German filmmakers, the embodiment of a continuity between significant epochs in German film history and the enduring resonance of this legacy. An awareness of tradition summoned forth a desire to preserve this past and one's own endeavors, to collect German films and use them as a valuable collective memory bank, as sights and sounds which tell one's own history in all its complexity and richness.

41. Alf Brustellin
The Other Tradition (1971)

Somewhere—pushed to the margins of society, outside of the distribution monopolies and the first-run houses, frustratingly dependent on the one subsidy board and beaten half to death by the other, one leg in the underground while the other still looks for firmer soil, relying casually on the television stations without trusting the seeming calm—somewhere, in any case, it continues to exist despite all: the German film. And perhaps it is this "Somewhere" which is the worst thing about it all, perhaps it serves as a fitting signal for the oppression centered here—this relegation to a space outside of history, to a climate of pure survival tactics without tradition, creating discontinuously and in the end simply involved with the production of proofs that one still exists which turn out more or less through no fault of one's own to be self-indulgent . . . an atmosphere, one suited well for the schematic, even for this schematic statue of liberty Rainer Werner Fassbinder which one has hydraulically lifted from the ground.

One has to stare a very long time and very carefully at this "phenomenon" German film, which refuses to die in order to find some sort of sign, any kind of signal which does not simply appear in the sky like a cloud to be blown away by the next gust of wind (and by the film industry in any case). A signal that indicates a certain stability. Now they seem to be there all of a sudden—the traces of another tradition, one eternally disowned, pulverized by a hammer from above and a school book literature from below: the tradition of heresy and rebellion, which also—as unbelievable as it always sounds—does exist in Germany.

It would seem, though, that we have no form, and here that can only mean: no popular form (as a priori film) for this other, profane, absolutely thieving and murdering tradition of insurrection; it would seem as if it were only—from Kleist's *Michael Kohlhaas* to Bloch's *Thoma. Münzer*—something to be sighted from the heights of literature and philosophy, to be admired, continued as a revolutionary mind game, clad in elegant formulations. And now something strange is brewing, something absolutely logical, but nonetheless something that sounds absurd, i.e., it has been boiling for some time now and we have before us the first results.

The impetus is genial and banal: in Germany we have created only one film genre which could be called specifically German, the *Heimatfilm*, and we have let it go to seed. But when you think about it, it is precisely this genre, starring the common people, which is the ideal medium for telling the other version of history, for taking up the alternative tradition, that of the people of humble origin, the lower classes, the exploited, the forever defeated and the rebellious—for that reason we're creating the new German *Heimatfilm* which takes the "literary provinces" not as a model, as an exotic reflection of society's constraints and urban conditions, but rather as a historical space which seems to have been banned from reality thus far.

Schlöndorff, well-versed in dealing with rebels, but only now at ease, has made a start; the result we can see now could be much more than something noteworthy, simply an interesting attempt, something beyond an anti-Fleischmann conception; this is to be sure not a historicizing neo-realistic "documentary feature film" in a documentary play and theater style, but rather—perhaps, let us hope—the new beginning of a "popular" (film) tradition.

The film *Der plötzliche Reichtum der armen Leute von Kombach* (*The Sudden Wealth of the Poor People of Kombach*) was first shown on television, hardly distinguishable and perceivable in the crowded culture programming. Now it's playing in Munich, in the wrong cinema. It tells the story of seven farmers and day-laborers who plan an attack on a "money coach" transporting tax monies, clumsily failing again and again, finally succeeding before being caught with no great trouble—a police official only has to figure out who has money, which given conditions one couldn't otherwise have—in the end being forced to repent their sin and having done so, now ripe for execution. A single culprit escapes: the Jew David Briel, a traveling salesman who doesn't own land or have a house, who can take off simply and without much ado. (Wolfgang Bächler, not an actor, but a poet, shapes this figure into something incredibly fascinating in two scenes.) This is all told quietly and in a distanced manner, completely in the style, consciousness, and "atmosphere" of a handwritten chronicle, one whose elaborate phrases and complicated formulations draw attention to themselves and to the reality lurking behind them.

Perhaps that is the only problem in Schlöndorff's direction: the prototype of an official commentary and the prototype of anachronistic writing lead to embellishments with a new exclusivity, one above and beyond the images, awakening the impression of artsy intentions, a stylizing penchant equally at work in the chronicles. Nonetheless Schlöndorff's guiding principle is much more honest, effective, and completely spontaneous: he sought the images that were obscured in the reports and fictions; one feels the energy and the commitment bound up in trying to break through an incredibly thick wall of cultural reproduction to find an authentic piece of history.

This effort above all is apparent in the use of language. One can see how it can lead to the real state of affairs. Stylization and journalism, cultural and official reworking of history dominate the film's commentary and the simple language of the farmers appear next to all this like images appear next to "the image" which one makes out of such criminal cases.

All of this has nothing to do with archaeology or reproduction; it is not because the film pretends to be authentic that it is so interesting and unnervingly honest, but rather it is because it takes the energy to imagine something lying beyond accepted notions of "cultural heritage": imagination that does not end in a "popular" vision, a sense of history that can do without kings, and finally the courage not to put together generalities in whose constraints the images become reduced to pure evidence.

Schlöndorff's film doesn't work like a contrived and researched montage of things worth knowing and thinking about; it's not as easy to swallow as most of the information we receive about society in general. It's more like a *démontage*, a destruction of myths and comfortable notions. A raw gathering of ideas from another tradition in which many players and a few actors played a glowing role. Perhaps the impetus for a popular film, if one means by "popular" not a bargain basement ideology or a cheap sentimentality, but rather something simply "nondominant." Because: "We've seen enough world history, it was also enough, too much, much too much form, polis, construction, deception, culture that closes things off . . ." (Ernst Bloch, *Thomas Münzer*, 1921).

The complete title of Ernst Bloch's study is Thomas Münzer als Theologe der Revolution *(1921).—The Fleischmann film referred to is* Jagdszenen aus Niederbayern (Hunting Scenes from Lower Bavaria, 1968), *prototype of the so-called* "Anti-Heimatfilm."

42. Wim Wenders

Death Is No Solution: The German Film Director Fritz Lang (1976)

"Death is no solution," says Fritz Lang in Jean-Luc Godard's film *Le Mépris* (*Contempt*, 1963), in which Lang plays an old director—himself. That is, I read an interview with Lang, published in *Cahiers du Cinéma*, in 1966, in which he recalls how this phrase occurred to him and he inserted it himself into the dialogue of *Le Mépris*, in a completely different context. Thereupon I feverishly spend half a day phoning around Germany, moving heaven and earth to find out whether there's a print of this film around somewhere. I want to hear him speak this sentence which I can't remember, I want to know the context in which it is said. But it turns out that there's no longer a print of the film in Germany. In England perhaps, in France certainly, but it would take too long to get it over here. I'd set my heart on hearing Fritz Lang speak that sentence, "La mort n'est pas une solution," and now I have to come to terms with my helplessness. I'd been reading everything I could lay my hands on by or about Fritz Lang, and the more I got involved in it, the more angry I grew at this schizophrenic state of affairs. A man who had been ignored while he was still alive was going to be acclaimed now that he was dead. It seemed to me that there was something not quite right about the obituaries on television and in the newspapers. I couldn't help feeling that there was an element of relief in them or else, conversely, of discomfort. And although what they said about Lang's importance for the development of the cinema and of film language was in itself entirely appropriate, somehow the sentence took on an assertive quality. Now that he's dead they want to turn him into a myth as fast as they can. Shit. His death is no solution.

What is true is that Fritz Lang has been treated badly in Germany. "Having come from Germany—after running out on Goebbels, who had offered me the leadership of the German film industry—I was very, very happy to get a chance to live here and become an American. In those days, I refused to speak a word of German. (I was terribly hurt—not personally—about what had happened to Germany, which I had liked very much—my roots are there . . .—and about what had been done to the German language.) I read *only* English, I read a lot of newspapers, and I read comic strips—from which I learned a lot."[1]

Fritz Lang made not only his first films here, but also his last ones, between 1958 and 1960 (*Der Tiger von Eschnapur/The Tiger of Eschnapur*, *Das indische Grabmal/The Indian Tomb*, and *Die tausend Augen des Dr.*

Mabuse/The Thousand Eyes of Dr. Mabuse). He made them under a misapprehension: "I didn't make these pictures because I thought they were important, but because I was hoping that if I made somebody a big financial success I would again have the chance as I had with M to work without any restrictions. It was my mistake" (Bogdanovich, p. 116).

In a French book on Lang, there is an article by Volker Schlöndorff about this period: "Fritz Lang lives in Berlin at the Hotel Windsor. He has lived for three years in hotels in Berlin and Munich. He has found no friends and no audiences. Germany does not forgive her emigrants. They are only allowed to return posthumously, preferably with a Nobel Prize. . . . Because he can't go out without feeling like a foreigner, Lang shuts himself up in the international anonymity of a hotel room. In order to find this country which he still loves, he has to leave it again, rejoin the other emigrants in France and America."[2]

Fritz Lang himself says: "After working there for fourteen months, that's two years ago now, I finally gave up once and for all the idea of making another film in Germany. The people you have to work with there are really insufferable. Not only because they never keep their word, in writing or otherwise, but also because the film industry (if it's possible to describe as such the miserable remains of what once made the country's film production world famous) is still controlled by former barristers, SS-men or exporters of God knows what. Their main activities consist of arranging co-productions under conditions such that their account books show a profit even before work has started on the film."[3]

Maybe conditions in Germany really are unfavorable for this art that is also an industry, maybe that's what the problem is. Lang wrote in 1924: "With the Germans' unique capacity for making the simplest things as complicated as possible, they have now tried to attack the cinema for being easily understandable and to describe it as a product for the masses. This attitude seems to me a gross injustice, both toward the masses and toward the cinema. For film is a strange hybrid form, an industrial product that can by its very nature be made cheaply and easily accessible to the masses without doing prejudice to its artistic vocation."[4]

Probably this is the only way to explain why the first German-language book on Fritz Lang didn't appear until 1976, at least ten years too late. In spite of this, or perhaps precisely because of it, it's a good and accurate book, loving, well-informed, provided with a detailed filmography and bibliography.

"During the filming of *Dr. Mabuse* Lang lost an eye. On April 27, 1942, Brecht made the following entry in his diary: '. . . he went to the oculist who covered one of his eyes and asked him to read out some figures. Lang said: but first you must turn on the light. The light was already on. Now he knows or suspects that his other eye is also threatened with blindness, like his father.' The single, steadfast camera eye sees more than a pair of eyes which react to every stimulus. Henry Fonda complained that while Lang was shooting his films, he looked through the camera more often than directly at the action. Having one's own vision, one's own perspective and being able to make distinctive images of processes that had previously eluded representation. Lang claims that he had never given any information about his private life in interviews. But he doesn't rule out the possibility that attentive eyes might find traces of it in his films. The reasons why he made films. When you look intensely at photos of Lang, when you hold them back far enough away, at the end all you see is a sparkling, glittering monocle."5

Fritz Lang had to have the book read out to him. He is said to have leafed through it, often holding it up to his eye in order to make out the outlines of the images. That reminds me of how he said in an interview that his hands appear in every one of his films. Probably in most cases in inserts where a hand is shown holding a newspaper or a book. Since then it is easier for me to imagine him. I haven't seen many of his films. The very first time I saw any was in Paris, when I found them very strange. Stranger, at least, than the American cinema, or the French, or even the Russian. Because: these films were German films and couldn't get through to me, my head was always full of other images and other enthusiasms. For fathers other than this one. Everything in me struggled against these cool, sharp, and analytical images, these thoughts made visible. The concept of *point of view* became clearer to me than ever before from other films. Someone had a point of view of things, someone adjusted his point of view, a point of view imposed itself, a point of view was shown: things and time. Often something seems strange when we're too close to it.

A newspaper advertisement for a new German film contains a quotation from *Der Spiegel*. The proofs read, "One of the most important German films since Kubitsch, Lang and *Muranu.*" The letters had refused to have anything to do with this sentence, or perhaps it was the printer who didn't want to be associated with that sheet. And with good reason, because this connection with the past doesn't exist. I don't believe that in the films of Herzog, Fassbinder, Schroeter, Miehe or any one of us there is a tradition which leads back to that era. Our films are new inventions. They have to be. Thank God. I think I know why *Der Spiegel* suggested I write about Lang; he's there in *Im Lauf der Zeit* (*Kings of the Road*, 1976), there's a reference to *Die Nibelungen* (*The Nibelungs*, 1924), we see two photos of him, one of them from *Le Mépris*. I didn't do all that intentionally. In this film about the consciousness of the cinema in Germany, the father who left us, no, the father we let go, imposed his point of view, slipped in of his own accord.

What do I know about Fritz Lang? One sentence spoken by Barbara Stanwyck in *Clash by Night* (1952): "Home is where you get when you run out of places." In my helplessness I place a call to Los Angeles, to Samuel Fuller, whom I've met once, and who helped me very much in another situation. He lived not far from Fritz Lang and I knew the two were friends. He cuts short my stupid questions about Lang with a laconic "I liked him." But then he tells me how he heard the news of Fritz Lang's death shortly after it happened, because he met Gene Fowler Jr. in the street. Fowler had often kept Lang company during his last days and had edited many of both Fuller's and Lang's films. "So what Gene is going to do, because there isn't going to be a big funeral, is he's going to get all Fritz Lang's old friends together, and we'll all have a lot to drink and have a wake." In answer to my question he explains, "Wake is an old Irish expression. When you talk and have fun and laugh and tell stories about the dead man. We'll do that sometime soon." After the conversation I feel relieved. A few old men on the West Coast were going to put it all right, those obituaries and all that shit. They'd get drunk and remember all kinds of stories. Death is no solution.

---

1. Lang quoted in Peter Bogdanovich, *Fritz Lang in America* (New York: Praeger, 1969), p. 15.

2. Luc Moullet, *Fritz Lang* (Paris: Seghers, 1963).

3. From an interview recorded by Gretchen Weinberg in New York in 1964, published in *Cahiers du Cinéma*, August 1965.

4. "Der künstlerische Aufbau des Filmdramas," *Filmbote* (Vienna), no. 20 (1924).

5. Frieda Grafe, "Für Fritz Lang: Einen Platz, kein Denkmal," in *Fritz Lang*, ed. Peter W. Jansen and Wolfram Schütte (Munich: Hanser, 1976), p. 82.

The sentence playing on the phrase "point of view" turns on the double meaning of the word "Einstellung," which means both a shot or a framing of the image as well as an attitude or a moral stance.—In his discussion of the ad in Spiegel, *Wenders modestly does not mention that the New German Film in question here is his own* Falsche Bewegung (Wrong Move).

43. Volker Schlöndorff
Rereading Kracauer's *From Caligari to Hitler** (1980)

It was my very first film book. A Yugoslavian friend, the director Bostjan Hladník, gave it to me as a present in May 1959 in Paris, while we were sitting in the Cinémathèque every evening watching old German films. Fritz Lang wrote me a dedication over the picture of Peter Lorre framed by knives (in M).

The meanwhile much-yellowed, slim Rowohlt volume, a product of a still existent rotary press, has accompanied me everywhere since, and is now being replaced by the new Suhrkamp edition, this time bearing the correct title, *From Caligari to Hitler—A Psychological History of German Film* by Siegfried Kracauer.

Twenty years later I have reread the book, now much more voluminous and complete, with the same enthusiasm, one that can be explained by simply citing the first sentence: "When, from 1920 on, German films began to break the boycott established by the Allies against the former enemy, they struck New York, London and Paris audiences as achievements that were as puzzling as they were fascinating."

What has taken thirty years in the wake of the Second World War succeeded after the First in only two years. The history of German film after the First World War constantly forces one to draw parallels with that after the Second. And this is what preoccupied me more in my rereading than the many precise synopses and the thesis summarized by the editor Karsten Witte in his afterword, namely that the collective consciousness of a people, its needs and its secret desires can be clearly seen in the films of this time: that for instance the *Caligari* film mentioned in the title anticipates Hitler with its deference to authority and its submission mechanism.

"Because the unseen dynamics of human relations permeate both the stories and their visuals, they are more or less characteristic of the inner life of a nation." This axiom, seeing feature films as the privileged expression of a society, shaped our film criticism in the fifties and sixties, including, with good reason, the *Autorenfilm*, which although seeming to be in opposition to society, actually contains a protest characteristic of the collective consciousness. Kracauer applies this analysis to German films of the Weimar Republic, not to provide some kind of basic typology of the German national character, but rather to analyze history through the psychological development of a people. He claims this procedure can be used for every other people and their intellectual history.

He focuses his attention, however, on this chosen time period, starting with the failure of the November 1918 "revolution," which he sets in quotation marks, and ending with the submission to Hitler. His audience consists mainly of the young white-collar workers, a group he examined in great detail in his book *Die Angestellten* (*The White-Collar Workers*). "Instead of realizing that it would be in their practical interest to fight for democracy, they lent an open ear to the promises of the Nazis.

Their surrender to the Nazis was due more to emotional fixations than to an appraisal of the actual situation." He continues: "Uncovering these inner dispositions in the medium of the German film could contribute to understanding Hitler's rise and seizure of power." In a letter to Hermann Hesse he recapitulates his procedure: "I am analyzing German films from 1918 to 1933 to obtain precise information about the predominant psychological dispositions of the Germans during this epoch. The whole thing is an attempt to grasp the decisive psychic processes at work at that time far under the surface of Germany's diverging ideologies."

So much for the theoretical presuppositions. Kracauer wrote his book in New York during the war, and if one wants to trace his steps accurately, his reviews that appeared in the *Frankfurter Zeitung* from 1924 to 1933, printed in the appendix of the new edition, are indispensable reading. His insight that the German cinema reflects the political development of the German people does not stem from a sudden inspiration during exile in New York, but is a perception that he felt and gave voice to in writing daily film reviews over the years. Already in his daily notices he warned of the political consequences of the films under discussion.

This was, for instance, the case with Luis Trenker's *Der Rebell (The Rebel)*, released shortly before the seizure of power on January 24, 1933 and, for our edification, recently aired on television. It was Kracauer's next-to-last review in a German newspaper and is worthwhile looking up and comparing with recent reactions to the film in the cultural section of newspapers if one wants to grasp how his understanding of a critic's role was much more political. Admittedly, a critic who always found fault with everything. Except for *Kuhle Wampe*—even here he found much to criticize—he left next to no film untouched, and only once did he actually surrender to writing a hymn to Asta Nielsen, on the occasion of a film, one probably and justifiably long forgotten, called *Unmögliche Liebe (Impossible Love)*. These forgotten films, however, are the ones that come to life again in his precise descriptions of them, and through the vividness and wit of his language reading his book is something like an imaginary trip to the movies during which several hundred films light up our consciousness.

Then as today, the German film could only survive through export, and then as today, the rule held that the more typically German the film is in theme and design, the more likely it is to arouse interest abroad. "Either it presents significant national characteristics or things of interest to the whole world." Kracauer calls international coproductions "shallow cosmopolitanism." Even then the New York and Paris premieres of, for instance, *Caligari* established the international reputation of films that only later found acclaim in Germany. Then, as today, foreign audiences search for the "ingenious" in German film, and not for a realistic image of Germany, which, in turn, had devastating consequences for the production of German films, where expressionist and exotic elements were cultivated, and not only because they fulfilled the mass need for repression, but also because they lent themselves so well to export. In the light of this, a realistic tradition only came about with some difficulty toward the end of the twenties.

Caligari, Dr. Mabuse, Nosferatu, The Golem all feature a tyrant who triumphs over chaos, and to whom we Germans willingly submit ourselves. "The Germans evidently thought there was no voice open to them between devastating anarchy and dynamic leadership." Even today this is the basic premise of all parties with a middle-class orientation, as is particularly clear in the well-known slogan of the chancellor candidate Strauss.

All of these films are rife with deeper meaning and fatalism. There are almost no comedies and only in his assessment of Friedrich Murnau's *Die Finanzen des Großherzogs (The Finances of the Grand Duke)* does Kracauer ease his critical stance in elation: "At last a film without deeper significance!"

Next to the tyrant films there was the melodrama, and in this genre, Karl Grune's *Die Strasse (The Street)* is the archetype of all German films. It is the story of a Babbitt who is enticed by the shadows cast by the street onto his apartment ceiling to seek out unknown adventure, only to return home after a few disappointing encounters—from which the prostitute with a heart of gold is never missing—and drop to his knees in front of wife or mother and throw his head onto her lap.

The main figures in German films (from time immemorial) are the eternal adolescents, who briefly revolt before submitting to authority. Later, at the end of the twenties and the beginning of the thirties, these heroes no longer return to wife and mother in plush living rooms, but instead find refuge in the bosom of sport associations and youth movements. They may submit to the fatherland and its new Nazi order, but the basic pattern is the same: it shows people who do not want to grow up, and the same infantilism of an epoch is to be found again in Adenauer's postwar Germany, whose films once again repeat this master narrative of escapism and faith in authority.

Have films changed since then? Perhaps since and because of '68? I believe and hope so. Recently, however, when the "television drama of the present" ran on ZDF, I suddenly came upon the familiar story line. *Das Ziel (The Goal)*—the story of an engineer who suddenly slips away from home to fulfill a dream of freedom. He meets the girl Marietta who lures him into undertaking increasingly daring escapades which finally land them in the hospital as psychological and physical wrecks. In the end he finds his way back to his job and the petty bourgeois life he so much wanted to escape.

Perhaps we do have this cursed national character Kracauer did not want to accept and therefore only ascribed to the period after World War I. Even the audience's reaction, as Kracauer knows well, is symptomatic. One comes to the cinema to be moved, to have a good cry, Böll writes in *Gruppenbild mit Dame (Group Portrait with Lady)*, to feel pity for oneself along with the hero, and to be reassured that destiny is omnipotent. Films presenting a different, a realistic image, like Pabst's *Kameradschaft* or *Mutter Krausens Fahrt ins Glück (Mother Krause's Trip to Happiness)*, may receive critical praise but are shunned by audiences. "In Neukölln, one of Berlin's proletarian quarters, it [*Mother Krause's Trip to Happiness*] ran before empty seats, while some dull comedy in the immediate neighborhood attracted huge crowds," claims an enraged Kracauer.

His account of German film of the period still praised today as its golden age evokes little nostalgia, but rather sorrow, rage, and the wish that films like these should never be made again. That is in fact exactly what Kracauer wants to accomplish. After all, Kracauer is not writing as a dispassionate commentator, but as someone who had to flee Germany and who sits in exile in New York, and from there charging that the German film he had written about for fifteen years was an accomplice in Germany's development. He is angry that film was not any different. He even wants his book to serve as a primer for making other, better, and more socially conscious films.

To be sure, he often goes too far, simply reducing cinema to a dream factory, recounting stories so that escapism is present in them all, and never doing justice to the poetic dimension, especially in the case of Murnau's films. Sometimes he simply presents arbitrary rules, for instance: "The masses are irresistibly attracted by the spectacle of torture and humiliation," as an explanation for the popular success of *Der blaue Engel (The Blue Angel)*.

But what constantly forces one to read on are the wealth of firsthand details and recollections, meticulously described shots, actors' expressions, script tidbits, and camera angles.

His description of the film *Überfall (Accident)* whets one's appetite to see this film which rarely is shown anymore even in cinémathèques. In this sense the book challenges one to search for the films Kracauer describes. Where can we even see these films? Where can we investigate the details he described and appropriate them in our own work?

Accident, he writes, "shows chaos without accepting submission to authority as the way out." "It was prohibited for its allegedly 'brutalizing and demoralizing effect.'"

If Kracauer could say of the first silent films that "they reveal the proceedings in nearly inaccessible layers of the German soul," then how much more difficult his analysis became with the onset of the sound film, which, by the way, as one of the few critics of the time, he championed without reservation, although it did not serve his own approach.

"To be sure, the new sphere of articulate reasoning enriched the screen; but this gain hardly compensated for the reduced significance of the visuals. While verbal statements more often than not express intentions, camera shots are likely to penetrate the unintentional. This is precisely what the mature silent films had done. They came upon levels below the dimension of consciousness, and since the spoken word had not yet assumed control, unconventional or even subversive images were allowed to slip in. But when dialogue took over, unfathomable imagery withered and intentional meanings prevailed" (Kracauer).

But even in the early silent films composition was much more dominant than it is today. While looking at the many film photographs in the book, one at times gets the impression that the films were in fact shot to illustrate Kracauer's theses, so overexplicit is the pictorial symbolism, so overstated are the basic visual patterns. A similar analysis would not be possible of the American or the French cinema, because neither is, put simply, as clearcut, or stated more precisely, as simpleminded. Kracauer also never maintains that directors, authors, or even audiences were aware of these meanings. "The less someone knows why he prefers one object to another, the more certain one is in assuming that his choice was determined by powerful forces beneath the conscious level," he declares, and this is perhaps why all of his analyses are of little use as a prescription for a different German cinema, although he hoped "that studies of this kind may help in the planning of films."

Distribution and exhibition—even at that time (there are many constants in German film)—depend on the maintenance of basic guidelines, and Bertolt Brecht's fight over *Kuhle Wampe*, a film initially banned by the censors, is exemplary. Slatan Dudow's film has the classic voluntary death episode; the suicide as submission is typical of many melodramas. But something here bothered the film industry: instead of the suicide taking place at the end of the film as a ritual of submission, it occurs right at the start. It is a complete reversal and no longer a submission, but rather a call to action. "Forward without forgetting," declares Brecht/Eisler's song at the end of the film at the point where other melodramas concluded with suicide.

Kracauer knows that the reality and possibly seductive force of authoritarian desires cannot be simply overcome by analysis. "Considering the widespread ideological opposition to Hitler, there is no doubt that the preponderance of authoritarian leanings was a decisive factor in his favor. Broad strata of the population, including part of the intelligentsia, were psychologically predisposed to the kind of system Hitler offered. . . . Irretrievably sunk into retrogression, the bulk of the German people could not help submitting to Hitler. Since Germany thus carried out what had been anticipated by her cinema from its very beginning, conspicuous screen characters now came true in life itself."

All of a sudden reality was like a film. And do we not find again the same submission directly after the Second World War, with the exception that here one submits to the democracy of the victors—here an American, there a Soviet one—but never truly emancipates oneself and establishes a republic of one's own?

Is there no alternative? Do all of our tales have to be "escapes to the realm of the soul" (today one says inner world, that is to say, subjectivity)? Do actors have to act "as if they were standing in an imaginary space, because there is, at present, no social reality"? Is it true "that the living space we are occupying is wavering, the air is rife with ideologies, and the ground under our feet is giving way"?

These are the questions we ask ourselves today while reading an article from 1931. At issue is *Berlin-Alexanderplatz* and Kracauer talks about what he considers to be an alternative: the epic narrative. Not in the sense of Brechtian theater, but as a technique of free association, which makes its way across the length and breadth of the world, rather than clinging to some narrow ideologically circumscribed action. "That is how every film that is a real film ambles along. It draws its suspense from the largeness of the camera, which only fulfills its task when it conspicuously kaleidoscopes its way through the environment, and draws in the world around us piece by piece." Kracauer is talking not only in terms of space, but also those of time. He points to Döblin and the social novels of Balzac and Zola as examples of an epic narrative style missing in German film.

Schlöndorff's mention of the change in title reflects the older expurgated version circulating as Von Caligari bis Hitler—ein Beitrag zur Geschichte des deutschen Films. *Karsten Witte notes in the afterword to his and Ruth Baumgarten's retranslation (now with the more accurate title* Von Caligari zu Hitler—eine psychologische Geschichte des deutschen Films) *that the earlier edition's title suggested a closed historical period rather than the inevitable conclusion to a political development—as well as suppressing the psychologi-*

cal implications of Kracauer's methodology in the subtitle.—The quote attributed to Kracauer regarding The Finances of the Grand Duke *is imprecise. In fact, Kracauer cites a critic from* Licht Bild Bühne, *the source of this judgment. See footnote number 9 on page 102 of the English original edition (Princeton: Princeton University Press, 1947).*

44. Alexander Kluge
The Early Days of the Ulm Institute for Film Design*
(1980)

The Oberhausen group had a three-point program. Its first product was the Oberhausen Manifesto, which only contained a general declaration. It was the result of a certain mood and was written the night before it was announced. Afterward we sat down together and asked ourselves: what is our program really? Three main points came out. The first point was the training of newcomers—the establishment of training sites, of film academies or institutes. This was coupled with the idea that we needed a theoretical center for film. This idea came from Fritz Lang. We thought that Fritz Lang, who had just finished *Der Tiger von Eschnapur* (*The Tiger of Eschnapur*) and had been very frustrated by Artur Brauner and the production style in the Federal Republic, should be a sort of guiding light. Lang sent his co-worker and companion Lilly Latté to Munich to talk with the filmmakers. She then went to Ulm and made contacts with the successor institute of the Bauhaus, the *Hochschule für Gestaltung* (Institute for Design), in the hopes of establishing there a training and theory center for the study of film, and Fritz Lang was willing to remain in Germany and head the new institute. That all fell through due to Lang's health and the fact that Otl Aicher (one of the founders and head ideologues of the Institute for Design) didn't understand Lang: the whole feature film business sounded fishy to him.

The second point had to do with the subsidy of debut films. This led to the founding of the *"Kuratorium Junger Deutscher Film."* And the third point involved a clear and continuing support of short films as a constant experimental field for filmmaking in general. These three points were presented in 1962 during a meeting with "Group 47."

Later on there was fierce infighting among the Oberhausen group. It looked something like the end and only a kernel of the group worked toward fulfilling the three program points. Norbert Kückelmann, Hans Rolf Strobel, and I looked up Hermann Höcherl, the Minister of the

Interior at that time, and in a twenty-minute meeting he promised us five million marks. With that money the *"Kuratorium Junger Deutscher Film"* was founded.

Detten Schleiermacher, Edgar Reitz, and I banded together to work in Ulm. At first we had negotiations with the governing group in Ulm. In the Institute there was an oppositional faction and a governing faction and there were battles for instance over whether one can study design in a scientific manner or whether there should be a strong emphasis on its artistic aspect. And a third faction claimed this is neither an artistic nor a scientific question, but rather a political one. Among representatives of the Institute for Design who knew that the Bauhaus had had a center for film there was a clear desire to include film in the course of studies. . . .

The curriculum was worked out by people who hadn't made any feature films yet, only short films. It contains impulses from Edgar Reitz, Detten Schleiermacher, and myself. Soon Vlado Kristl appeared on the scene and during the semester break he made the film *Der Damm (The Dam)* with his students. That caused a total disruption of the entire program. The film forms that he brought to the school proved so fascinating for the second-year students that our curriculum already was under intense discussion during our second year of operations. This discussion still continues and later led to the founding of an assembly and to the self-determination of students. That is to say, the conception was thought out by Edgar Reitz, Norbert Kückelmann, Haro Senft, Christian Rischert, Detten Schleiermacher, Enno Patalas, H. D. Müller, H. R. Strobel, myself, a large group. One did not turn to foreign film academies for orientation. One has to realize that our program was not based on any academic considerations. One component was Critical Theory. The second component: montage and camera. Beate Mainka-Jellinghaus and Edgar Reitz were above all responsible for this. Films were always conceived in terms of their editing; variations in camera perspective were less important. Third, we thought much more of musical and literary models than filmic ones. Insofar as filmic professionalism was a concern, we looked back only to the films of the twenties. The feature film more or less was rejected. In our minds a new beginning in German film could not stem from what had been done already.

45. Edgar Reitz

The Dream of a German Film House* (1981)

The situation in the cinemas has become more wretched, brutal, and alienating for the film art than ever before. There are fewer and fewer cinemas. I noticed with horror that the good old Lehnbach Cinema in which over the years we had so many premieres—*Abschied von gestern* (*Yesterday Girl*, 1966) ran there, *Mahlzeiten* (*Meal Times*, 1967) ran there, recently even *Der Schneider von Ulm* (*The Tailor of Ulm*, 1978)—doesn't exist anymore. It has become a bar. It makes me sad that this cinema doesn't exist anymore. Instead, a return to soft-core porno and brutal slugging matches in the cinemas. New discoveries are *Children of Paradise* or Walt Disney's *The Jungle Book*, and when one takes in a film, several hundred rowdy, mostly young people sit in these cinemas, whistling and booing loudly at a film like *Children of Paradise*, as if it were a film made yesterday which one can piss on like one pisses on everything that one comes across. There is no reverence, there is no respect, there is no history, there is no love for that which has been made, there is no desire to retain that which has been made, there is no pride about what we have or have done. No doubt I say all of this with a certain bitterness, but then so many years of work and film politics have led to nothing. Film politics are apparently not politics at all. One tries to carve out a small corner of humanity. And this is not possible when everywhere one turns respect for life diminishes, when the life of people means nothing, when those who control the larger world ignore human lives.

In the next days the annual meeting of the *Arbeitsgemeinschaft* is taking place. I cannot be in Munich to attend, although I would very much like to revive the *Arbeitsgemeinschaft*, to work together with a few friends and at least make this organization become what it actually always wanted to be, namely a homeland for the art of film, which in fact has been betrayed in recent years by the so-called producers among us. The task of the *Arbeitsgemeinschaft* today should be finally to establish the Munich Film House that we wanted to create already in 1971 when the Occam-Studio was closed. The work of twenty years and many generations of newly arrived German filmmakers lies in a large cemetery. Season after season there are films that are not distributed, ones that are treated miserably by their distributor, films that run in the wrong cinemas, wonderful films that one recalls and will never get a chance to see again, films so personal that their makers didn't dare to show them publicly. We are perhaps the only country in the world which for over two decades now has produced unshown films, expressions of entire realms of life and existence, done with more or less skill, with more or less talent, but in any case films to which people have devoted their lives, these films which have been banished prematurely to the cemetery of the "no longer current" films, as if there were something like seasonal currency in matters of art. All of this hits us altogether harder than we might realize right now, because the life's work of many lies there and cries out to be noticed. I recommend therefore once again that we create a place in

Munich under the title House of German Film, where all of this is available on a day-to-day and ongoing basis.

What is needed is a beautiful, large, old-fashioned screening facility, rooms where one can house exhibitions and sales booths and an archive. A large archive, in which we will gather every German film, every single German film since 1962, since Oberhausen, one copy of each on hand and where we can organize an ongoing program in which we will show these films one after the other throughout the entire year, every day, two, three, or four films, short films, long films, documentary films, feature films, everything that has been made, and there are in my opinion more than one hundred films from our generation alone which we could bring together, which could be kept on hand there, to be looked at, to be retained as a daily reality in people's consciousness; interested parties could have all of these films shown to them once again on video cassette copies. This would be a place where film research could be possible, where journalists could gather information, as well as foreigners, importers, exporters, but also the filmmakers themselves, who know too little about each other's work.

What has to be found would be a house in which there is a marvelous screening facility, enough other rooms, and above all rooms in which the copies could be stored and gathered. The daily program could for instance be such that in four successive showings a different German film would be shown each time, that each German film could be seen again in the course of a year, and that one could upon request view every title, all of which would have to be listed in a large catalogue. The daily presentation of a film program in a city like Munich would provide a real enrichment and above all give us the self-conscious feeling that we have made twenty years worth of film history. It is completely irrelevant how good the individual films are. I would include everything in this program, even the soft-core pornos, school girl and German weepy wares. Here it is a matter of having everything at one's disposal, in order that one can gauge the relative importance of single works in the context of other works. It won't hurt if there are no qualitative guidelines, because the battle for quality is a concern of the filmmakers and not the concern of those who gather films.

One could also organize auctions in this film house where the filmmakers could sell off objects after completing a film, e.g., costumes, props, film apparatus that was no longer needed, but also publicity stills, illustrations from the film, posters, scripts. Particularly valuable objects would be, for instance, the director's copy of the shooting scripts, the copies of the director's assistants with the attached polaroid photos, etc. One could also collect such objects, they would some day take on great interest for film history. Further, one can have a film library there with a circulation desk for film literature, periodicals, one could sell posters, publicity stills, press booklets, etc., leftover publicity posters from films that have already run in the cinemas. One could organize exhibitions and write monographs devoted to single films that were being presented or were running at the time in cinemas. One could support activities originating in other cities meant in a similar way to keep the German film alive as well as through a distribution service. The whole thing need not be done on a commercial basis, the admission prices would have to be kept low so that one could finance the continuing operations from such funds and not pass on the box office take to producers or distributors. Every film would be shown which either already had its public run behind it or has not found its way previously into cinemas. Films produced in cooperation with television, but produced as films that take their shape from a film-historical consciousness, should also be gathered here. Because there are hardly any German films nowadays which have not in some way been coproduced with the television networks.

It's easy for me to make such plans because they all can relate to plans that I have been thinking about for some time now. The difference between today and yesterday is perhaps that we now actually do have a fantastic mass of films we can look back on, films that have almost all been prematurely cast aside and which have not deserved the status of simply being labelled depleted or dead.

46. Werner Herzog
Tribute to Lotte Eisner* (1982)

Today we are here to honor Lotte Eisner, *die Eisnerin*. Bertolt Brecht, who in his brash way usually was right, was the first one to call her that, and it's caught on.

Die Eisnerin, who is that? I'll make it clear at the start: she is our collective conscience, the conscience of New German Film, and since the death of Henri Langlois, probably the conscience of world cinema. A fugitive from the barbarism of the Third Reich, she survived, and is now among us here, on German soil. That you, Lotte Eisner, ever stepped again into this country remains one of the miracles granted us.

Blessed are those hands which presented her the Helmut Käutner Prize, blessed is the seat on which she sits, and blessed be, ladies and gentlemen, the affection which your presence expresses.

Langlois, the dragon who guarded all of our treasures, the brontosaurus, this marvelous monstrosity, has left us and now we only have *die Eisnerin*. Lotte Eisner, I greet and honor you as the last mammoth on earth, as the single living person in the world who knows the cinema from its earliest days on, or to be more exact: you knew everyone of importance from the beginnings of cinema, you knew them personally and often supported them: the magician Méliès, who made his films between 1904 and 1914—of course, you only got to know him later— then Eisenstein, Chaplin, Fritz Lang, Stroheim, Sternberg, Renoir, everyone. And there was not a single person who did not revere you.

And it was the same with following generations as well as the present one, my own. *Die Eisnerin* is the goal of our pilgrimages and in her small apartment in Paris one finds almost only young people who gather around her, because her spirit has remained young. Only your body has aged and become a burden and a bother to you, who would much rather go mountain climbing with us. Lotte Eisner, I won't remain silent about that shameful moment when you were cowardly enough to try to steal away from this life. It was 1974 and we, the New German Film, still a sensitive organism, still not firmly rooted, still scorned as the "young film." We could not allow you to die. I myself tried at the time to appeal to fate: I wrote you a letter, please forgive me that I quote from it: "*Die Eisnerin* must not die, she will not die, I won't allow it. She will not die, she will not. Not now, she cannot. No, she won't die now, because she won't die. My steps are steady. And now the earth trembles. Mercy! She cannot. She won't. When I arrive in Paris, she'll be alive. It won't be different than that, because it can't be. She cannot die. Maybe later when we allow her to."

Lotte Eisner, we want to have you among us when you are one hundred, but for the moment I will free you from this horrible spell. You may die. I say this without frivolity, in all respect to death which is our single solid certainty. I also say it knowing that you have made us more secure, because you have enabled us to find a link with our own history, and more important than that: because you have given us a legitimacy.

It's strange that the continuity in German film was torn by the catastrophe of the Second World War. The thread was worn away, actually even a bit earlier. The road led to oblivion. And with the exception of a very few films and directors like Staudte and Käutner there was no real German film anymore. A gap of a quarter century opened. In literature and other areas this was by no means as dramatically apparent. We, the new generation of film directors, are a generation without fathers. We are orphans. We only have grandfathers, like Murnau, Lang, Pabst, the generation of the twenties.

Your books, above all your book about German Expressionist film, *The Haunted Screen*—I'm certain it will remain the definitive and final study about this epoch—as well as your book about Murnau and the one about Fritz Lang, besides your activity in the Cinémathèque in Paris and your participation in our fate, that of us young filmmakers, all of this has spanned a historical, a cultural historical bridge between us and the past. The meaning of this will never be grasped by the French, who though struck by the same catastrophe were able to go on without a break, nor will the Italians, who created their own neo-realism right after the war, much less the Americans, the Soviet Union, no one. Only we ourselves can gauge the meaning of this.

Once when I was at your apartment, feeling exhausted, scorned, and desperate, you said in an off-the-cuff sentence: "Listen, film history won't allow you young German filmmakers to give up."

The second thing that is particularly important to us is the question of legitimacy. I have been declaring and insisting, for many years now: WE HAVE LEGITIMATE FILM CULTURE IN GERMANY ONCE AGAIN. In order that you understand me correctly, ladies and gentlemen, I mean this in contrast to the barbarism and horrendousness that Nazi Germany brought over us. We have not become legitimate because of a simple declaration, through a self-empowering decree, so to speak. We have become legitimate by virtue of the Final Authority, *die Eisnerin*. Through her we have been declared legitimate. I might explain it in this way: during the Middle Ages when someone was crowned as emperor, this was a matter of succession and above all political power, but one had to go to Rome to obtain the necessary legitimacy. Because *die Eisnerin* has declared us legitimate, we have become so. And it was this act that has allowed us to find audiences abroad. . . .

With your permission, Lotte Eisner, I will read to you, ladies and gentlemen, what I wrote at Christmas 1974, on the day my harrowing pilgrimage reached an end:

"Paris, Saturday, 14 December.

"Afterward one more thing: I went to *die Eisnerin*, she was still tired and drawn by her sickness. Someone must have told her on the phone that I had come on foot, I didn't want to tell her. I was embarrassed and laid my weary feet on a second stool which she pushed over to me. In my embarrassment a word went through my head and because the situation was strange anyway, I said it to her. Together, I said, we'll cook a fire and hold fish over it. She looked at me and smiled very tenderly and because she knew I was on foot and therefore without protection, she understood me. For a tender short moment something calming went through my dead-tired body. I said, please open the window, I learned to fly a few days ago."

Lotte Eisner, I'm not the only person whom you have given wings. I thank you.

Lotte H. Eisner was the first recipient of the Helmut Käutner Prize, an award endowed by the city of Düsseldorf to recognize individuals "whose work has supported and influenced the development of the German film, making a contribution to the understanding and acceptance of the German cinema."—Herzog's famous trek in the snow from Munich to Paris is documented in his book Of Walking in Ice, *trans. Martje Grohmann and Alan Greenberg (New York: Tanam, 1980), a volume from which Herzog quotes here.—Herzog's* Jeder für sich und Gott gegen alle *(The Mystery of Kaspar Hauser) was dedicated to Lotte Eisner, "and the better part of Germany that had to leave." Cf. as well Sohrab Shahid Saless's documentary of 1979,* Die langen Ferien der Lotte H. Eisner *(The Long Vacation of Lotte H. Eisner). The final shot of Wim Wenders's* Paris, Texas *reads, "For Lotte H. Eisner."—Lotte Eisner died on 25 November 1983.*

47. Christian Ziewer

Last Words for Wolfgang Staudte* (1984)

Why is it so hard for me to write something after the death of Wolfgang Staudte? Why the difficulty reflecting about my relationship to this—next to Konrad Wolf—most important director of postwar Germany?

I think, as strange as it might sound, it has to do with the great affinity and, at the same time, great distance.

The great affinity: here was someone who after the end of the Third Reich refused to resign himself to forgetting, who didn't let himself be pacified by the round dance of the weepy cartel. Who posed incisive questions about the past and present and thereby hoped to influence the future. Who, as he said of himself, "took an active part in public life." When we as film students in Berlin met Staudte in 1966, such activism was for us the be-all and end-all for our future film work. But it soon became clear that neither a productive mentor-student relationship was to be nor a collegial cooperative endeavor. We responded to Staudte's attempts to transmit his opinions, experiences, and working methods with distance and misgiving. Not that misgivings toward our elders, especially teachers, were illegitimate, but the tenor of this rejection, the coldness of argumentation toward a man whose commitment after all was so close to our own appears to me in retrospect incredible. And a good decade later, after Staudte, accepting our invitation, became a member of the *Berliner Arbeitskreis Film,* no active contact ensued which might have had an effect on our own film work. A few intimate conversations, his active participation in a *Filmvolksfest* we sponsored—we left it at that. We responded with indifference to his attempts to encourage us. And yet we younger ones wanted to change the world as much as he did, to defend ourselves against the bureaucratic and economic suppression of film, just as he had, because he wanted to survive as an artist.

The great distance: after Staudte left DEFA, where very different production conditions rule than here in the West, he had to work in a film industry in which money governs the minds and imaginations of authors and directors. The young German directors of the sixties no longer were willing to subject themselves to this commercial system of producers and distributors. They distanced themselves from *Opas Kino*. Support systems like the *Kuratorium Junger Deutscher Film* and later television made these independent endeavors a reality as well as the *Autorenfilm* and a different public sphere, one that did not only expect new talent, but also produced it by propagating a new image of "film-makers."

Given this radical break with the old system, Staudte could not be included among the "new." Instead he, who in his struggle against the old order had constantly run up against vestiges of the old, was thrown into the same pot as the other old fogies, the ones who had continually tried to keep him down: the reactionaries, militarists, anticommunists, in-triguers, rabble-rousers and denunciators, soft-steppers and conformists (many of whom will probably honor him enthusiastically now that he is dead). Just as he did not belong among their ranks because he did not share their hypocrisy, so he also remained cut off from the others, the younger generation, because they did not accept him as one of their own, because he did not share their ideas without reservation. They had their (qualified) solidarity and their group identity—he was alone. Is it so strange, then, that in the end he completely went over to television and in so doing fully disappeared from the sight of the younger colleagues?

The protest against the "fathers" also makes one blind toward one's friends. The fact that Staudte, with his resolute insistence on "an active part in public life," was our forerunner, left in us, if we recognized anything at all, no feeling of affinity which might carry and stimulate us.

It seems to me that the unfinished and problematic element in our relationship to Staudte has a lot to do with our broken relation to the German past in general. We young directors who wanted so much to come to grips with this past have in fact completely and neurotically cut ourselves off from it, so much so that we have destroyed the necessary connections to it. No other country has robbed itself of its own tradition, no country has in this manner destroyed its own film history because of the burden of its past. Even the "angry young men" and the new English cinema remained closer to their colonialist fathers, drew on them in the most vehement spirit of contradiction, not to mention the French and the Italians. Staudte's great DEFA films? They remained something talked about in film societies and in no way a part of our present. At the time when I made my first films, ones that Staudte liked a lot, I explained to him with a smile and a certain smugness: there weren't any German influences, no Dudow, no Jutzi, no Pabst (I didn't need to say "no Staudte," that was understood!), but rather English, Italian . . . and my own experiences. The latter in particular: we had to discover everything for ourselves, to reinvent, to formulate filmically, because the past was garbage—or ideology. The romanticized search for a German Hollywood and its directors is only the flip side of the same coin, and Staudte hardly makes a good cult figure: someone who possesses the ability to depict social inequity under such a harsh light does not lend himself easily to transfiguration. But I have the feeling now that the political and cultural development of our country is bringing us closer to Staudte. Gradually we're coming to realize what kind of films he made and under what sort of pressure they came about. How much energy and artistic power he had to mobilize in his energy- and imagination-robbing battles with those people who financed his films.

As the spectrum in which we today make our films becomes increasingly narrow, we recognize all the more the rebellious spirit of this man and its expression in his films. His victories will become more apparent. And his defeats? We will understand them better when we have our own behind us.

A few days ago I received word from the Film Subsidy Board that financing for my film about the German Peasant Wars was rejected due to its "wanting economic potential." To judge film art according to its economic potential and the box office—this is the one, still living tradition in our country. The other, related to it like Scylla to Charybdis, is the demand to avoid any political controversy and to try to please mass tastes. Remembering Wolfgang Staudte and his films should help strengthen us in our fight against these traditions.

Ziewer did go on to finish the film mentioned in the last paragraph. Its title was Der Tod des weissen Pferdes (The Death of the White Steed); *it received its premiere at the 1985 Berlin Film Festival.—For another West German filmmaker's reaction to Staudte's death, see Helma Sanders-Brahms, "Wir haben ihn allein gelassen: Für Wolfgang Staudte," in Jahrbuch Film 84/85, ed. Hans Günther Pflaum (Munich: Hanser, 1984), pp. 23–32.*

48. Robert Van Ackeren
How a Film Classic Becomes a Video Clip (1985)

One fine day a friendly man, who introduced himself modestly as Giorgio Moroder, appeared in the office of Enno Patalas, head of the Munich Film Museum. He related that he was a composer and spoke of his interest in writing music scores for silent films, if only he could find the right film. Unaware and overjoyed, for such interest comes rarely, Patalas, believing in the composer's good intentions, spread out the pearls of cinematic art before his guest and suggested he work with *Metropolis*. The sound-drama took its disco-course.

With *Metropolis* Fritz Lang created an evocative expressionistic masterwork of silent cinema in the twenties. Giorgio Moroder has now managed to pull off an even larger feat. With a clever coup he has turned film art on its head: music no longer accompanies the film, the film is degraded to an accompaniment for the sound mix. Moroder uses the classic in this way, as a vehicle for the lucrative reproduction of his disco music. With this in mind he has, working with love, but above all moved by commercial instincts, taken various versions of the film and come up with his very own "reconstruction." Moroder has managed to do something that very few filmmakers bring off: one sits in the cinema and is at first incredibly taken aback.

He did not even take the trouble to run his version at silent speed and thus forces it to unreel onscreen too fast by a third. Moroder "reconstructs" *Metropolis* according to his own editing principles. From long scenes he deletes entire passages, he adds new footage, and throws out the intertitles, and in so doing destroys all silent film rhythm.

His hammering synthesizer sound takes care of the rhythm as well as an electronic noise backdrop, orchestrated as if this were a comic film. He embellishes the silent work with seven songs and without trying imparts the impression that the projectionist has forgotten to turn off the upbeat intermission music. He spreads airy cloaks of color over the black-and-white images. In this way the film is made palatable to "our little ones" as a sort of gigantic feature-film-length video clip for the Walkman generation: sing along with Fritz Lang.

"An entire generation now has the chance and the motivation to discover a masterpiece which it would otherwise not bother to see" (Moroder). Only what we have is no longer the masterpiece that once was; little remains to discover from Fritz Lang's vision of the future, for *Metropolis* has become "Giorgio Moroder's fantastic rock vision" (in the words of the distributor).

The process behind all this was equally fantastic and simple. Moroder elicited audience wishes in small test groups. After a handful of private screenings he passed out questionnaires and found out his audiences wanted rock music and a lot of songs to accompany the silent film. Without hesitation he responded to these wishes, remaining faithful to his tried-and-true disco recipe: "a little Philadelphia sound, a pinch of this, a pinch of that, all mixed in my own inimitable manner."

To seal his pioneer accomplishment, Moroder awards himself a cinematographic medal of honor. He styles himself a cultural guardian angel and presents the bastard child as the "resurrection" of a forgotten masterpiece. This sort of resurrection in fact more resembles a cultural burial; it presupposes that one first eulogizes the film as a dead body one wants to rescue before going on to violate it. Moroder is clever enough to know where the pitfalls lie and, with calculated laments, anticipates future detractors: "Some will reproach me for exploiting the film commercially, above all German film critics."

His comment that the old version still exists for "purists" along with his patchwork one is pure hypocrisy, especially given his attempt to "motivate" an entire generation to partake of his product, to tempt people with his musical sugarcoating. Above all he forgets to mention that it is practically impossible to see the old version, for only few copies still exist, incomplete and spread all over the globe, and, besides, every single showing must be cleared by him.

In a generous appreciation of his own accomplishment with the "dusty" film, Moroder finally speaks as an artist about the artist Lang: "Lang surely would have used the same acoustic means if they had been at his disposal." A truly audacious legitimation. The Lang whom I met shortly before his death was an embittered Lang, who had fought for his rights as a director his whole life long, a perfectionist who tolerated no outside interventions in his work, but who had to suffer them throughout his entire career. Lang no longer can defend himself against Moroder's underhanded tactics in the battle over the copyrights to the film.

To avoid any misunderstanding: my objections are not directed against Moroder's music—I regard him highly as the composer for films such as *American Gigolo, Scarface, Cat People,* and the songs of Blondie—but rather against his way of abusing a film. Under the cheery motto "modern and up-to-date," Moroder stands as a vanguard figure in an American film industry just about to conquer the last holy bastion and to plunder the film archives. For the first time heads of companies can be found wiping off the dust in their archives. The "Metropolizing" of film art has begun. This will cut down storage costs and should provide compensation for the lack of original ideas, so that the Moloch of a medium can be fed with new software.

Out of the old make the new, Hollywood as an optical-acoustic recycling center, celebrated by the press for "pointing the way," for now the possibility poses itself of dressing up long-since written-off white elephants "in a new costume in step with the times" (Moroder) and making a profit. Just like cutting off the legs of worn-out pants, sewing on a few colorful splotches, and passing them off as trendy bermudas.

There are no limits to the ingenuity of artistic intervention in an industry that apparently is not able to accept the silent film as a form of its own, but rather simply sees in it a film that lacks sound, and sees in black-and-white film a film that lacks color.

In the meanwhile other old films are being redone via a special process, "modernized" with completely new framing; black-and-white film classics are being re-released in glaring color, for instance, *Casablanca* in "living colors." Proudly the head of the U.S. color firm declares: "How a film was once shot is no longer visible." After Moroder's trendy refurbishing, there is not much left to see of Fritz Lang's masterful film *Metropolis*. It used to be that old films were destroyed to regain silver worth pennies; in the process celluloid was made into combs. Nowadays films are being "restyled" in a speculative fashion. The process is different, the destruction is the same. I think films were better off as combs.

VI

Collective Memory and National Identity

From its inception, Young German Film was a cinema concerned with the past and wrapped up in the present. The initial breakthrough in 1966 came as the result of films that explored the past with an acute retrospective awareness (Schlöndorff's *Der junge Törless/Young Törless*) and surveyed the present as the function of a still operative authoritarian legacy (Kluge's programmatic *Abschied von gestern/Yesterday Girl* and Peter Schamoni's *Schonzeit für Füchse/Closed Season on Fox Hunting*). In years to come, critics and spectators in West Germany would gauge the state of the nation's film culture in terms of its ability to function as a mirror of history, a critical reflector of current events, often in terms reminiscent of Kracauer's call that films should serve as a register of a nation's psychological life, its collective dispositions, and mental processes. More often than not, West German films did not, at least in the minds of journalists and critics, stand up to this imposing challenge. They took refuge in literary adaptations, private reveries, stylistic flights of fancy, and impersonal entertainments. A closer look at West German films from the late sixties and early seventies reveals, however, that the concern with past and present and the fatal continuities between the two abided, no matter what many pundits were fond of saying. Toward the end of the seventies, the resolve to scrutinize German history seemed stronger than ever. Spurred by the disturbing events of the fall of 1977, a period that gave rise to recollections of war and a nation under siege, stimulated by the broadcast on the third channels of the American popular series *Holocaust* and irritated by an increase in Nazi memorabilia and Hitler literature, West German filmmakers reacted to, and in some cases, unwittingly participated in, a "new discourse" on National Socialism, a public act of exorcism whose acme came with the ceremony staged at a small military cemetery in Bitburg during the spring of 1985. The responses ranged from attacks on those who sought to whitewash the past to attempts at finding new routes of access to this sector of German history. The activation of memory, the catalyzing of sorrow, the liberation of otherwise repressed associations, the healing of wounds: these approaches toed a tenuous line between problematizing and neutralizing the legacy of National Socialism. (Saul Friedländer would argue that these reflections *on* the Third Reich were unwittingly also reflections *of* the Third Reich, films that took recourse to the same phantasmic appeal and a similar aesthetic *frisson*.) Making critical films in Germany has always been difficult; producing works that provide a running commentary on the state of public life in the Federal Republic remains to this day an often-expressed and widely desired resolve that quite regularly has met resistance and occasioned debate.

49. Wim Wenders
That's Entertainment: Hitler (1977)

> Obscenity, who really cares?
> Propaganda, all is phony.
> (It's All Right, Ma) Bob Dylan

The Hitler film by Joachim C. Fest and Christian Herrendoerfer was premiered at the Berlin Film Festival. With a set of program notes in hand chock-full of explanations I awaited the film with great expectations. In the notes I read: "This film depicts the Hitler era dispassionately, objectively and rationally. It conveys the fascination of Hitler's career without in any way being tempted to fall prey to this fascination.

"This film does not manipulate our history. It does not transfigure either. It explains." Why all these words of defense for something one hadn't even had a chance to attack yet?

My consternation became all too justified, however, when the film started, and it soon grew into an incredible dismay. At the end of the film a short applause, then the otherwise so outspoken festival audience headed for the exits, perplexed and disconcerted. Someone cracked, *"That's Entertainment, Part 3,"* but that didn't make things any better. Something had happened here almost beyond belief, no, it was not so much a matter of what we had seen as much as the way, HOW we had seen all this. It was hard to sort out, to be sure, for that reason the difficulty and the reluctance to give it a name.

With growing exasperation I followed the discussion about the film over the next few weeks: frivolous or impudent acclamations for the most, inoffensive cultural page rhetoric (in *Stern:* "If the Führer were to find out") or the positivism of *Der Spiegel:* "He has moved the filmic coming to grips with recent German history in a new direction."

You can say that again.

Then the first decided rejection, with no ifs, ands, or buts, in *Die Zeit,* where Karl-Heinz Janssen expressly terms the film dangerous and also carefully explains his judgment.

Finally, in the *Frankfurter Rundschau,* the most painstaking analysis by Wolfram Schütte, who shows "how greatly this film's aestheticization of reality resembles a similar penchant inherent in fascism."

Of course the film is doing well. To expect anything else would be childish. This is how fortunes are made.

I finally become furious last week after watching the wretched performance on television, the program *Aspekte,* where the Hitler film was supposed to be discussed. The good will behind this boomeranged. The program devolved into an extended advertisement for the film. As soon as the evening news was over, we were already graced with clips from the film as a trailer, and Janssen repeated his theses from *Die Zeit* sitting in front of a studio wall draped from top to bottom with the Hitler poster. At least one should have learned one thing from this film: you cannot show something at considerable length if you want to distance yourself from it. In film (in television no doubt as well) what we see is above all the crucial representation, only secondarily what we think about it. And instead of discussing the formal means of the Fest film, HOW this film had been made, one limited the debate to matters of content and historical fact: WHAT the film was about or was supposed to be about. The same old television setting, then, diverse OPINIONS and the historian Fest could be seen in the circle, smiling forbearingly. Whether Lubitsch emigrated in 1923 or 1932 ("change the two and the three around!"). Passed off as a bit of trivia, "a give-away." One didn't even get around to talking about Fritz Lang. Taking up their side, however, I would like to say a few words about this nonfilm (*Unfilm*), as someone who makes films in Germany. I speak for everyone who in recent years, after a long drought, has started once again to produce images and sounds in a country which has an unceasing distrust of images and sounds that tell its story, which for this reason has for thirty years greedily soaked up all foreign images, just as long as they have taken its mind off itself. I do not believe there is anywhere else where people have suffered such a loss of confidence in images of their own, their own stories and myths, as we have. We, the directors of the New Cinema, have felt this loss most keenly, in our own persons in the lack, the absence of a tradition of our own, as a fatherless generation, and in the spectators with their perplexed reaction and their initial hesitation. Only gradually has this defensive attitude, on the one hand, and this lack of self-confidence, on the other, broken down, and in a process that will perhaps take several years more, the feeling is arising here again that images and sounds do not have to be only something imported, but rather can be something concerned with this country that also comes out of this country.

There is good reason for this distrust. Because never before and in no other country have images and language been abused so unscrupulously as here, never before and nowhere else have they been debased so deeply as vehicles to transmit lies. And now a film comes along which, with an incomprehensible thoughtlessness, wants to sell exactly these images as the heart of the matter and as "documentary footage," SOLD, and in the process once again, ONCE AGAIN, several lies are transmitted. "Having come from Germany—after running out on Goebbels, who had offered me the leadership of the German film industry—I was very, very happy to get a chance to live here and become an American. In those days, I refused to speak a word of German. (I was terribly hurt—not personally—about what had happened to Germany, which I had liked very much . . . and about what had been done to the German language.)" (Fritz Lang in an interview, 1965.)

The "career" that Fest and Herrendoerfer wanted to investigate was above all possible because there was a total control of all film material, because all of the images of this man and his ideas were made in a clever manner, were chosen skillfully and used tactically. As a result of this thoroughgoing demagogic treatment of images, all of those people in Germany involved with the conscientious and equally competent production of film images left this country. Fest and Herrendoerfer, almost without exception, can therefore only cite the images of Nazi sympathizers in their "comprehensive documentation," the gaze of the complicitous, in a phrase, propaganda footage, the most despicable meters of celluloid ever shot here. They use all of this in an uncritical fashion, not bothering in the least to draw the necessary consequences for their presentation, not even stopping at making the claim at the start: "This film contains no dramatized footage," dressing things up even more (which moves the producer to proclaim proudly, "No expenses spared"), heightening and replicating the propaganda value in so doing and making themselves in the process once again accomplices after the fact.

To repeat myself: because of these images we see before us for two hours there was a hole in the film culture of this country which lasted thirty or forty years. Fest and Herrendoerfer, smiling the whole while, tear it open again, proud of their gruesome discoveries. As a dam for all

the things that come gushing out they only have a commentary. Does this
suffice to stop the flow of these images, which are anything but innocent
and harmless?

Where is the author of this film if not in this commentary? Or, more
precisely: in the VOICE that speaks this commentary. Because it is its
USE which causes a reaction in the spectator. I watched the film a second
time, armed with a cassette recorder. Free of the tensed-up agitation of
the first viewing, I am this time more able to comprehend what is going
on here. And that is the voice. It leads the spectator by the hand and
seduces him in a way that is not much different from the other voice one
constantly hears. In the same way it is less and less important what it says
and more important how it says what it does. It too gradually pulls the
spectator in and puts one to sleep. Which I only gradually am able to
perceive: it in fact does not stand "soberly and objectively" above its
object, but rather tries to illustrate it, to enter into it, to change its
modalities: sometimes reverent, sometimes casual, sometimes mournful,
then suddenly hopeful, occasionally amused, occasionally angered, also
bold or mocking. . . .

Sometimes a subterranean tone of sympathy or comradeship re-
sounds: "Everything Hitler hated: bickering between parties, communists, Jewry . . ." or even: "He couldn't stand the countenance of party
comrades who had grown corpulent while in office." Or a sympathetic
recognition: "He could neither be bought nor was he in league with big
business." (I am only talking here about HOW things are being said.)
The voice is at its worst when it says: "In the early part of '33 the first
concentration camps are established. No one at the the time wanted to
see such images. There were reasons: embarrassment, fear, shyness."

The voice goes silent, one sees the front of a KZ accompanied
suddenly by a glockenspiel playing the melody, "Freut euch des
Lebens" . . . (Can I believe my eyes and ears? I look around in the
cinema: no one really seems to be getting what's happening here. What
sorts of MEANS are these anyway in a film made "without emotion, with
almost scientific reserve"? Irony, perhaps? Or pure mockery?), and then
this infamous voice actually goes on to say in a RELIEVED tone, I swear
it, in a relieved tone, I repeatedly listened to it on the cassette player,
continues in a relieved tone: "What happened behind the barbed wire
was obscured by popular amusements and all sorts of simple pleasures.
The Germans were among themselves." The embarrassment, fear, and
shyness mentioned several moments ago are here no longer a matter of
content, but rather a form of speech, here the repression of a theme has
become a method and has only joined together with arrogance. . . .

Given the way this film is organized, quite simply due to customary ways of seeing and the most simple patterns of identification, one has to be frankly relieved, for instance, that Hitler survives the assassination attempt of July 20. I too notice how I respond to this with a certain, so to speak, completely formal satisfaction as Hitler reports to a just arrived Mussolini about the great bit of luck he has just experienced. Given the way this film is organized the assassins remain exactly that: assassins. The narrative stance, emanating from Hitler, makes us see them as such. This film about the "career" comes at the cost of all those who suffered because of this career, who were murdered or forced out of the country. For this reason they only are marginal presences here.

This film is so fascinated by its object, by its importance, in which it takes part ("He gave truth to the phrase that history on occasion loves to take shape in a SINGLE person"), that this object again and again takes control of the film, becoming its secret narrator.

Here someone thought, arrogantly and with outrageous stupidity, having already tested the waters successfully with a best seller, that his language was superior to the language of demagogic images, thought that with a superior commentary he could put everything in its correct place, like a god from on high.

Blindly he stepped into all the traps that a much more clever god from on high set for him forty years ago. Without noticing it, he performs the same acts of homage as did all of the sorrowful masses from whose reproduced faces he cannot tear himself loose. At one point we hear the phrase: "He who had let out the cry knew the magic of simple images. He loved to come down to his people like a kind of god." I have a hard time understanding this except as a description of Fest's own method.

During the second viewing I am occasionally so overcome by nausea that I leave my cassette player running and go out. On the toilet wall in the cinema a couple of dumb phrases are scribbled on the wall, a swastika as well. Of recent vintage. I sit there numbed by it all. A bit of graffiti occurs to me, a stupid wordplay using "business write-off company" (*Abschreibungsgesellschaft*): that one could write off this film as a film about fascism. And right away then the next step: that this film was copied (*abgeschrieben*) from the fascists, every single image. Somewhat relieved I go back into the cinema, just in time to change the cassette.

At one point toward the start the authors seemed to have realized something. "Scores of cameramen constantly surrounded him. Their photographs stylized him into a sort of monument." But this film stylizes every bit as firmly (*feste*). "As a monument, that's how he wanted to go down in history." What is this film if not a monument?

I think I am in my own way too only advertising the film. NOT to see the film is perhaps the only recommendation one can make. Or, if one wants to see it *partout* with one's eyes and above all: to hear it with one's own ears, then only as a testament of the kind of fascination which this film succumbs to and reflects.

Wait for Theo[dor] Kotulla's film, *Aus einem deutschen Leben (Death Is My Trade)*, which has more to say about this fascination by refusing to share it. I hope this film will soon come to the cinemas as a sort of correction. But even if there were many other sensible films like this: one does not so easily make up for the set-back which the film by Fest and Herrendoerfer has brought to cinema in Germany.

I am ashamed of the decision of the FBW, which deemed this film PARTICULARLY NOTEWORTHY and allowed it to be played on holidays and for youths twelve years and older. On the other hand, films that are so peaceful, careful, and humane as Wolfgang Berndt [and Doris Dörrie]'s *Ob's stürmt oder schneit (Whether It Storms or Snows)* are denied such a predicate for purely formal reasons and there are others which are forbidden to youths under eighteen *(Im Lauf der Zeit/Kings of the Road)*.

These, too, are reasons to emigrate, Rainer Werner.

(I'm only bleeding.)

The complete title of the film under discussion is Hitler—eine Karriere *(Hitler—A Career). Fest, one of the editors of the conservative daily newspaper, the* Frankfurter Allgemeine Zeitung, *was the author of* Hitler, *translated into English by Richard and Clara Winston (New York: Random House, 1975). Fest played a very prominent role in the campaign against Fassbinder's play,* Der Müll, die Stadt und der Tod *(Garbage, the City, and Death). He would coin the phrase "left-wing anti-Semitism" to describe the director's drama. See Fest's article, "Reicher Jude von links," FAZ, 19 March 1976.—Janssen's article appeared as "High durch Hitler: Das neue Werk des Führer-Biographen Fest entpuppt sich als ein gefährlicher Film," Die Zeit, 8 July 1977.—Schütte's notice bore the title, ". . . seine energischen Gemeinplätze: Joachim Fests und Christian Herrendörfers Filmfeature* Hitler—eine Karriere," Frankfurter Rundschau, 8 July 1977.—The Lang quotation comes from Peter Bogdanovich, Fritz Lang in America *(New York: Praeger, 1969), p. 15.—The final invocation of Rainer Werner Fassbinder refers to the director's plans at the time to leave Germany and work abroad.*

50. Alf Brustellin, Rainer Werner Fassbinder, Alexander Kluge, Volker Schlöndorff, Bernhard Sinkel

Germany in Autumn: What Is the Film's Bias? (1978)

One can rightfully assume that the nine of us who collectively directed this film have different political views. In one respect we are in agreement: we are not the chief justices of contemporary affairs. As filmmakers it is not our concern to provide another statement about terror here and abroad, about "the penal role of the state from a to z," to add to the hundred thousand theories the first correct one. That would be a film without images anyway.

It is something seemingly simple which roused us: the lack of memory. First the news blockade, then the imageless verbal usages of the news media. After the fall of '77—Kappler, Schleyer, Mogadischu, the Stammheim deaths—followed, like every year, Christmas '77 and New Year. As if nothing had happened. In this traveling express train of history we are pulling the emergency brake. For two hours of film we are trying to hold onto memory in the form of a subjective momentary impression. As best we can. No one can do more than he can. In this regard our film is a document—this too is another weakness that we do not want to hide.

In a certain sense we are counting on the spectator's patience. Other similar films will follow this one—collective films. The success syndrome and cooperation are mutually exclusive. The film is the first anti-subsidy board film. We're completely fed up with the public pampering and the subsidy boards. We want to concern ourselves with the images of our country.

We have tried hard, we cannot do any more than we have. We expect from the spectator the following: that he looks calmly and carefully, that he doesn't let himself be confused by the fact that this film has been edited differently than TV films or films that are shown in commercial cinemas, that he confides in the images—despite pressures of time and trouble, that he puts up with confusion and weak passages which truly belong to us, to him, and to the autumn of '77.

"When brutality reaches a certain point, it doesn't matter who started it—it only must stop."

Frau Wilde says this, a woman with five children, buried in the rubble in April 1945 after a bomber attack, to a psychologist of the occupying American army, an individual entrusted with finding out

whether people who have been tormented in this manner are still capable
of vengeful feelings toward the Allies. It's somehow striking: tools of
torture are industrial products of modern society; but the protest against
these tools of torture—in the form of imagination, memory, "revenge"—
still remains human products. In this way an apparent imbalance holds
sway: the overwhelming presence of the world of facts, the impotence of
humans in the face of it. But the point is not to let this apparent state of
affairs fool us (Adorno).

The point is instead to seek the material core in human feelings and
that means: when brutality reaches a certain point—when it is no longer
bearable for normal working, living, nonspecialized human beings, then
a tower of cultural values collapses: logic, judicial authority, eye-for-an-
eye, tooth-for-a-tooth, etc. What remains are the living eyes. And these
eyes (or ears or other senses) say: as a human being I don't want to suffer.
That above all. Only then the question, who started it all, who's right,
what does reason say, one's ancestors, the whole "nightmare of dead
generations" (Marx), who also are partially responsible for all of this?

This quotation stands for this material core. It refers to the spring of
'45. What it means for autumn '77 is mysterious (schleierhaft). We are not
smarter than the spectators.

A fool, who gives more than he has. Autumn 1977 is the history of
confusion. Exactly this must be held on to. Whoever knows the truth lies.
Whoever does not know it seeks. Insofar our own bias, even if we have different
political views.

For a background account of the events surrounding the "German autumn,"
see Tatjana Botzat, Elisabeth Kiderlen, and Frank Wolff, Ein deutscher
Herbst: Zustände—Dokumente, Berichte, Kommentare (Frankfurt am
Main: Verlag Neue Kritik, 1978). For a summary in English, see Miriam
Hansen, "Cooperative Auteur Cinema and Oppositional Public Sphere: Alexander Kluge's Contribution to Germany in Autumn," New German Cri-
tique, nos. 24–25 (Fall/Winter 1981–82): 44–46.—Deutschland im
Herbst (Germany in Autumn) received no government subsidy money or TV
support.—Frau Wilde is a character who appears in Kluge's collection of
stories, Neue Geschichten. Hefte 1–18. "Unheimlichkeit der Zeit."
(Frankfurt am Main: Suhrkamp, 1978), pp. 313–15.—For a lengthier account of the deliberations among the filmmaker collective during the making of
Germany in Autumn, see Alexander Kluge, Die Patriotin (Frankfurt am
Main: Zweitausendeins, 1979), pp. 20–37.

51. Rainer Werner Fassbinder

The German Feature Film and Reality (1978)

In contrast to Italy where, for instance, Francesco Rosi, Damiano Damiani, and others make films—one could almost say—so close to the reality of their country that they and their films have a tangible effect on this reality and all of this even under the decidedly commercial dictates of a film industry; in contrast to America, where continually films are also produced which in a totally critical manner insinuate their way into the world of current events, here as well, not oblivious to the commercial aspects of an industry, which, how could it be different, is after all a commercial one; in contrast to France, Spain, even to Switzerland, where Jonas will be twenty-five in the year 2000; in contrast to almost all of the Western democracies, there seems to exist a clandestine common interest among the different groups in the Federal Republic of Germany concerned with film to make certain that this kind of film will not be produced in our country.

For many years this interest in not producing a German film that deals with German reality was justified by nothing less than the simple assertion that the German public was not interested in "this kind of film," an assertion which the already confused and timorous German producers simply believed and accepted. Reality, they all seemed to agree, was a matter for the television stations, which for their part, fortunately, are networks governed by the laws applying to public bodies and to that extent at least duty-bound to a balanced coverage of reality—or is a balanced coverage a gross pluralistic one, one rather where everything somehow has its own special laws, especially the Law?

In order not to be misunderstood, it is of course clear to me that— with whatever limitations there might have been, this varies more or less from one station to the other—critical films in the Federal Republic of Germany have only been possible on television or at least in cooperation with television. But I also know in what context this critical content reaches the TV watcher and that it—the critical content—is effectively eliminated on the one hand through the special way in which an evening's schedule is organized, how sad is one supposed to be about something, when almost exactly at the same moment Peter Alexander or Anneliese Rothenberger are formulating a sentence on a talk-show, I know, it almost can't be any worse than this, but for the most aren't things like this (the sentence is correct, you can believe me, I mean grammatically, that is), and that on the other hand, more and more directors are coming close to being captives of an aesthetics characteristic of television, and there really is such a thing, put in another way, people who make films for the cinema usually do not take the medium television, which puts bread on their tables, quite so seriously. In this manner sloppiness takes over in many, many minds and it has without a doubt its ultimate consequences, this sloppiness, in the subsequent feature films these directors might make, which at least the audience will notice and hence can only be detrimental to cinema as a whole.

No doubt this set of problems is as a whole considerably more complex than I have outlined things here, you know what I mean? But up until the very recent past it seemed to be a foregone conclusion that German reality in German films could at best take place in more or less successful translations from the nineteenth century perhaps or in the twenties, if it all, films received the warmest reception when they were able with much dexterity to prevent the danger that the spectator might be reminded of his own reality. (This sentence contains by the way much more truth than one might initially suspect. For safety's sake read it again before the thought that I might be unjust becomes even more firmly ingrained in your head than it already is.)

Anyway, I could at this juncture already quite easily switch to a concrete discussion about the theme of my film *Die dritte Generation (The Third Generation)*, because the denial, and, indeed, perhaps that of the media to confront reality, is for me at least also one of the reasons why precisely the reality, this specifically West German reality, has not managed to do something which I assume to be a basic premise for any democracy, has not managed to reach the individual citizen so that a real democracy might have arisen, one not democratic in name only and one in which the phenomenon of an almost inexplicable escalation of violence would never have been able to arise. But, in my customary straightforward manner, I will talk about this later.

Before I do that I would like to express my hope, as best I can, that all of these omissions or exclusions or desired and rewarded acts of cowardice now, and this increasingly so, soon cease, that a situation arise for German film that one could not imagine to be more liberated, joyous, fruitful. I think, and I hope you will excuse me if that is the case, that I let the last sentence take something of a cynical turn, but only a very, very little bit of one, don't you think? Or is it the case that I might have drawn a false conclusion from the "critical successes" (and commercially things went quite well, unless, of course, the rumors this time around are even more inaccurate than usual) of the films *Das zweite Erwachen der Christa Klages (The Second Awakening of Christa Klages)* by my colleague von Trotta and *Deutschland im Herbst (Germany in Autumn)*, a film, by the way, which for me, and I made no bones about saying this openly again and again, from the very start, seems with every minute to become more and more terrible, but nonetheless a film which I have decided to defend with my inimitably large amount of Parsifal-like naïveté, that it wasn't the obscene moments that made this film become an important and for many people interesting and important film (and for those who perhaps don't know, I don't think it's obscene when I play with my prick in front of the camera, I think it's obscene that some people masturbate who would rather pretend to themselves that they didn't have a prick, and also don't have a firm enough grip on their brain so that they could give it a good yank and at least jack off with it. There has been, and that is at least some kind of accomplishment, a surprisingly large amount of masturbation done with mouths, which, speaking for us sisters of the revolution, in fact is impossible, with mouths, you know, with mouths. . . ?). (This sentence is correct as well, in any case, at least grammatically!) A conclusion, besides, additionally supported by the actually quite large commercial success of the movie *Die verlorene Ehre der Katharina Blum (The Lost Honor of Katharina Blum)*—yes, yes, self-liberation can also demand sacrifices, even those of the spirit, "God grant" that this is not one of the unpardonable sorts, one of those that can be punished with indelible marks on one's soul.

A commercial success, then, for three films, which in three absolutely different ways confront the reality of the Federal Republic of Germany here and today, a success finally which leads me to the conclusion that it now seems to have become possible even here to pose concrete political questions with the medium film, also and especially with the feature film, and that the potentially interested audience for this film is large enough so that these three films mentioned above might give way to further films of this sort, and so that these films, in contrast to previous experience, might also have the chance to find an audience. One thing above all seems important to me, namely, that one remain, so to speak, on the ball, so that in the future these films can be produced widely and that one doesn't allow the enemies of this desire to view cinema as a site of communication the opportunity, precisely because of the lack of such films, to turn things around and say that this lack automatically proves there is no popular interest.

This is one reason among many why I am determined every so often to make a film that deals with topical political questions. I think one can also make these films increasingly attractive through casting and styling and I think that for this sort of "speculation" there are more than sufficient moral reasons. When one thinks for instance about Italian cinema, one thinks among other things again and again about well-known stars, like for instance Franco Nero in Bellocchio's films, Gian-

Maria Volonte in Damiano Damiani or Rod Steiger in Francesco Rosi or, or, or . . ., this list could be continued at length and in *All the President's Men*, it was Robert Redford and Dustin Hoffman who brought to the filmic adaptation of the Watergate case not only their dramatic talent but also their glamour. I don't think I need say any more about the potential question why I want to make *The Third Generation*, a film that deals with a problem, that is to say with terrorism and the terrorists today, which one could say remains at the point in time during which this film is being made a problem that the inhabitants of this country and those people who represent this country have in no way at all, be it practically or even only intellectually = ideologically, begun to comprehend.

Fassbinder refers in the first paragraph to Alain Tanner's Jonas, Who Will Be 25 in the Year 2000.—*The second half of Fassbinder's essay, "Ein Film—ein Titel," goes on to discuss more specifically the socio-historical backdrop to the problem of terrorism in the Federal Republic.*

52. Edgar Reitz

The Camera Is Not a Clock (1979)
(Regarding My Experiences Telling Stories from German History)

Film has much in common with our ability to remember. It is not just the capacity to retain images and events, to salvage them from the march of time, but also the possibility to mix past and present in a way that causes them to permeate each other. Many people in our profession make the mistake of confusing film images with reality. But what the camera captures on film is already at the moment it is screened part of the past. The filmmaker should develop a feeling for the fact that when he is filming, what he sees, what he hears, is being transported into the past. The sorrow we feel about the transitory nature of happiness can never be greater than in the moment of filming. When we remember previously lived images and replay memories, we are like magicians: we call up the dead and let them appear before the camera. The film image allows something already past which only floats about in our memory—connected by associations with a thousand other memories—to become once again present, recallable, actualized, an integral part of our life today.

Over the years I have increasingly come to use film as a vehicle for memory work *(Erinnerungsarbeit)*. History, as we learn it in school, or as it is practiced by historians, attempts to generalize, to order events, to disclose cause and effect. Our capacity for making judgments is trained in this fashion. In the history of the century we live in, the world of images stored up in our memories, the actual living substance of history, are repressed in an irretrievable manner. To counter this abstract system that confronts us in the course of our lives as "school," as "education," as "politics," as "psychology," etc., we have to defend ourselves with a powerful weapon. This weapon from time immemorial has been art, especially narrative art: literature, poesy, film.

It goes without saying that the demarcations I'm making here are equally abstract. But what is not abstract is the work in this realm. When a philosopher, a teacher, a lawyer, or a businessman uses stories (something that happens daily, e.g., when stories are told in a court case or in a psychological report or in a speech in front of parliament), these people, having cited these stories and examples, drop them just as quickly and go on to make their ultimate point, one connected with an abstract decision-making process, without themselves suffering in the least. When a story-teller, on the other hand (and as a filmmaker I see myself as a story-teller), takes something in hand, picks it up, be it a small event, a figure, a certain glance, a smile, a gesture, a word, he can never again put these things down when he has no more use for them, because when they are used in his art they are never only the means to an end, they never *merely* prove or illustrate something beyond their own existence. When we tell stories, everything we take in hand is indestructible, it demands its own life, it cannot simply disappear again in the course of a film, it assumes a magical existence and becomes stronger than the will of the story-teller. Once one has grasped this it is a question of developing a certain sort of sensibility. Kafka once wrote: "Repetition is the only artistic principle we recognize." For years now I have pondered this sentence again and again and think I understand it now. Every object used by an artist at one point will return again insistently in the course of his work, will want to show itself, will also appear when it has long since lost all meaning. This holds in music for tones and sounds just as it does in painting for colors and lines, in film for situations, images, and movements. The old discussion about content and form is beside the point when we see things in this way because form is nothing more than the manner in which every single thing we conjure up demands eternal life, not reconciling itself simply to disappear within a given work.

This notion of filmmaking gives rise to difficulties when one wants to work with stories that occurred in the controversial epochs of this century. In our television networks and the state film subsidy boards there are people driven by a sense of responsibility, be it pedagogic, political, humanitarian, commercial, or otherwise, people who want to justify their decisions to themselves and to others. Of necessity they see in each project the "message," the "relevance," the abstract sense of the undertaking, because only these sorts of things can be published in newspapers or sent on in the form of memos to the desks of their superiors. In fact, however, artistic practice tends to disintegrate sense, to combat all forms of abstraction. Art is ambiguous, an eternal mystery for schoolteachers.

Die Reise nach Wien (The Trip to Vienna) and *Stunde Null (Zero Hour)* are set in an era about which people have hard and fast prejudices. The war, the Nazi-Reich, and its collapse in the year 1945, all of these are historical phenomena over which schoolmasters and political parties have long since passed judgment. This works against the telling of other stories whose nuances retain a mystery of their own. German film critics are in a frightening way devoid of aesthetic understanding and producers depend on films being interpreted correctly.

Die Schneider von Ulm (The Tailor from Ulm) can serve as an example. In this film (1978) I drew on a story from the end of the eighteenth century. The story of an artisan in Ulm who constructs wings and devotes his life to the dream of flying like a bird. This world of images and atmospheres was not understood in the FRG. The press, film critics did not accept this film whose mysteries cannot be articulated in accepted terms and concepts.

I worked on this film almost three years. The cinemas do not show it because no one can explain to the public why it is a wonderful film. We have to fight with determination against an abstract system of communication.

Right now I am working on a project that once again will probably occupy the next three years of my life: under the title of *Heimat*, a many-hour-long film epic about a family, a village, a landscape is taking shape. It is about the region in which I was born and in which I grew up, the Hunsrück, west of the Rhine, located between the cities Mainz and Trier, a ramshackle hilly area.

In our German culture there is hardly a more ambivalent feeling, hardly a more painful mixture of happiness and bitterness than the experience vested in the word "*Heimat.*" Throughout the history of German culture one has been continually plagued by this feeling. Heine was almost driven crazy by it, Hitler tried to turn this word into a political precept. The story I want to tell, with all of its innumerable sidepaths, takes place between 1918 and 1980.

Here I see an answer to my theory: what must be for artistic reasons, namely that the things one picks up dare not disappear, all of this becomes confirmed in reality. I come across, for instance, a story that has to do with the construction of a telephone line in 1933.

While writing the screenplay, I know I will have to seek out this telephone line with my camera again and again, that there is no way I could simply leave it out, that at best I would have to take recourse to a poetic metamorphosis. After working on the screenplay for three months, I finally go to the Hunsrück in person and, lo and behold, find an actual counterpart in reality for this telephone line just as I had described it for poetic reasons in the present. Apparently history takes its course with the same regularity which it shares with poetic story telling. Professional historians, even today, still have not recognized this and learned to deal with it.

I must at this point bring a moral concept into the discussion. It is "the respect for things." A society that treats itself and nature according to abstract principles of instrumentality, profit, and intellectual legitimation, is no longer capable of summoning up this respect for things. Things are nonetheless not dead just because this is so. They take their revenge on us. There is no art that does not have this respect for things. To that extent it remains the only humane method known to me. Working with a camera demands the same sensitivity. Even the camera and our entire cinematographic apparatus are things for which we must have respect, because they, regardless of how one uses them, have their own lives. The camera is an instrument of magic. It transforms every place to which one brings it. It takes things out of time, tears their sensual appearance out of the banal present, making them available, granting them a chance to survive. In this way the film camera is a dangerous toy. Even if we are not aware how it functions, it nonetheless functions in this way. The entire lot of terrible television programs and commercial offerings in cinemas is in reality the revenge of the camera on those stupid abusers who think they are reproducing reality. The result is a haunted semblance of reality. The independent existence of camera and apparatus has started to work against us.

I think it's a lie to say that time is a smoothly flowing stream in which all of us and all things move at the same speed. Time as we measure it with clocks, as we register it in calendars, or as we define it in meters of film, does not exist. Every living thing and every object lives in its own time and this personal time does not flow continuously, but rather stands still at times, proceeds only haltingly, sometimes with incredible velocity, that is to say, it is irregular. What is past is not past, the future does not lie before us, but just as much behind us. The present is not the time in which we live. Anyone working with the medium film has to deal with the problem of time.

I think it's fantastic that the film camera is not a clock, not an abstract instrument for telling time. One can live with a camera in a familiar common time just as one does with one's favorite things. I will always hold onto the old 35mm film, onto the Arriflex camera, onto this mechanical principle that has long since been declared technically behind the times, which itself is a bit of history. (I say all of this as the son of a watchmaker who grew up in a mechanical age and grew sceptical in the age of electronic media. Love always has something to do with memory.)

53. Hans Jürgen Syberberg

Mein Führer—Our Hitler. The Meaning of Small Words (1980)

Hitler was proud that no foreigner, not even a sympathetic or a vanquished one, would ever have the right to say, "Mein Führer," that would remain a privilege of the Germans for all time, much like a citizen of Rome during the golden age of the empire. The Americans are now saying, "Our Hitler." And in talking about this Hitler which has now become a film, this Hitler suddenly and quite naturally is becoming "their Hitler." A German coming to America who knows little or nothing about the strange change in the film's title which exists only in America, will be surprised or shocked to hear people in discussions or dialogues, Americans, talking about this man as "their" own. Imagine the uncanny situation when an American can speak of "our Hitler," e.g., "How would you explain that our Hitler has in Germany today, within this German postwar intellectual establishment, no chance to be understood? Our Hitler is suffering under the hostile indifference of certain German media which do not want to know him . . ."

Addendum: How much I would have liked to have named the film in the manner Coppola saw and understood it. He thought at first it was a film with the title: The Grail.

The quoted passage appears in the original in English—Francis Ford Coppola's Zoetrope Studios handles the American distribution of Syberberg's Hitler—Ein Film aus Deutschland (Our Hitler).

54. Eberhard Fechner

The Experience of History (1984)

"Oral history" is the English term for the representation of contemporary history through the description of ordinary people's personal experiences. There is still no appropriate German phrase for this new form of historical reflection, one that is increasingly aligning itself with objective historical analysis and supplementing it with subjective recollections.

Since 1969 I and others have made a series of films dealing with the individual destinies of people from various levels of German society during this century. They are eyewitness accounts in which German citizens tell about their lives and thereby about the age that has shaped their lives.

These people include proletarians, low-level white-collar workers and craftsmen, public servants and industrialists, academicians and artists, the poor, the rich, Christians and Jews. They all relate their childhood experiences, how things were at home with their parents and at school. They talk of how they chose a profession, of their plans, hopes and disappointments, of love affairs, marriages, children, of death and birth.

And everything they relate is couched in historical events that have unceasingly influenced their lives: World War I and Germany's defeat, the disorder of the early postwar years, the inflation and unemployment later in the twenties, January 30, 1933 and the consequences of Hitler's policies, World War II with its conquests and war medals, the Gestapo, concentration camps, nightly bombings, flight or emigration, and, in the end, the all-consuming collapse. Then, life in the postwar period, a life that for many consisted only of hunger, cold, and worrying about one's next meal. Finally, an account of the last thirty years, with the division of Germany and the step-by-step economic recovery of the Federal Republic. Each person with a voice in my films—*Nachrede auf Klara Heydebreck* (*Testimonials for Klara Heydebreck*, 1969), *Klassenphoto* (*Class Picture*, 1970), *Unter Denkmalschutz* (*Under Landmark Protection*, 1973), *Lebensdaten* (*Life's Key Dates*, 1975), and *The Comedian Harmonists* (1976)—experienced these times differently and thus has different recollections. None of their private lives, however, remained unaffected by historical events. Hardly anyone paid much attention to politics during their life. Politics, on the other hand, did not go unnoticed in any of these people's lives.

From each of these life stories it becomes clear that the private existence of each of these individuals was determined by contemporary history and social constraints. This is true not only in the sense that people endured and tolerated politics as an inexorable fate, but also in the way it shaped personal decisions, attitudes, and reactions during changing political periods.

Hardly anyone among those interviewed was aware to what degree their life was dependent on the course of history. At the end of each of these films, however, the image of an epoch from Germany's recent past takes shape in the mind of the viewer, as seen through the eyes of the filmed witnesses, as the sum of various experiences, even when these were, in part, interpreted in a contradictory manner, sometimes even at odds with everything we know about history. As noted earlier, though, the representation of individual destinies is at the same time of necessity a subjective form for the presentation of contemporary history. In the course of these past years, regardless of the material with which I started or what theme I treated, it invariably resulted in a description of the political developments in this country.

I took, for example, the photograph of a graduating class from 1933, people I had never met who lived in a house in Frankfurt, or the wedding notice of an engaged couple I did not know as occasions to seek out people found in such a coincidental way and to ask them about their experiences, their lives, what they had learned. It quickly became apparent that almost all of these lives were ones that you would generally describe as normal, average, inconspicuous, common, and insignificant.

But exactly this seeming insignificance makes these life stories become significant, noteworthy, and edifying for the normal viewer.

People like to be told stories. Literature, as well as the theater, has been living off them for thousands of years, and the cinema for nearly a hundred. How can television do without them? These stories do not in any way have to tell about extraordinary lives, about exceptional people and their unusual experiences. On the contrary: precisely the presentation of average fates, those shared by most viewers, imparts to this sort of identification the possibility of evoking sympathy as well as understanding of social relations.

Every one of the millions of television viewers can find themselves mirrored in these destinies, or can discover differences between these experiences and their own under the same circumstances.

The description of an "average" fate during the last war or the postwar years does not only interest me more than presenting the career of a man like Adolf Hitler; it also says more about the times then, it is richer in insights and more accessible to every viewer. I do not believe that the depiction of extraordinary fates—from Frederick II to Wernher von Braun or Albert Schweitzer—can disclose the true meaning of a particular time. It is reflected above all by the lives of those who are its victims. . . .

What other approach could provide a better account of the consequences of the course of history on the lives of German citizens, how they acted in response to it and what kind of people they were, living in those times? They talk about their own thoughts, their feelings, and their actions, in this way bearing witness to themselves and their contemporaries. History seen from below.

With the film *Im Damenstift* (*The Old Ladies' Home*, 1984) I am thus continuing my efforts to impart a picture of German society in this century through the recollections of those who experienced it firsthand. This time around they are not from the middle class, but rather nobles living in the Castle Ehreshoven located a half hour's drive from Cologne.

The shooting at Castle Ehreshoven took place during the summer of 1983. In the autumn and winter of 1983–84, the filmed material was screened, choices were made, and finally the single interviews were edited so that the different testimonies appear like a mosaic, a sort of jigsaw puzzle, providing in the end a sort of imaginary dialogue which never took place in reality. That is to say: the dramaturgical construction of this film only took shape at the editing table after all the shooting was finished.

In conclusion I would like to touch upon one frequently recurring misunderstanding that apparently can only be resolved with some difficulty in talking about my films.

Like the five other productions in this series, *The Old Ladies' Home* does not pretend to be a documentary, even if some people gain this impression. The fact that documentary elements such as old photographs, letters, and other authentic memorabilia are used in no way means that these films as a whole become documentaries. Rather they should be seen as a particular form of television drama and they simply draw on stylistic elements common to the documentary, much as the way in which an author of short stories or novels works, who also utilizes and manipulates parts of reality, eventually assembling them in a new and synthetic pattern.

I am trying to tell stories in this series of films in a comparable way; but not on paper, with a ballpoint pen or a typewriter, but with the help of a camera and a tape recorder, with the aim of adding to the verbal track a second one, i.e., the optical one. The manner in which the material captured on film and tape is already highly artificial and makes it clear that the "laws" at work in the so-called "documentary" film are only applicable here to a limited degree.

55. Hans Jürgen Syberberg

The Abode of the Gods (1984)

In 1976, when my first book was published, instead of raising my fist in protest in the tradition of 1968, I spoke of home, or "Heimat," or the place where one belongs. At that time it was quite a bold thing to do and something ridiculous as well, rather like a call to deny the very things that were identified with revolution. For the New German Cinema had started as an uprising against the *Heimatfilm* (those often sentimental films of idealized rural life); and the word "Heimat" itself had become debased since Hitler. Nevertheless, Germany was and still is a country of "homeless" people, people without a "Heimat"—in a deeper sense of the expression as well—where more than a quarter of the population is unable to live in the place where it was born.

At that time, I was of the same mind as Ernst Bloch, who defined "Heimat" as a place no one had yet attained, but for which everyone yearned; rather like a psychoanalytical projection, a process of hope and utopia. Now that the word "Heimat" has suddenly become fashionable again, I think more in terms of the "Heimat" of which Heidegger spoke, when he quoted Hölderlin and understood the word as meaning the abode of the gods. And I am concerned that those who now speak so glibly of "Heimat" again penetrate as far as this as well, for up to now they have not been very successful in their quotation of poets in Germany.

Strangely enough, the three most striking films by German directors this year (1984) are distinguished by the fact that the two less important ones were made in America and Australia, and that the major achievement is precisely that mammoth work in which the author and director cautiously try to take a closer look at "Heimat" again, even down to matters such as dialect. It is also striking that the other two, both made in English, range from alien uprightness to the kind of heartbreaking sentimentality for which the old *Heimatfilm* was notorious in the past; now it comes from outside Germany, has become international. Striking too is the fact that it is precisely the minute detail and remoteness of this new film *Heimat* that helps it to attain something that has been needed for a long time, something that is probably only possible after a defeat. What is possible in the art form of film, however, would seem to be lost in reality, where the answer to the big question of our ability to feel and find "Heimat" must be a sad one.

The three films Syberberg mentions are Wim Wenders's Paris, Texas, *Werner Herzog's* Wo die grünen Ameisen träumen (Where the Green Ants Dream), *and Edgar Reitz's* Heimat.

56. Jean-Marie Straub
Bitburg: A Text* (1985)

The truth is that this old crocodile Reagan had wanted to manifest and celebrate there over dead bodies the solidarity and reconciliation of American capitalism with the capitalism of those who under the direction of Adolf Hitler launched a crusade against what they called Bolshevism.

For those who, like Syberberg or some Americans, even Jews, do not wish to see this truth, six million Jews, twenty million Soviet citizens, died in vain; and how many Germans and young Americans?
May 1985

Straub discusses the meaning of President Reagan's controversial visit to a small cemetery in Bitburg, Germany, one containing the graves of former SS soldiers, on the occasion of the fortieth anniversary of V-E Day.—The Syberberg essay on the same event appeared in English translation as "Bitburg," On Film, no. 14 (Spring 1985): 37.

57. Josef Rödl
In Search of the Lost Heimat* (1986)

I try to look at things with a completely naïve gaze. "That's the way the world is. Boomboom. Always boomboom. Burned out, shot up. No peace. Always," are lines spoken by Jack in the script. Training grounds are the same everywhere. Internationally. Secret lands. Cain lands [Kainland].

I stumble through the country further. I'm searching for Bavaria, it's a search in the interior, in a hidden, forbidden country. Gun shells on the grass, wires for small missiles, tank ruins are my destination and churches without towers accompany my trip as well. This is the shooting site for my film: a shooting site has to please you like a lover and promise secrets, to emanate seduction and to elicit the desire to come closer. This lover offers the temptation of forbidden lovers, dangerously seductive and at the same time hostile. This lover has affairs and remains a stranger, but also pulls at you, sucking you in, dragging you in, deeper and deeper.

And suddenly before me: a pile of stones. Incredibly large. That is the village. Not the one I want to film, but another village: here is where my grandfather once lived. I had wanted to see it while it was still intact, but it no longer exists, images from old photographs crumble into a gigantic pile of stones, a massive tower, almost as high as the church steeple that used to be here. It's here, under this pile of stones, where you were born, Josef Rödl, the oldest son of a farmer and a blacksmith, someone who rose from a prole to a craftsman to a master journeyman.

I am going to make a film. In the deep interior of Germany, 1985. In these deep reaches Germany is dead, Jack says in the film. I am going to make a *Heimatfilm*, a regional film, in small spaces that have a wider application. Here in the provinces where the country still is alive.

Here in this country at the margins, at the border of a world divided between East and West, in this no-man's-land of the troop training ground, this is where I want to make the film. Here, in this land in East Bavaria, is where they all come, the small soldiers as well as the military leaders, from Europe and America, ministers and chancellors, here to this tiny world that means so much.

And they come from all over Germany. This small country that one condescendingly calls the provinces is full of motion: atomic dumping sites, the Rhine-Main-Danube canal, the largest troop training grounds, dying forests and nuclear reactors, atomic missiles between America and Moscow. Everything is there which moves Germany: an unsettled, protesting, agitated Germany watched over by police and military. Provinces? I call for the provincial film: full of spots, dirt, rough edges [*fleckig, dreckig, eckig*]. It contains (folk) theater, (folk) music, as well as (peasant) painting, local dialects, the faces and gestures of the provinces, the dreams and fears and joys. All of this on film. Small, distinct, bearable, lively and nonetheless still a "large" provincial film. I demand it—above all from myself.

The problem of German film is not the provinces, but rather its short-sighted provincial minds.

Germany is not America. America is admirable, for it is more agile, a fascinatingly better "America," Germany admires America, it needs America, but it needs itself as well, just as, for instance, France needs its France or the Russians their dear Father Russia. Young German filmmakers are searching for identity, Germany is in search of its identity—for this reason Bavaria is more alive than Germany, because it has a more distinct cultural and political self-consciousness. Germany, that sounds to me like Denver and Dallas. A synchronized Germany, one that allows itself publicly to suppress its greatest filmmaker/writer, (Herbert) Achternbusch. For years now. Instead everywhere you look more or less successful imitations. And imitation is a perfect definition of . . . Germany as the provinces.

I'm still standing in the village ruins in the troop training ground. . . . By nightfall I have to leave this training ground, otherwise it could be dangerous. Maybe I should go into the American settlement not far from here, go see a movie there, or go to a club. There, over the valleys, lies America, you can get there on foot. Or, maybe I'll walk to the north, to Franconia. The Hof Film Days themselves are like one gigantic, exciting mammoth film. With all the scenes, hopes, successes, disappointments, for beginners and luminaries from all over, everyone intoxicated by images and beer. The first beginnings and great beginnings. Football and film and everything is animated: the provinces. The Hof Film Days are like this. They don't just act like it—they are this way. Like that! Unmistakable. That's how it's done. Just like that. It's good that way.

But now I walk on toward America, between untouched, maddeningly beautiful innocence and disquieting, voracious violation.

Images of America, my first impressions as a child: soldiers, tanks, chewing gum, and powdered milk. Our cows at home also gave milk, but the soldier's milk is a powder. Sweet, enticing, white-powdered America, friendly and foreign to us village children.

"Amis kommen"—that was a signal in the village. We ran through the forests to the soldiers, through the winter cold and snow, a long way, in hope of presents and leftovers, of chocolate, ice cream, and canned food. NATO olive cans were the first magic receptacles before we figured out what "jam" and "meat" meant. Everyone had enough to eat at home, but this was America. America out of the can. And America had everything for our own cowboys-and-Indians games in the forest: tents, camping stoves, knives, guns, and armed men who spoke a foreign language. We accepted gifts and pilfered things. We smoked our first cigarettes with you Indians during maneuvers as if they were a peace pipe, coughing, coughing dizzily until the world went round, dizzy and pale, but high. We learned quickly to pick out the German phrase "Fräuleins" from your foreign words and to nod energetically. Village boys promised their sisters for a stick of gum, even if they didn't have any. Little procurers, who with their child's hands drew the "Fräulein" with some curves in the air, because we had seen older boys do the same while they made finger signs showing eighteen years. Americans on maneuvers, that was the annual event we all looked forward to in the village and for them we provided a break from an otherwise boring life in the woods. America, that was the first temptation of a world with more adventures and more riches, the first signs that far away from here there is a much bigger world than one's own village; because for us our village between the forests was the middle of the entire world.

We walked around America in the woods, excited by this first short friendship, by sweet powdered milk, by cigarettes that made us dizzy. America came into the village.

The first sticks of gum, the first tanks, the first atomic bomb, the earliest signs of America in my head. It has the brightness of unloved beautiful women and the seductiveness of forbidden lovers. Troop training ground. This land here has an undertow and it can kill, everyday and everything. Training area for freedom and for death. Black, beautiful, deadly, American Germany.

These comments were written as program notes published in the festival brochure of the 1986 Hof Film Days, where Rödl's film, Der wilde Clown (The Wild Clown), was shown. Rödl's first public success dates back to another screening at the Hof Film Days, the showing of Albert—warum? (Albert—Why?) in 1978. The Hof gathering celebrated its twentieth anniversary in the fall of 1986. It remains the most significant annual meeting of West Germany's film culture, now taking place over five days each year in late October, under, as ever, the guidance of the redoubtable Heinz Badewitz.

58. Martin Theo Krieger
Finding a Home in Berlin* (1986)

I've lived in cities and villages, their names are Lingen, Neuss, Bremen, Hildesheim, Ottbergen, small places where you know your way around. Places in which I quickly found a place, that is to say: problems, goals, tasks, plans, recognition, enemies, resignation, consolation, love. I was lost in these places, but I also was at home.

Now I've been living in Berlin for eight years. Berlin, for me that meant at first an undefined hope for something different, a hope fed by all the things I had read in newspapers, seen on television, and heard from friends. All these undefined hopeful images, half-truths, and clichés were at the time reason enough to make a decision: I'll move to Berlin and see what happens. At first there was a lot to see, and it was exciting, stimulating, frightening. The almost daily experience of being in some way impressed was oppressive—and fantastic. Oppressive because noise, light, tempo, waste and development, garbage and construction pass by you so quickly, and one is nonetheless forced to take notice of them; oppressive as well because there does not seem to be any continuity, any feeling of recognition and familiarity. And fantastic because things lose their familiarity and one seems constantly to have the "chance" to take part in life directly. Cinemas, theaters, concerts, readings, exhibitions, discos, sects, sport clubs, citizen initiatives, political groups, flea markets, demonstrations, places to talk about relationships and to get advice, Ku'Damm and neighborhoods, Berlin argot and Istanbul flair. For all of this there is a "scene," and one is in the thick of things, alternately hyper and stunned, and one pants hungrily and contentedly, free and alone on the trail of the self-satisfying pleasure of licking the city's blood each day.

There is hardly another city in Germany which at the same time attracts so many people and repels so many others. Berlin is an island. Every day people are stranded on the shores of this island. Dreams and hopes are bound up in this city. But every day just about as many people seem to notice that the wishes and hopes with which they came to this city have not been realized. Suddenly they feel the many walls, experience the narrowness, and wish they could go away again, dreaming of new shores. Some people do not even have time to dream.

The difficulty of finding firm ground in Berlin, that's what my first feature film is about: *Zischke*. *Zischke* tells stories—interwoven and interrupted—about people who have lost their home: about "middle-class" boys and girls and "lower-class" teenagers, about "foreign" refugees and "domestic" pursuers. . . .

A lot of figures, then, a lot of stories. Nonetheless, *Zischke* does not linger on one theme, but rather tells about a handful of people and follows them for a while as they try to get situated. This happens in a quiet and a loud manner, with excitement and fun, sorrow and hope, with a blend of politics and poetry. But the stories also tell about me as well: I like living here. Nevertheless: I miss so much living here. Nevertheless: the city makes me sick. Nevertheless: I don't want to leave. Everything remains open: everything is a matter of searching and finding.

Krieger's debut feature, Zischke, *premiered in German cinemas during the fall of 1986. Numerous critics in the FRG spoke of it as one of the most noteworthy films screened at that year's Hof Film Days.*

VII

Filmmakers and Critics

When foreign commentators discuss the difficulties encountered by the New German Film at home, they regularly mention the harsh treatment directors and films have received from domestic critics. Film journalists thus figure in a nation's overall disinclination towards individuals seeking to provide a running chronicle of public life and private dreams, of the sights, sounds, stories, and myths of a country. Hans Jürgen Syberberg's ongoing battle with film critics, so vehemently dramatized in his *Hitler* film and his various books, has gained much attention in the foreign press. His colleague Margarethe von Trotta, the victim of a fierce series of attacks after the premiere of *Heller Wahn (Sheer Madness)*, argued in 1983 that West German film critics do not take part in the growing and learning process evidenced by filmmakers, that pundits instead limit their activity to grade giving and nitpicking. In some ways, these bitter responses, so often recounted in popular tales about New German Film, do have a basis in reality. Film criticism in general remains a minor pursuit in the Federal Republic, a country lacking the vital network of film periodicals one finds in Great Britain, France, and Italy. Books on film for the most part remain limited to mass-marketable items; serious and sustained works on film history and individual directors are rarities. Among publishers one continually hears the stock phrase: "Filmliteratur geht nicht," i.e., it does not sell. As a rule discussion about film takes up little space in the otherwise so voluminous culture pages of Germany's daily tabloids. Outside of scattered reviews, there is no continuous discourse about film, much less German film, in the Federal Republic. Here, too, it is a question of a lacking public sphere. Nonetheless, certain other factors also deserve consideration, lest the situation appear as a one-sided conspiracy against the filmmakers. ("Everyone for Him- or Herself and the FRG against All" would be an apposite title for this paranoid scenario.) Many filmmakers have gained markedly from the assistance of certain critics: the championing of Achternbusch by a gathering of supporters has helped him through a series of crises, for instance. In fact, one can point to certain voices that have consistently spoken up in favor of the *Autorenfilm*, difficult filmmakers, and controversial works, individuals writing in the *Frankfurter Rundschau, Süddeutsche Zeitung, Jahrbuch Film, Die Zeit, epd Film, Reihe Film*, and other outlets. Further, filmmakers themselves often slip into the role of critics, not simply to further their own cause (even if that is a partial motivation), but also to speak out for important films, to address compelling political issues, to engage in polemics. Making films and writing about the films one makes remain inextricably bound activities in West German film culture: it only stands to reason that directors quite frequently also reflect on the nature of film criticism in Germany, couching their responses invariably in quite personal language.

59. Wim Wenders
Learning to Hear and See* (1976)

I am a filmmaker. Until about six years ago I wrote film criticism, but I stopped doing so when I was able to make films. To do both seemed to me a contradiction. At the time, towards the end of the sixties, there was even less German film than there is now. Nonetheless, in the daily newspapers and in two film journals, there were serious, attentive, and no doubt even competent film critics. If I want to find out something today about one of the most important new directors from America, Robert Altman, I have to read foreign periodicals, for instance one of the five English film journals, which you find over there even if next to no one makes films in England anymore. If I now write about a film by Robert Altman, want to write about it, I do so ultimately out of anger about the state of film criticism in the Federal Republic, out of anger about the climate in which one writes about films, out of anger about the reputation writing about films in general still has.

It is different than at the end of the sixties; films are being produced in the FRG which are finding international attention. And these are to be sure not one-shot successes anymore, but instead films by a large number of people who make one film after the other. On the other hand, though, there is not a single film journal anymore which comments on the development of this "New German Film" like the *Cahiers du Cinéma* accompanied the "nouvelle vague." There are several enclaves of film criticism in the large daily and weekly newspapers. There are the more recent cultural guides like *Szene, tip, Blatt, Hobo,* which serve as an ersatz for the lack of real film periodicals.

But these film criticism preserves are oriented toward everyday pragmatics: they provide in the main critical judgments, opinions about films. Things are written here that distributors can quote, but one doesn't find any sense of film as a language and a culture unto itself. This type of criticism comments on individual films, but it does not compare anymore, neither with the history of cinema nor with the situation of cinema in the world today nor even with the situation of the world. In only writing about film as something one should or should not watch, this criticism loses sight of the fact that cinema has something to do with our lives, that cinema provides a more exact and comprehensive documentation of our times than theater, music, or the arts, that cinema can be detrimental when it estranges us from our real desires and fears, or that it can be beneficial, opening up people's lives and showing them freedoms, in short, that cinema is more than an industry that produces films.

At the same time I don't want to be unjust toward the very few people in this country who write about film. It's not their fault that the status of their work stands in direct correlation to the status of film culture in general, and this film culture has over the last thirty years been thoroughly purged in the American colony FRG, even worse than the twelve years before wiped out German film culture in an unprecedented way.

At the same time there are plenty of people writing in the regional newspapers with profound insight and a great love of cinema, but even they are not allowed to write in the culture pages: these are reserved for culture. Film criticism is found in the local section.

Often enough I have heard how film reviews were condensed, rewritten, or even deleted by these dumb but for that reason all the more arrogant idiots who control many editorial offices.

In the national weekly journals, especially and conspicuously so during recent months in *Spiegel,* film criticism, the writing and thinking about films, has given way to a sort of film journalism which I consider to be particularly depressing: because one takes oneself more seriously than what one writes about, one either raves about or ravages films, but always from on high, and not with any knowledge of the works in question. This kind of journalism is without character, conviction, that is to say without any real opinion and it willfully serves nothing other than its own image. In *Spiegel* a cover story appears about the Young German Film, *Wunderkinder;* several weeks later appears a completely different story: a crass retraction, "Film: A Branch without a Future." As if one had built something up so that one might all the more effectively tear it down. This doesn't help the status of cinema and writing about cinema. I don't mean to say that there should be more accolades—on the contrary, over the past couple of years there have been more than enough acclamations of new German films, probably for political reasons, so as not to endanger what has come about in the process. One consequence of this is that now every other film is being launched by its distributor as "the great international German film." False hopes have been stirred up; no: hopes have been stirred up falsely.

There are not going to be any German films capable of competing with the international and mainly American large-scale productions. Given the production situation this is not possible. But instead of that there could be a specifically German film, that is to say a film that is not vaguely international and conventional, which at least could gain a part of the German film market.

To help realize such an idea, to convince others about it and to win, or win back, an audience for this idea could be the task of film criticism. Or of a journal that does not exist. . . .

Wenders's early film criticism has been collected in the volume, Texte zu Filmen und Musik *(West Berlin: Freunde der Deutschen Kinemathek, 1975).—The remainder of this lengthy essay is devoted to a close discussion of Altman's* Nashville, *an example of precisely the kind of film criticism Wenders sees as lacking in West Germany.—A more comprehensive anthology of Wenders's writings on film appeared in late 1986:* Emotion Pictures: Betrachtungen eines beteiligten Zuschauers, *ed. Michael Töteberg (Frankfurt am Main: Verlag der Autoren).*

60. Rainer Werner Fassbinder

Public Statement Regarding *Garbage, the City, and Death* (1976)

One has reproached my play *Der Müll, die Stadt und der Tod (Garbage, the City, and Death)* for ostensibly being "anti-Semitic." Under the guise of this reproach certain parties have presented theses and interpretations which have nothing to do with me and my play. Regarding the play: among the figures in this text there is indeed a Jew. This Jew is a real estate broker; he contributes to changes in the city which are detrimental to how people live; he makes deals. The conditions governing these deals are not his creation nor his responsibility; he uses these conditions. The place where such conditions can be discovered is called Frankfurt am Main.

The matter itself, although on a different level, is a repetition of developments from the eighteenth century, when Jews were only allowed to deal with money and this dealing with money—often the only way in which Jews could make a living—in the end only fueled the arguments of those who had forced them into this activity and who actually were their adversaries. It is the same situation with the city in my play.

Put more accurately: the motivations of those who resist any discussion about these matters deserve some attention. They are the real anti-Semites. It would be worthy of consideration why one, instead of looking at the real state of affairs, attacks the author of the play with sentences which he—in order to throw critical light on certain circumstances—created for his figures.

There are also anti-Semites in this play; they do not only exist in the play, though, but also for instance in Frankfurt. It goes without saying that these figures—I find it truly superfluous to repeat this—do not represent the opinion of the author, whose own stance toward minorities should have become clear enough in his previous work. Particularly some of the cheap shots in the discussion make me all the more concerned about a "new fascism," which was one of the reasons I wrote this play.

The controversy over Fassbinder's Frankfurt project would rage into the mid-eighties, stimulating a fierce international debate about the representation of Jews and the presence of anti-Semitism in postwar Germany. For a comprehensive documentation of this discussion, see Die Fassbinder-Kontroverse oder Das Ende der Schonzeit, *ed. Heiner Lichtenstein with an afterword by Julius H. Schoeps (Königstein/Ts.: Athenäum, 1986). See also the collection of critical essays,* Deutsch-jüdische Normalität . . . Fassbinders Sprengsätze, *ed. Elisabeth Kiderlen (Frankfurt am Main: Pflasterstrand, 1985). In English, see "Special Issue on the German-Jewish Controversy,"* New German Critique, *no. 38 (Spring/Summer 1986).*

61. Herbert Achternbusch
Letter to Wolfram Schütte (1979)

Dear Mr. Schütte,

In the Graz publication *manuskripte* you claim to have read a good text, good prose of mine. A short time after this I wrote the attached text. It's completely harmless but I cannot bring myself to throw it away.

Perhaps you might see your way clear to publish it. On the telephone you spoke to me about my talents as a writer; they are, you claimed, quite extraordinary, indeed singular. Yes. I've always tried to move my readers. That sentences are things. Perhaps objects of exchange. But they still remained only sentences and no one was moved and the certainty that I moved no one made me even more lonely. In my impotence I made films, which is terribly hard work, but work with other humans, and only in this work do I find hope that I am getting somewhere, which is the most important thing for me. Your encouragement on the phone that I once again write prose and your claim that you in fact "also" like my films is insofar unjustified because my films are more advanced as creations and do not stand aside from my other work, because to me the classical notion of a closed single work meant to please the audience is a repugnant one. You of course can use this letter as a prologue to the text, which has no title.

Wolfram Schütte is a critic and editor of the culture section in the Frankfurter Rundschau.—*The attached text Achternbusch mentions appeared as "Text ohne Titel" in the* Frankfurter Rundschau *on 22 September 1979. It is reprinted in* Es ist ein leichtes beim Gehen den Boden zu berühren *(Frankfurt am Main: Suhrkamp, 1980), pp. 129–34.*

62. Helma Sanders-Brahms

My Critics, My Films, and I (1980)

Said now, about *Heinrich,* to German film critics, and to myself.

Self-Appraisal

That's me,
Doing the splits,
One foot straight up
The ladder to the light
(Is that where it's really pointed?)
The other foot down
Dans la merde
The great hope
The great flop.
Again and again
Allez hopp!

I say to you:
Those who hope for me,
Receive derision,
Those who wrinkle their noses
(Because of la merde),
Will be well rewarded.

On the occasion of a retrospective of my films in La Rochelle, I recently saw *Heinrich* again. Almost simultaneously it was also screened on German television, in the summer program, shoved to the side almost as if one were ashamed of it. Worse than this, the ARD, usually so eager about feature films, rescheduled the film five times, announcing it numerous times in the winter and even once before last year in June, as if it would be better if they were to hide this film. But it isn't even a question of politics. It's only a film about a German who killed himself.

There was enough of this talk in the summer of 1977 when *Heinrich* was shown at Cannes, and *Le Monde* wrote: "Kleist—notre contemporain,"—"Kleist, Our Contemporary." But *Heinrich* was ripped to shreds by the German press because people thought it was too unpolitical. One of the survivors of the German urban guerrillas, who in 1977 had already been in jail for six years, told me that he could hardly watch the film because it had touched him so deeply.

"My soul is so sensitive, I almost want to say, that when I put my nose out the window the sunlight that shines on it hurts me . . . Many will think this sick or exaggerated . . ." That's how the film begins, with these strange German sentences which had the watchdogs of German criticism in Cannes climbing the palm trees.

La Rochelle was the personal—if you can put it this way—festival of the pope of French film critics, Jean-Louis Bory. After the same screening in Cannes which had the entire German press cooking in anger and scorn, he came to me, in the foyer of the "Miramar" in which *Heinrich* had just been shown in the section "Les Yeux Fertiles" and while the German watchdogs and prethinkers came streaming by me in a fit—which I didn't notice—Bory embraced me and said: "C'est un chef-d'oeuvre, Helma." The retro for me was one of his legacies. When I came to La Rochelle I thought I would see him. I didn't know that he had committed suicide over a year ago after he had celebrated the fate of homosexuals in his book *Le Pied*. Bory, the first Frenchman to win the Goncourt Prize since World War II.

When I was told that he was dead, a suicide at that, I was overcome by a feeling of horror. Because of this strange nexus. As if some sort of witchcraft had been at work.

I had really looked forward to seeing him in La Rochelle. He was one of the most brilliant critics I knew and he fought for the things he loved. La Rochelle, his festival, was a strange orphan without him and his following of cultivated and glowing, flashy homosexuals, who gathered around him, the small, rather ugly, and already aging man.

In Cannes at the time *Heinrich* was shown in the "Miramar," I went to dinner with the widow of André Bazin, Janine Bazin. And at the same moment the thumbs of the prethinkers in the "Majestic Bar" all were pointing down. Two days later I read in *Le Monde* and elsewhere what a great film it was, and I read in the German press pans, pans, pans. Such a deep shock that I was hardly able to be around people anymore. Why did I take things so seriously? Because this really murdered the film. Not completely, it's still there, it still remains. They're going to have to use it as a standard in the future.

In fact it almost had become the German selection for the main competition in Cannes, it already had been chosen, so one claimed at the time, but then the festival committee had to give in to the demands of United Artists, who were only willing to let the American selection run in Cannes if the German selection were also a United Artists film: in this case Petrović's *Gruppenbild mit Dame (Group Portrait with Lady)*.

The major reproach of the German critics at the time was that I had set my sights too high—a bit more modesty wouldn't hurt was something I heard again this year on the occasion of the Berlin festival screening of *Deutschland, bleiche Mutter (Germany, Pale Mother)*. But can it actually be the case that the same film which is declared in France, Italy, and the USA similarly as a work of great beauty and exactness (not to mention the hymns of praise which went even further!) is in truth a failure? Or perhaps it was a matter of being too close to see things clearly?

The second reproach was that the film was another literary adaptation made for the screen. And with costumes to boot. At the time there were a lot of literary adaptations. And a lot of costume films. But *Heinrich* is not a literary adaptation. There is no novel entitled *Heinrich* which I might have adapted. What we have is the description of a broken and torn life, in scenes lined up associatively, much like memories.

It is therefore not a film about a writer, but a film about the process of writing, about everything that leads to writing, what happens when one writes, and what is done with what is written. In that sense a film about the production and consumption of literature. But not a literary adaptation. A literary adaptation is something like *Die Blechtrommel (The Tin Drum)*, *Group Portrait with Lady*, or, if you will, even the never-ending *Buddenbrooks* travesty made for German television. But in this sense *Heinrich* is not one.

When the German critics heard that the entire foreign press had judged differently than they had (which now after *Pale Mother* is the case almost to a greater degree), they simply declared that the foreign critics were all dopes, especially in France where people go nuts over everything from Germany—they had to read the appropriate notices to see that journalists from Spain, Italy, and USA, etc. had made this distinction quite clearly. In Spain where *Heinrich* on the one hand received the Culture Prize of the Basques (who normally do not award their prizes to unpolitical films!), it also was honored on the other with the Critics' Prize for the best historical film. The honor, awarded also because the Spaniards, well schooled under Franco, knew how to read metaphors, above all stressed the mosaiclike broken form of the film in which historical events are not told in a linear manner, in the way of "he was born then, then he did this, and then he died," but rather in leaps, as memories, thoughts, and emotional identifications work in an individual's mind.

The film begins with the bed, the soiled bed that looks like a snowy mountain from such a close distance, also like a funeral shroud. Death bed. My deathbed, Heinrich's deathbed.

There is where all of my thoughts about Kleist begin, with this bed we have in common, with this yearning for death we have in common. Then also the child at the door, the one you can find at the end of *Germany, Pale Mother*. Only the image of the mother is a marble statue in the *Heinrich* film. Cold Mother Prussia. Heinrich didn't know his mother.

Yes, my God, one of the watchdogs faulted me for daring to identify with Kleist, for daring to have problems in common with him. (One common problem I have for certain: Kleist never had an easy time with critics and he didn't even find consolation abroad. . . .)

Then the writing. In *Pale Mother* the child is always writing between the horror scenes with the parents.

Heinrich writes after the child has beaten on the door, silently, one doesn't hear it anymore because the window is closed. Writing as something that keeps you afloat, that allows you to exist.

Then he writes and it is a letter of supplication. Humiliation. Starting over and over again, out of shame, out of anger. Then the result of eternal exertion lands on the table of Hardenberg and he's already dead. A black feather writes: "To the files, because the person von Kleist no longer is living."

The plea becomes a document and lands in the Prussian archive.

It occurs to me that in the entrance to the Prussian State Archive, in which among other things the only remaining picture of Heinrich is preserved, that in this entrance the same Herr von Raumer still stands, a plaster bust, cold bureaucrat who caused Heinrich to grind his teeth and whose absence from the court gave him hopes of new favor.

Heinrich's letter disappears from sight, it's dead, part of a dead file, there's nothing deader than this. And then you see him lying there dead, among the leaves, on a cold November day, the Wannsee, and this is where everything starts. A single shot of the dead Heinrich, of the dead Henriette, into the trees and up to the sky, and in the meanwhile the actors run under the camera and when the camera returns to the shore the two stand there alive once again, throwing small stones into the water. "In the middle of the triumphant song which my soul takes up in the moment of my death . . ."

But I don't want to recount the entire film. One can read through the script version which will soon appear, one can go to the movies when the film shows up again. And that will happen, sooner or later. I'm absolutely certain of that.

I let myself be driven crazy by the watchdogs and the prethinkers, I believed them, when they said: "These Frenchmen, they have a weakness for this kind of stuff, but it nonetheless still is shit."

I neglected my film, didn't want to see it anymore, and was ashamed of it. When they awarded me a State Film Prize I grinned from ear to ear, because I thought you've got to with a child in your belly, how would it look if you made a long face, but I was ashamed nonetheless. I would have much rather sent the whole business over to Herzog, because everyone was saying he should have gotten the prize. And I stood there feeling so stupid. This eternal outsider, which I am, always only TV films, and now a feature film, and so heavy-handed at that. But damn it all, why not? Now, in La Rochelle, I sat in front of my own film, and once again when it was shown on TV, this above-described survivor from 1977.

And I thought about a poem which I wrote to one of the great watchdogs of German criticism when I was in Cannes.

> Why don't
> we punch each other out?
> Clean up
> Clear the air
> You're not going to
> Beat me
>
> Why not
> Duke it out

Like the boys from the US
—It's too quiet here too quiet—

And there they all fly
Like rags:
Brahms with the beard,
The smashed Kleist,
Lying prostrate
Poor B. B. and
Laurence Sterne embryonically.

And we thrash each other
On the Croisette.
That would be great,
Pound the mug
Until it becomes a face.
(You don't understand
Any other language!)

Don't be scared
That I'm just a girl
Who you're not supposed to hit.

I'll get
Up again and again.

Or perhaps I'm only wearing a disguise?

Nevertheless the negative notices in the German papers led to the
ARD treating *Heinrich* like a piece of shit, even though it had received
the highest Federal Film Prize that the Federal Republic has ever awarded
and the ARD had always fetishized Federal Film Prizes.

This led to next to no runs in the cinemas or, if at all, very short
ones. Because it's clear that a film like this needed the support of film
critics.

Recently in the *Spiegel* description for the TV screening, I read that
the film was supposedly "overadvertised" when it first came out—no, this
was hardly the case. I still respect the small distributors who dared to
release the film, at the risk of their own money, who had copies made and
posters printed—even though it was clear that none of the German film
critics would help the film.

And then one thinks about all of the mediocre stuff that gets praised to the sky. But this situation has very much to do with the situation of a film critic in general, with the hard facts of that profession, the pressure always to be finding new trends and constantly to have to condemn new films, and all of this overnight. At least I and my film can wait, because the film remains after all. But the critic cannot escape the momentary impression, he's got to use it as best he can, he has no time to rethink his position, and, above all, he may not and cannot contradict himself too often, otherwise he will lose his credibility.

To contradict oneself is at best the privilege of a chosen few. What a job.

A CIRCLE OF CRITICS

Hello! I think,
There sits one of those people
Who have to market their
Sensitive soul everyday.
Don't know their name,
Only know, he too
Isn't having much fun and
Can't understand those who are.

The script to the film under discussion appeared as Heinrich *(Freiburg: Panta Rhei, 1980).—See also Sanders-Brahms's review of Klaus Kanzog's edited volume* Erzählstrukturen-Filmstrukturen—Erzählungen Heinrich von Kleist und ihre filmische Realisation *(West Berlin: Schmidt, 1981), in* Kirche und Film, April 1982, pp. 22–23.—The Buddenbrooks *film referred to is Franz Peter Wirth's eleven-part version made in 1979.*

63. Hans Jürgen Syberberg

Media Response to Fassbinder's *Berlin Alexanderplatz** (1980)

Why an irrationalist is accepted today by the supposed rationalists in Germany. Because their response is a guilty one.

A unanimous yes from all of the German film critics. The *Bild-Zeitung* doesn't like it, claims the *Spiegel* triumphantly, its sole recommendation for the intimidated reader. It's clear that any enlightened citizen has to be for the film. The *Bild-Zeitung* immediately turns against anything that moves the comradely ranks of German film journalists to sing hymns of praise. The game is simple and so are the business arrangements. If *Bild* doesn't like it, then an obligatory show of solidarity is in order. Someone once called F. the "Messiah of New German Film," someone else dubbed him "the thermometer up the ass of our culture," which prompted *Spiegel* to the premature conclusion: a controversial phenomenon. The only thing that is controversial about all this is the audience's response to these critics, assuming that it even has a chance to make up its own mind and to think for itself after this media onslaught, without which the series *Berlin Alexanderplatz* would fall under the magic ten-percent viewership and catastrophe would ensue—which does not necessarily mean that one side is right, the audience or the critics, or, to be sure, the film.

So are we just standing in the deluges of those who control our opinions, shivering in the cold of exposed responses? One hundred percent voted for Hitler and Stalin and Ulbricht, and *Holocaust* was loved in Germany, in keeping with this law. A gay drama based on a famous novel by a Jewish author, one banned by Hitler. And then take a look at those, those people writing for our television audiences, dear Fassbinder! They're forcing you into the obligations of an arid love relationship, one that is going to kill you. A gay outsider in the guise of a proletarian hooligan, raised to the status of a myth for the masses and hero of a title story of the highly influential manager magazine of a technocratic society, this all cannot end well.

Cf. the title story, "Fassbinder: 'Der Biberkopf, das bin ich,'" Der Spiegel, 1 October 1980, pp. 224–47.

64. Christel Buschmann
Response to H. C. Blumenberg (1983)

Hans-Christoph Blumenberg is upset. About the "new 'we-feeling' among German filmmakers" and the "revolt of the running board riders." Apparently once again untroubled by any regard for the history of New German Film and beyond any possibility of thinking in political terms, not to mention of acting in such a manner, he denounces the solidarity among filmmakers with clumsy arguments (of course, selectively, for it is

easier to malign solidarity than to foster it, especially in the case of
Achternbusch) and doesn't comprehend that there are political situations in which the question of community can and must take a back seat
to a common and more important political interest. It's a matter here
after all "not of details, but rather the concept of a direction" (Kluge).
And it's a matter of solidarity, and to denounce it only can prove a
person's unspeakable stupidity. Because it was this solidarity that brought
about the New German Film and perhaps will enable its further survival.

Wenders: "I hope that something comes about again which we
surely had at the time, fifteen years ago. I mean, the New German Film
only existed because of the great solidarity at the time among filmmakers
and perhaps there will be further survival if there is such solidarity once
again."

What kind of claims does this person Blumenberg dare to make
anyway?

He dares, stuttering feebly and impotently, ignoring the minimal
requirements of journalism, that is, to write names correctly, to tell us
what filmmakers should and should not do, how they should feel and
think, and this in a fashion that is feeble, journalistically, intellectually,
and humanly. A playground for any psychiatrist or even for any layman
with the least interest in psychiatry, including the self-portrait that was
apparently provided by Blumenberg himself, an artistic one, shrouded in
dark tones. Attacked publicly for the first time in his life (two short
sentences)—something that has been happening to all directors in much
different proportions for years now—he drops his trousers and there he
stands: a wretched, powerless worm, who thrashes blindly around himself—the eternally frustrated, cowardly, narrow-mindedly arrogant know-
it-all Blumenberg. The film critic for *Die Zeit*. And only in this regard
does he take on the importance that he otherwise would not have.

Not how he writes is interesting nor what he writes, these fickle,
unfounded and slobbering arbitrary opinions lacking any knowledge of
film politics, these after-the-fact, cramped trend reports (and everything,
you can count on it, without a trace of original thought), what is
interesting is only *where* he writes. And only here is a reason to invest
once again more than a weary smile in this gentleman.

As long as the editors of *Die Zeit* do not tire of granting H. C.
Blumenberg unlimited space for his highly stylized personal frustrations
which have become the measure of film criticism, one can demand as a
reader of a weekly newspaper with a circulation of more than 400,000
copies that *Die Zeit* not allow a film critic to write who uses his position of
power to further his own private interests.

Now I don't mean Blumenberg's tactical behavior in the light of recent political changes. That he is a film critic, the likes of which Zimmermann can only be happy with, the enemy of all politically engaged films and at the head of the silent majority, is well known, even if it is becoming even clearer now. I mean Blumenberg's tactical behavior in the light of his private change from a film critic to a director.

Something has happened, that which he regretted so deeply in his 1982 interview in *Filmfaust:* ". . . In the meanwhile everyone wants to make films and right off a feature film at that." And now even he is making a feature film, his theme: peep shows. Recently he has been desperately applying for subsidy support, and one wonders why someone in precisely this situation allows himself to reproach other filmmakers for doing the same thing. But presumably he thinks it wise to speak out against all of those who—to spare the names of several authorities seemed appropriate to him—are likely to be cut off by Zimmermann. Blumenberg still has not found complete financing; the Script Commission of the Ministry of the Interior in its present form, one not well regarded by Zimmerman, has rejected his project, the strategy seems to be: prepare yourself for the future. Blumenberg still wants to have subsidy support even after Zimmermann works over film subsidy arrangements, even if most of us will have to do without such support or even want to out of film political considerations, because subventions under Zimmermann's conditions are not acceptable to us.

Everyone who wants to and is able to find the means should make films. I don't see things as narrowly as Blumenberg, even if I do think it unacceptable that a film critic, someone who for months now has pursued his own interests as a director and is planning a feature film project, at the same time in a prominent position with security of employment, quite selfishly denounces his momentary and future competitors in this public forum. Private interests as a standard for film criticism. I demand he either quit his job or remain silent.

Having said this, I now retreat again from an admittedly not completely unimportant but still secondary battle site, knowing well that Blumenberg, thanks to the possibilities still open to him, can defame me further at any appropriate or inappropriate moment according to his desire, whim, or tactical interest. I am emotionally prepared for this; even when you write about kangaroos in Australia, for instance, you can surely imagine how unprofessional a kangaroo Christel B. would be, how clumsily she would hop through the desert, in contrast to the casual elegance with which you would. And if in the coming years I should continue to speak of "we," consider yourself not included. And don't worry anymore about the things that troubled you in *Filmfaust* in 1982, namely that people always only want to make films and don't want to write reviews. I want to do both.

See Blumenberg's polemic, "Der Aufstand der Trittbrett-Fahrer," tip, 12 August 1983, pp. 34–35. Blumenberg was film critic for Die Zeit *from 1976 to 1983. He went on to become a director; his debut film premiered in 1984 with the title* Tausend Augen (Thousand Eyes).—*The* Filmfaust *interview appeared in numbers 28–29 (1982), 28–39, "Ein Gespräch zwischen Hans-Christoph Blumenberg/Bion Steinborn, Köln, den 30. April 1982."— The sarcastic reference to Blumenberg's writing about kangaroos is directed toward his lengthy sojourn in Australia which gave rise to a series of articles about that country. See the section entitled "Antipodische Bilder" in Blumenberg's second collection of film criticism,* Gegenschuß: Texte über Filmemacher und Filme 1980–1983 *(Frankfurt am Main: Fischer, 1984), pp. 135–58.*

VIII

Directors and Players

The initial rejection of the old German film meant that the young directors remained unwilling to people their films with the well-known faces from that heritage—or, if they did, only in a critical way such as was the case in Peter Schamoni's use of Willy Birgel in *Schonzeit für Füchse* (*Closed Season on Fox Hunting*) as the incarnation of a moribund past. The question was: where to turn in search of appropriate players? The advocates of the new cinema were skeptical about using stage actors in their films, fearing them to be too mannered and constrained. One could hardly afford international prominence—and, clearly, it was precisely this "glamour-at-any-price" ilk of filmmaking in their elders that they eschewed. What stands out in the early years of Young German Film is its found character—and its found characters. Directors ferreted out eccentric and surprising figures, in many cases individuals with little or no film experience. Fassbinder's "factory" would serve as the most famous and influential example; his colleagues Schroeter, von Praunheim, Kluge, Achternbusch, and others would develop retinues of their own. What is striking about the *Autorenkino* would not only be its distinct styles and its privileged set of themes, but also its motley collection of curious faces and engaging personalities: Rolf Zacher, Peter Kern, Hannelore Elsner, Hans Peter Hallwachs, Eva Mattes, Alfred Edel, Annamirl Bierbichler, Magdalena Montezuma, Marquard Bohm, Clemens Scheitz, Rüdiger Vogler, Gabi Larifari, Alexandra Kluge, Tabea Blumenschein, Tilo Prückner, Hanns Zischler, among a host of other stunning persistent presences. Much of the drama inherent in later New German films would come from the tension between the precarious destiny depicted onscreen and the vulnerability and fragility of the personage enacting it. Herzog's Bruno S. comes to mind in this regard, as do Reinhard Hauff's *Paule Pauländer* and the director's reflection on that film and on his behavior,

Der Hauptsteller (The Main Actor)—not to forget the many films in which filmmakers themselves embody their own dilemmas before their own cameras. Lisa Kreuzer would speak for many players circumscribed by a cinema of authors when she complained that this system tends to limit certain actors and actresses to certain directors, that one becomes all too marked by a particular filmmaker when one appears in several productions, so much so that other directors are then unwilling to cast players. In this sense actors become material that can, in the logic of this situation, be limited in its use value, simply used up or, indeed, abused. The real stars of New German Film would seem to be its directors; the few players who gained international renown (Edith Clever, Bruno Ganz, Klaus Kinski, Hanna Schygulla, Barbara Sukowa, Angela Winkler) are merely the exceptions that prove this rule.

65. Rainer Werner Fassbinder

Talking about Oppression with Margit Carstensen* (1973)

MC: Martha's behavior, it seems to me, is that of a sick person.

RWF: She's not sick, though, she's just like all other women.

MC: Not all women. Not me for instance. Or if I were like that, I'd fight back.

RWF: How are you going to fight back against something that's been done to women for a thousand years? And while this has been going on, they've become much too weak to fight back anyway, even if they wanted to try. Anyone who wants to fight back first of all has to know against what and then has to have the power to do so.

MC: You're mystifying things. There are more and more women who refuse any longer to let men victimize them.

RWF: Look at you, any man could do anything to you he wanted. I could oppress you . . .

MC: At work, but not now. Because I'm not dependent on you anymore.

RWF: That's a different kind of dependence, and it has nothing to do with you and me, but rather has to do with women's situation. A man can hurt you, he can humiliate you.

MC: A woman can do the same things to a man.

RWF: Sure. But a man can oppress a woman simply by letting her know that she's a woman. That's what so miserable about it.

MC: You couldn't do that to me.

Pause.

RWF: Women who let themselves be oppressed often are more beautiful than women who fight back.

MC: You think so? That's right, because they are probably more gentle. Because when you have to fight back you get tense. That's why I'm very ugly a lot of the time.

RWF: In *Martha* you're beautiful.

MC: What I've seen of the film has had a very strange effect on me; I like it, but I don't really think it's beautiful. If I do look beautiful some of the time, it's because Martha may be letting herself be oppressed, but she still lives with the feeling that she wants to start fighting back against this oppression. There is a tension in her between being oppressed and nevertheless wanting to let herself be oppressed.

RWF: Martha isn't being oppressed, but rather educated. And this education is the same thing as oppression.

MC: Life itself is one long education. I'm putting that in very reactionary terms, I know, but I've had a negative experience. That doesn't mean that I think it's right.

RWF: Don't try to fight back. You like it, don't you?

MC: I obviously can imagine another kind of education. But I know that the manner in which my father educated me has made me the person I am today.

RWF: At the end of the film, when Martha can no longer take care of herself, she has finally gotten what she wanted all along.

MC: I wouldn't go that far. I really think that this is a resignation on her part. Throughout the film she has made some attempts at fighting back, she reacts aggressively to her father, her mother, and her husband. Do you really mean to say that she is happy in the end?

RWF: Yes, isn't she? She wanted this resolution all along, secretly, and now she can really be the person she was the whole time.

MC: But she never wanted to do the things her husband demanded.

RWF: But she stayed with him.

MC: But she did run away from him, even if she was hysterical when she did so.

RWF: Exactly. She didn't even once try, consciously and clearly, to take a rational stand against her father or Helmut.

MC: She's too underdeveloped for that.

RWF: What is underdeveloped about her?

MC: Her self-awareness. You always live only in relation to others.

RWF: Everyone does that.

MC: One has to for the most part. But I think somehow she

completely missed out on becoming her own person. She probably learned to find her motivation only in negative energies. Like in the relationship to her father who denies her everything she wants.

RWF: Why doesn't she try, even once, to talk to Helmut?

MC: Maybe she's not able to, because she only endures everything, always only reacting to circumstances, thinking about them, but never about herself . . .

RWF: She's thinking about things?

MC: I mean, living with them.

RWF: Or from them.

MC: If you live from them, that's how she deals with her conflicts, even through hysteria. Only I really don't understand the ending: why is she supposed to be happy now?

RWF: She goes back to Helmut, doesn't she?

MC: Because she has no other choice, now that she's bedridden. When he appears she starts screaming and says, "No."

RWF: And then she accepts the situation. Because in the end she has gotten what she wanted.

MC: I don't know if I'd call fulfillment sitting in a wheelchair and not having to be tormented by him anymore because now one really is a tormented person.

RWF: But that would be the greatest masochistic fulfillment, not being able to take care of oneself anymore.

MC: From my point of view, I can't imagine how that can be the end of the story.

RWF: Sure you can. The film simply tells a story that goes like this: how does this woman find happiness?

MC: Yes, that's true in her case, given her limited possibilities. But she's limited both intellectually and spiritually in a way which one simply cannot be nowadays.

RWF: A way one cannot be, but a way that would possibly be wonderful if one were allowed to be like that.

MC: I think that's not enough for a human being.

RWF: She's not dumb: she's well-educated, it's not that you can say she doesn't know anything. She knows more than most women. Only she's daring enough to be what other women only want to be. Or are you perhaps in favor of emancipation?

MC: Of course I'm for emancipation.

RWF: Independent of your head? Even alone at home in your bed?

MC: Even there I'm for emancipation.

RWF: I don't believe that's the case with any woman. That would mean that women are smarter than they actually appear to be.

MC: When they're alone, they're in favor of emancipation.

RWF: Most men simply can't oppress women as perfectly as women would like them to.

MC: In any case, I'm not in favor of oppression. I'm perhaps occasionally in favor of conformity.

RWF: They're the same thing.

MC: Oppression means that it happens to you involuntarily, conformity means that you do it voluntarily.

RWF: That's even more terrible.

MC: One can base a life together on a certain degree of conformity which doesn't have to totally govern you. By the way, I can't do that. I'd rather oppress my partner.

RWF: Or perhaps he you. You only reversed it in your head.

MC: No. You know, I'm a person who has to live relatively alone.

RWF: That's true of Martha. She lives either to be lonely or to let herself be oppressed. And what lies between, that most people make concessions, Martha can't do that. Either to live and be lonely or to let herself be oppressed and be happy, that's the choice a woman has.

MC: Or as a woman you constantly have to be fighting back, something one doesn't like to have to do all the time. Nonetheless it's possible today to live in a different way with a man.

RWF: For that to be true, men would have to be emancipated. Do you know any emancipated men?

MC: I don't know a single man I would let myself be oppressed by.

RWF: But that's only a trick and one of your making.

MC: No, there's such a thing as a cordial commitment to another person. There are feelings that allow me to do things willingly for someone else. And I don't like to let people down.

RWF: Sure you don't.

Pause.

MC: You're really a wretched person.

RWF: That's what I've been saying all along.

MC: How am I supposed to pull myself together after this?

This dialogue took place after the completion of the TV film Martha *(1973).—For the reaction of another actress to the director, see two articles by Hanna Schygulla: "Wer wirft den ersten Stein?"* Konkret, *3 May 1973, p. 19, and "Ich will nicht länger seine Puppe sein,"* Zeit-Magazin, *8 June 1973, p. 14. See also "Frauen bei Fassbinder—eine Diskussion mit Ingrid Caven, Margit Carstensen, Irm Hermann, Helma Sanders-Brahms, Hanna Schygulla und Volker Spengler,"* Frauen und Film, *no. 35 (October 1983): 92–96.*

66. Wolfgang Petersen
Some Thoughts about Ernst (1977)

1. Who is going to play Thomas?

"Who is going to play Thomas?" This would be the main problem, that was clear to me when Gunther Witte gave me a copy of the novel *Die Konsequenz* (*The Consequence*) during the summer of 1975 and I decided shortly thereafter to do a film version of it. The other leading role, Martin—that was no problem. For a long time I'd been looking for a good role for Jürgen Prochnow. (After three films I still had not had my fill of him—on the contrary.) This was his role, no question, Jürgen would be Martin. But—who would play Thomas?

Thank God, I had a lot of time, during the summer I would write the script together with Alexander Ziegler, we would do the shooting in the spring of 1977. A year and a half, no problem, he would be found if we looked hard enough.

I finally found him—seven days before we started shooting, on March 1, 1977! The search leading up to this is almost impossible to describe. I had gone about things systematically, first inquiring in all the casting offices: do you have a boy, seventeen or eighteen years old, attractive, sensitive face, preferably blond (as a contrast to Jürgen), to play an important and extremely difficult role, the development of a young boy from a lively, enthusiastic, idealistic sixteen-year-old to a shattered, humiliated, wrecked twenty-year-old, who is driven to a suicide attempt. Preferably someone with experience in front of the camera, because what layman could take on such a role? Similar inquiries at all the agencies, theaters, and acting schools.

Mountains of photos arrive. We sort out the thirty-to-fifty-year-olds, then the ten-to-fifteen-year-olds, a first selection, a second—in short, about fifty are left. With these I do video-casting, i.e., I have a long discussion with every single one. Everything is recorded by a TV camera and afterward evaluated; the best ones are invited for further screen testing.

The screen tests take place—even the partner-to-be Jürgen Prochnow is there—but, no go! Not one of them fits the role, no one is the Thomas I have in mind.

Renewed attempts, further inquiries at all the likely places, TV editors, fellow filmmakers, film producers, journalists, friends and acquaintances, grandmas and aunts: "Do you have a Thomas for me?"

Mountains of photos, video-casting, screen tests—nothing. In the meanwhile we're only two weeks away from the start of shooting!

One last attempt. We print an article in the Munich *Abendzeitung*: a photo of Jürgen Prochnow, next to him an empty space with a question mark. Headline: "Male lead wanted."

We get about sixty responses. Maria, my assistant, makes the pre-selection, ten remain who might be possibilities. Again the usual tests—no, my Thomas is not there. In the production offices depression spreads. And then it happens, better than any scriptwriter might have imagined: the door opens and in walks a young man with a pile of photos. "A friend of mine. I think that's the boy you're looking for." He's seventeen years old, lives in Amsterdam (but is from Bavaria) and more or less has gone through the things that happen to Thomas in our film.

I look at the photos and am completely fascinated by this boy, by this face. This has to be the one!

2. Working with Ernst

Working with Ernst Hannawald was by far the most difficult experience I had ever had with an actor. (Given that *The Consequence* is my twentieth film I can lay claim to a certain amount of experience in these matters.)

The first time I saw Ernst, shortly before screen tests in the Bavaria Studio, he was trembling with fear and intimidated, he was so upset his stomach ached. There was no way we could do a screen test. So we took a walk through the studio grounds and had a chat. I told him about the role and asked him about his past. And it came pouring out of him: he told me about his father, a drunkard, about his mother who is completely overwhelmed by her thirteen children, about his sister who is a hooker, how he ran away from home, about the time spent in various reform schools, about all the times he escaped from these places, about the "teachers" who beat him, about the "nice old men" who chased after him, and about the officials who finally had him transferred to the notorious institution in Haar. About his escape to London, where he tried to be a musician and dreamed about becoming a famous rock star, about his girlfriend whom he met in London, and who took him with her to Amsterdam, where he now lives, without any real education, without a job, with a lot of dreams in his head, with a lot of anger in his gut, and with little hope. And all of this in seventeen years.

I have to say I was pretty exhausted after listening to his story and watching him cry and tremble like a little boy. He looked bad, sickly, very pale, lines under his eyes. Despite all he really has a pretty face, dark blond hair down to his shoulders, attentive, intelligent eyes, but his face had hard features, almost a little cynical, aggressive—he looks older than seventeen.

This is my Thomas—yes, this is how I had imagined him. I caught myself thinking this while he was sobbing and telling me his life story. I was a little ashamed. But for what reason? Things would be starting in seven days and I had found my Thomas . . .

And this work would help the boy. He would earn money, he would work, he would gain self-esteem and maybe become a bit famous, just as he had always dreamed. People won't step on him anymore, but rather respect him, he would show the world once and for all, he could work through all of his anger in the role of Thomas, work through it and stylize it. I didn't begin to imagine at the time the kinds of problems that lay in store for us.

The screen tests were short and painless. A few minutes into them I broke off, it was completely clear, I wasn't mistaken this time. He spoke quite simply, quite naturally, without any dramatic emphasis, he wasn't playing, he simply was, yes, he was our Thomas.

Final preparations. Ernst's hair was cut, bleached a bit blonder, he went to the swimming pool everyday, then to the solarium, he slept a lot, he was happy and pleased, he wanted to be in the best shape possible.

Then Jürgen arrived. Tension—how are the two going to get on, particularly because they're playing a "couple." Long conversations between the three of us. I think the modicum of inhibition we all felt—to depict a homosexual relationship without being homosexual ourselves, to show acts of tenderness and passion between two men—gradually lessened at the point when we decided to play things every bit as straightforwardly, naturally, and openly as we might in a film about a man and a woman. What is the difference anyway? That was in fact one of the reasons why we were making this film after all!

Shooting started and Ernst found himself in the company of thirty or forty people who were all sincerely concerned about him. Everyone knew about his past, everyone wanted to help him, everyone was impressed by his simple, honest acting.

But then the problems began and at first it was the simple matter that Ernst wasn't a professional, how could he have been? The whole film production machinery is set up in a way so that everything will run without a hitch, precisely calculated plans accord to a predetermined financial and temporal framework. This setup bothered Ernst. Discipline was anathema to him, he hated it—and who will blame him? When he was supposed to be concentrating and memorizing his lines for the next scene, one found him in a tree, caught up in his dreams, finally falling and twisting his ankle. When he was supposed to go to makeup, he disappeared instead into an underground tunnel on the trail of some untold adventure. I have no idea how many miles the production assistants put in chasing Ernst Hannawald. At first the profis laughed this off as youthful mischief, but this soon stopped—and who will blame them, the film had to be made.

Yes, Ernst was difficult, in every respect. He had totally identified with the role of Thomas, he didn't want to "play" at all, he didn't want to pretend, he wanted to be Thomas. Everything had to be real. He was radical in this regard—and that of course meant problems. If he was mad about something, he couldn't go on to play a "happy" scene. He had to feel everything exactly and authentically, otherwise it wouldn't work. Being an actor was the same as being a whore for him if one only faked emotions. If he wasn't in the right "mood," we had to stop and everyone had to wait. Anyone who has made films knows what this means. Kind words, threats, arguments, psychological tricks—nothing helped. When Ernst didn't want to, he simply didn't want to. We were dependent on him and he knew it.

And Ernst was suspicious. He didn't trust all the friendly words that came his way after the start of the production. He wanted to unmask them as "professional" friendliness. They weren't directed at him, at his person, but rather were directed at the male lead Ernst Hannawald, who will be stroked by everyone for six weeks so that he will do his job, who will later disappear and be forgotten. You're right, Ernst, but I didn't make this world and the film simply had to be made somehow.

Ernst found his suspicions confirmed by the growing anger of the crew toward him. He became even more aggressive, fighting back, he had the power to do so, he was the "star." The tensions escalated, a vicious circle, Ernst threatened to sabotage the film and to disappear without leaving a trace.

And then he changed his tune, he was sorry, he was nice to everyone, he recognized the necessity of "professionalism." He wanted to fit in, wanted to do his job, he wanted to be respected, accepted, liked, yes loved. Then the next day once again the star who savors his power, who resists, who fights back, who distrusts each and every one. Who will blame him: Ernst in search of his identity . . .

When he finally was in front of the camera, when he had memorized his lines, and—this above all—when he was in the mood to act, then he was marvelous, at times even moving. But, as I said, when . . .

Of course there are explanations for his behavior and we professionals who have to stay on schedule shouldn't forget them. Ernst took revenge—consciously or unconsciously—on all of us for the things others had done to him over the years in all of the reform schools and police stations. For the first time in his life he was the center of attention, for the first time he enjoyed something like power, for the first time he called the shots, he was the star on whom everything depended, he made up for lost time, now he could finally realize the kinds of things he had dreamed about in London with guitar in hand on some street corner, even if only for six weeks, nonetheless. And he relished this—that was the feeling we got at times—totally. Who will blame him . . .

We took him from one extreme situation and placed him in another one. That was our doing. But can one really do this? Is it really fair to expect that of another human being? Can he cope with this kind of challenge? What's going to happen to him now that the film is finished?

Let's forget this as quickly as possible, the crew has dispersed and gone on to other jobs. Who cares about Ernst Hannawald anymore now that he is back in Amsterdam at the unemployment office in search of a job, not finding one. I don't have time to think about him, the next film demands my attention, and besides—he was the perfect Thomas . . .

Alexander Ziegler is the author of the autobiographical novel, The Consequence.—*For an account of public reaction to the film, see* Die Resonanz. Briefe und Dokumente zum Film "Die Konsequenz," *ed. Wolfgang Petersen and Ulrich Griewe (Frankfurt am Main: Fischer, 1979).*

67. Volker Schlöndorff
David Bennent and Oskar Mazerath* (1978)

I stop taking notes. We talk about Oskar Mazerath, that is to say about David Bennent. Oskar Mazerath was my means of access to *Die Blechtrommel (The Tin Drum)* because I don't have the same history as Günter Grass and in order to be able to enter the book and its world, I had to find a key, something in common. It was childhood. I was a very serious child, not an *enfant terrible* like Oskar Mazerath. The film will be more the description of the relationship of a child to the adult world than it will be a description of a petty bourgeois milieu during the thirties, something I don't have anything to do with directly.

Sometimes during the filming I have the feeling that I am making up for a missed childhood or, at any rate, am now consciously reliving my own childhood. In this David above all helps me, David who for me is more than an actor: he is a medium. He himself has problems similar to those of Oskar Mazerath, which means that he brings an authentic element into the film. He isn't playing the role of Oskar Mazerath, rather he brings his own experience into the film, so that the film becomes at the same time a document about the singular child he is.

David has assimilated the book totally. We've read it to him so often, he's again and again worked it over so often with questions, so that on his own he smears his mouth with cake like a three-year-old and acts like a three-year-old. If he's playing the eighteen-year-old, he tries to copy adults he has observed and acts like an eighteen-year-old all day long. I've almost got to watch out that he doesn't hide behind the role, so that he himself, David Bennent, child, comes out as well. Oskar Mazerath is no doubt an exceptional child, but not an abnormal child. His gaze at the world of adults who become increasingly childish as they grow older and nonetheless never rediscover the earnestness of childhood. This earnestness of childhood is also something which the book and the figure imparted to me.

We produce situations in which Oskar experiences the events of childhood, and along with him David, who not only plays the role, but also experiences these events. Every shot has something of a happening about it. What strikes us in the process is how brazenly David behaves in front of the camera. Often and without doing so consciously, David obviously outshines the other actors. They always have to hold back before the camera, because as adults they cannot completely let themselves go.

David's lack of shame before the camera, in contrast, is much like the lack of shame Oskar Mazerath has toward his environment. And for that reason David is equally shocking. He is the opposite of a child actor who everyone thinks is touching. He has no pity, no tact at all, no sentimentality. He can catapult himself instantly out of the role, beating on his drum not as Oskar Mazerath, but as David Bennent, waking the whole team up; suddenly everyone is once again sober and attentive. He literally uses the drum to establish a distance between himself, David Bennent, and Oskar Mazerath and us—spectators and film team. The drum is for him a common bond between Oskar Mazerath and himself. He uses it as Grass uses his typewriter or as Oskar does his own drum. It is a common bond and at the same time a protective shield. A minute ago David too was unnerved in a scene, then all of a sudden he once again is the boy with the drum, who beats on it, who makes faces. Everyone laughs and we don't have unpleasant moments where one might feel like a voyeur watching a sick scene. He stylizes things and turns them into a joke and the danger passes.

In our work we are accomplices. He sees in me someone who helps him to get to know life, to try out situations that he as a twelve-year-old hasn't yet experienced. The film and the role are a sort of school of life for him. He doesn't simply follow my every suggestion, though, he has his own ideas. One either has to use these ideas or explain to him why we can't—otherwise one faces the spite of a child who won't listen to anyone.

68. Margarethe von Trotta
Working with Jutta Lampe* (1979)

The twenty-ninth day of shooting.

For the moment our last day of shooting. Over Easter we will take a six-day break. Most of us will go home, some are having their families or friends join them in Hamburg and will take off from here and do something.

Jutta and I are the only ones who are rather unhappy about this interruption and have the feeling that we will lose our steady concentration. We would much prefer to keep working and rest later. But over Easter we would have to pay triple-time for the technicians, and that of course is not in the budget, besides it might irritate people if they had to work over the holiday. As it is, they work all year long, almost without a break, moving from one film to the next. We, on the other hand (Jutta and I), only make this one film and for that reason everything is so very serious and important for us.

Maria and Miriam on an excursion steamer. Sun and wind. Jutta is disappointed: she had imagined playing this scene in such a subtle way and the wind destroys the intended nuances. She is used to the theater, to quiet spaces where there is no nature and natural light, and has trouble getting used to this added dimension in film, complains about having to change repeatedly in the bus, because we don't have time to go back to the hotel. She isn't used to film yet and only knows the less hectic conditions of the theater, ones not so bound to questions of money and time. And in fact this film is relatively harmless. How we froze when we made *Der Fangschuss (Coup de Grâce)*! Our faces were sometimes so cold and paralyzed that, outside of grimaces, we were unable to show any kind of reaction.

Film, that means life, exertion, torment, even physical exhaustion. In the morning Jessica shows the first sign of star pretensions. She moans and casts her eyes to the heavens even though she only has to carry several hard moments. Franzl Bauer wants to jump in immediately and take off the pressure. I get furious and prevent him from doing so, try to explain to her why this kind of exertion is also necessary.

In the afternoon the scene in the language school, i.e., the street in front of it. Maria awaits Miriam and asks her to move in.

A tracking shot, a relatively simple one, especially because the street is sealed off from the wind. Jutta cried after the scene this morning, out of disappointment. I think she feels better now.

In the late afternoon, rushes. Dialogue Maria/Fritz very good. Nonetheless, it seems to me that the images and the landscapes do not have the distance and the power which they should. What am I, what are we doing wrong? Once again my imagination was more ambitious than what I see before me on the screen. Everything seems to me tame, half-hearted, not extreme enough. Jutta fusses with her eyes much too much, not in an affected way, just nervously, she can seldom really hold her gaze, that destroys the tension. Franz [Rath] on the other hand is pleased because his problems with the lighting do not show up in the office scene. We will continue to work with long objectives in the executive offices. In the office scene Jutta is on top of things, sure of herself, in control, completely a head secretary. She wants to make a different person out of Maria in the office, with a different face than the one she has at home with her sister. . . .

When I actually do sit down and talk about my fears and doubts as a filmmaker, the others feel obliged to pat me on the shoulder, as if to say: you can do it, you have your insurance, etc. They don't understand that these moments of fear can be productive ones. Only doubt and anxiety bring me further, force me along . . . Why do they at all costs want to deny me these feelings?

Von Trotta describes the shooting of Schwestern oder Die Balance des Glücks (Sisters or the Balance of Fortune).—*Jutta Lampe plays the role of Maria; Jessica Früh plays Miriam.—Franz Bauer was the film's prop-man.—Fritz Lichtenhahn plays Fritz.—Franz Rath, who had worked previously with Schlöndorff, was the cinematographer.*

69. Rosa von Praunheim
Erika from Würzburg: A Portrait of the Actress Magdalena Montezuma (1981)

The pseudonym Magdalena Montezuma comes from the American photo-novel *Little Me* which Werner Schroeter and I discovered during the sixties. That's how Erika from Würzburg became Magdalena. In 1968 Werner and I got to know a dramatic waitress in a Heidelberg wine restaurant, someone whose intensity, inner tension, and enormous expression did not remain hidden to us young filmmakers. We had just come from Knokke, where the entire American underground film had made a large impression on us. A completely different type of actor was born. Already much earlier I had made a photo series in Berlin with Elfi Mikesch using wild, eccentric, crazy, exotic young people. Berryt [Bohlen], Steve[n Adamczewski], and Carla Aulaulau (whom I later married out of economic considerations) were our superstars long before the expression was first used.

Magdalena was the exact counterpart of the energetic, funny village-Monroe Carla. In 1968 Werner Schroeter made his first film (in normal 8-mm) in his home town with me playing the lead role; its title was *Grotesk—burlesk—pittoresk*. We engaged Magdalena as a partner. Our first scene took place in her apartment, where I right away, as soon as the light was turned on, stripped and was absolutely bare-naked, while Magdalena, somewhat surprised, peeled an orange. The way she peeled it was extraordinary and cannot be learned at any acting school. She was so different and singular, in a way we had never seen before in a living being. A charm, a magic emanated from her which enchanted us, which held us for days, years, and now over a decade, under its spell.

When Magdalena quite a bit later played her first theatrical role in a production of Werner's at the Hamburg *Schauspielhaus*, the well-known critic Friedrich Luft complained about her faulty s-es. He and many of his colleagues continue even today to confuse technique with personality. Theater must be a perfect lie. Humanity, warmth, and honesty can only be depicted in an oblique way, never directly and existentially. Lampe and Sukowa in *Die bleierne Zeit (The German Sisters)* are for me negative examples of overworked, vitiated, petrified, drained actresses, ones who have been broken by the sterile, academic German theater system.

Magdalena, on the other hand, shines, beams, vibrates, is so hot that you get burned if you come too close to her. Even Peter Zadek could not offer her much in the five years she spent at the *Stadttheater* in Bochum. If one does not know Magdalena from more than twenty Werner Schroeter films, one can now admire her in four new and forthcoming films.

In Ulrike Ottinger's *Freak Orlando,* where she at one point appears with two heads, in Werner Schroeter's new film, *Tag der Idioten (Day of the Idiots),* where she plays an introverted madwoman, in Elfi Mikesch's *Macumba,* where she functions as an enchantingly beautiful writer of detective novels, and in Schroeter's most recent opus, *Liebeskonzil*

(*Lover's Council*) based on a play by Panizza, where she plays an archangel.

Many film freaks also know Magdalena from a bit part in *Taxi zum Klo* (she plays the assistant of the dermatologist who takes a look at Ripploh's anal passage). Magdalena played in *Bildnis einer Trinkerin* (*Ticket of No Return*) by Ulrike Ottinger, in the wonderful short film *Execution* by Elfi Mikesch, and even flickered on the TV screen in an episode of *Tatort* (*Scene of the Crime*) next to Dieter Thomas Heck. Right now she is rehearsing her role in *Tartuffe* for the Berlin *Volksbühne*.

Despite all of these appearances, Magdalena's qualities have only been noticed in passing by academic critics. Quite justifiably one is afraid of her, because she plays without reserve, at one with her own joy and suffering, something that's not always amusing, usually in fact repulsive and dangerous. One prefers to admire the art of being different, the others are always the pigs. Actors, questioned about their profession, often give the answer: I want to act on the stage because I can't do so in real life. The imagination which one does not have should be supplied by the director. Magdalena is different, she's intense in real life as well, regardless of whether she's shopping at the supermarket or standing before the camera as a tragic figure. That's indecent, an actor is supposed to be ice cold and professional. A fart behind the curtain and a shining Hamlet before the curtain. Art is not a ghetto, but rather life, but that only applies for very few, most people have become artificial. Magdalena never wanted to become an actress, she was more interested in painting, but when Werner Schroeter starting working with her in his early films *Argila*, *Neurasia*, and *Eika Katappa*, she discovered that she could not only work with colors and lines, but also with herself. She has only worked with people who respect her creativity.

I can't imagine any director capable of topping her suggestions. She understands everything about makeup, and that helped in *Freak Orlando*, where the makeup took hours. She was told her positions and decided herself what her gestures would be. She knew exactly when she had to be sad or happy.

Magdalena is introverted, shy and hides this behind burning eyes that spit fire when someone steps too close. She used to suffer when others were able to be entertaining, funny, and loud, but she has discovered all the more the opposite for herself. She seldom has outbursts, but when she does they're violent. It doesn't make sense to throw dishes out the window anymore, she says today. I reminded her of some time we spent in Los Angeles. Werner married his stewardess in Las Vegas while Magdalena made plastic of the window screens.

Magdalena reminds me of Garbo, she can be extremely beautiful.

She is passionate in a way that becomes stronger the less she is fulfilled. She is a saint and the price she has paid is too dear to use her as a model.

Magdalena Montezuma, born Erika Kluge, died in West Berlin on 15 July 1984.

70. Herbert Achternbusch
Annamirl Bierbichler* (1984)

After Annamirl had inimitably played her role, "my" wife, in my 1977 film *Servus Bayern (Bye Bye, Bavaria)*, she visited us at the end of the year in Navis, where [my wife] Gerda was a ski instructor, along with her brother Sepp, who skied like a madman. After Annamirl, with some trepidation, also rode away from me, I gave up this sport. Only recently in a dream I stood at the valley stop of the Navis ski lift and waited and waited for one of my children to ride down the slopes in quick swirls. Many skiers plodded down, but they, my elegant experts, didn't come. Once when I was in the "Altwirt" restaurant in Holzhausen, sitting as a frozen father of a family, and Annamirl by chance showed up, I was surprised how quickly her presence warmed me up. When, a year later, she adamantly refused to play in *Der junge Mönch (The Young Monk)*, I was very disappointed. She simply would not change her mind. So I was unable to get to know her better. But no matter how commanding she was as an actress, she never was lacking in private either.

For a summary of Achternbusch's longstanding relationship with Annamirl Bierbichler, see Herbert Schödel, "Das Ende des Volksstücks. Der Beginn des Präsidententheaters. Anmerkungen zu Achternbusch, seiner Arbeit und zu Annamirl," in Jahrbuch Film 83/84, *ed. Hans Günther Pflaum (Munich: Hanser, 1983), pp. 15–20.*

71. Jean-Marie Straub
Fire: Alfred Edel (1986)

Alfred exceeded all of our expectations. When working with actors we have no expectations. We simply expect that something will happen and with Edel it did. He came to two different sets of rehearsals in

Frankfurt and Hamburg and tried the whole time to prove to us that he is a classical improvisational actor who cannot memorize a single line. He's always worked like this. After the fourth session we told him, Alfred, that's impossible, everyone is capable of memorizing lines. And then we thought up something for him, like children we worked with him, we wrote down his lines like a poem, drew them out, something like a musical score came about in the process. One could work well with Alfred, he always came on time to the rehearsals in Hamburg.

Then it was a matter of making the lines stick in his head. They can be said to be firmly in place only at the point when they come out perfectly even upon the hundredth repetition.

Then Alfred broke into a gallop, his fire broke out, he has fire, a lot of fire. To make an internal fire out of this galloping, and not an external one, was our task, we practiced, rehearsed for a long time, a very long time, as long as we took with the other actors as well. Gradually we worked out small gestures and gazes. During the shooting his fire took on something statuesque. Everything is a question of time and patience, one has to have both. Everything was just the opposite of what Alfred had done before. He respected the rules of our game.

In 1972 we met him in Frankfurt, in the Communal Cinema, our film *Chronik der Anna Magdalena Bach (Chronicle of Anna Magdalena Bach)* was running. Alfred was excited about the film, which he had just seen. I fell "in love" with him at the time in 1972 in Frankfurt, again and again I recalled his fire. If you give Alfred the chance, he produces this fire, he is capable of mighty things.

The advantage of his role in *Klassenverhältnisse (Class Relations)* in comparison to his other roles: this role is more dialectical, it emanates from the intellect, and Alfred is more confident, more self-confident. The human being Alfred comes out in this role, lets himself be discovered. Alfred has a concrete kind of intelligence, not that of an academician. Nowadays there are hardly any academicians who can still think clearly.

He respected the rules of the game, he didn't change a line, he memorized the Kafka text.

He always arrived in Hamburg punctually, we picked him up at the train station, then we chatted for a while about Reagan, rockets, politics. Then came the hard and intensive work. We said goodbye in the evening, everyone spent their evenings alone. Alfred wanted things that way, it made a lot of sense, otherwise one just blabs on and on, and one has to catch one's breath for the next day's work. One can see that Alfred possesses a lot of sense and wisdom.

Edel played the role of the "Oberkellner" (Head Waiter) in the 1983 production, Class Relations, an adaptation of Franz Kafka's Amerika.—See also Alexander Kluge's short tribute to the actor, "Blindflugintelligenz," epd Film, February 1986, pp. 21–22.

IX

Filmmakers and Colleagues

If New German Cinema, according to many foreign observers, is a cinema of authors, then its directors above all stand out by dint of their idiosyncratic willfulness, their denial of shared assumptions, and their ardent zeal to remain distinct. These individuals thus have little in common, no program, political or aesthetic, no organizing emphasis, formal or thematic. As John Sandford puts it, "Their interests are disparate; they are not close friends." Clearly, this rhetoric sanctifying the self-dependent and self-serving *auteur* makes these filmmakers into anchoritic super-stars. The price of this canonization and mythologizing has been considerable. It has obscured the numerous bonds that have existed between filmmakers over the years, the ways in which so many Young and New German directors have worked together. It also has concealed the many group allegiances within West German film culture, the multifarious factions and alliances and the resultant clashes of interests. In some cases filmmakers have suffered painful breaks with previous cohorts which have given rise to bitter altercations or silent hostilities. In any case, rather than a collection of monads, a gathering of self-involved navel-pickers and solipsists, West German film culture is a place where people watch people carefully and closely. (In this regard, an hour spent in the press center café at the Berlin Festival or a night out in the *Galeriehaus* after the evening's final screening during the Hof Film Days can be remarkably instructive.) When filmmakers go public about their feelings regarding a particular film or a certain colleague, they are always impassioned and never impartial, either a partisan or an adversary. The personal nature of one's own films finds an extension in the very private and subjective character of one's responses to the work of colleagues, responses in which the other becomes a site of projection and a mirror for one's own doubts, fears, and aspirations.

185

72. Hellmuth Costard

A Call to Revolt: On *Particularly Noteworthy* and *Chronicle of Anna Magdalena Bach* (1968)

There is a wonderful custom in the Caucasus, where on their twenty-first birthdays young Russians have all of their body hair burned off. Of course this is accompanied by a wild orgy and of course the Party has taken over this custom and infused it with an ostensibly new meaning. From a Western point of view this singular ritual of the Caucasians seems repulsive, but in its origin this custom is a triumph issuing from perverse fantasy.

This seems to me worth mentioning because my film *Besonders wertvoll (Particularly Noteworthy)* has as its motto the quotation from Goethe, "Only perverse fantasy can save us." At the same time *Particularly Noteworthy* is also dedicated to Anna Magdalena Bach. (This "at the same time" refers only to physical occurrences. In terms of psychic occurrences during the film, the above-mentioned sentences are not positioned at the same time in the film, because German readers in any case read from the top down.) My dedication of course does not refer to the historical Anna Magdalena, but rather to that which comes to mind since Straub's film when we hear "Anna Magdalena Bach."

Straub's *Chronik der Anna Magdalena Bach (Chronicle of Anna Magdalena Bach)* for a very long time made me sad. I have the feeling that Straub made the film by tearing strips of flesh from his body, that he made this film at great physical cost to himself.

We hear of Bach in two regards: his music and (from the chronicle of Anna Magdalena Bach) that he obediently and naïvely accepted his social situation. Bach remained quiet his entire life long. Instead of throwing bombs, he contented himself with writing respectful petitions to his sovereign. With his music he created a private space of his own and the greater his suffering under the political order became, all the clearer and more mighty his tone mountains had to become. No doubt Bach did not perceive his modesty as such, for he saw the source of his suffering and discontent in the will of God and not in the wretched governing order.

My films are not meant to be my private space. Jean-Marie Straub's *Chronicle of Anna Magdalena Bach* was for me a call to revolt, whose means of resistance will also become my films. And in order to spur on the Anna Magdalena Bach who never existed, I have dedicated *Particularly Noteworthy* to her.

Costard's name appeared at the top of the original article as CostARD, an irreverent play on the call letters of the First German Television Network.

73. Wim Wenders

"*Red Sun:* Baby, You Can Drive My Car, and Maybe I'll Love You" (1970)

In the back pages of many daily newspapers one finds comics which always consist of three or four images so that a coherent story takes weeks and months to develop. If one doesn't buy the newspaper regularly, or occasionally misses a day or two, and doesn't keep up with the stories, then the individual episodes become totally unintelligible, so much so that the straightforwardness which these images emanate starts to give one a scare.

A long time ago I cut out the stories from the newspapers and pasted them together in notebooks. Just like these homemade Phantom and Blondie books, that's how *Red Sun* seemed to me: I saw something very simple and very inexpensive and unpretentious which had been taken seriously and treated with care.

Red Sun is one of the very rare European films that do not simply want to imitate the American cinema and show that they actually should have been made in New York with Humphrey Bogart, but rather have instead borrowed an attribute from American films, the ability to display for ninety minutes without any sense of urgency nothing more than surface appearances. This POINT OF VIEW becomes visible in every image of the film: it's there in the constant flatness of the shots, in the monotony of the optics that only uses a handful of focal lengths, in the banality of the camera movements that are never more elaborate than absolutely necessary, in the strange colorlessness of the colors which is just like in Mickey Mouse comic books: no one would be surprised if the walls which were yellow a minute ago suddenly became blue, that happens.

The story is totally in keeping with this. Although no one pushes it and it still always somehow keeps going, it nonetheless comes to a conclusion and to a FINAL IMAGE that seems completely consequential. The sun sets. Or rises. TV series and westerns end like this: with an image that apparently signals an ending. The economy of film, to come to a conclusion in ninety minutes, is also exactly the economy of its story.

In *Red Sun* people continually talk as if they didn't care about the further course of the film. They talk unabashedly in their respective situations. They are always only present there, where they are. They don't know what comes next: the film concerns itself with their story, it doesn't intrude upon them. The film takes place in Munich. It isn't ashamed of that.

> I like the way you walk
> I like the way you talk
> Oh, Suzie Q.

Rudolf Thome's Rote Sonne (Red Sun) *was made in 1969.*

74. Doris Dörrie
Searching for Stories in a Gray Germany* (1978)

Godard once said: "Cinema—that's truth 24 times a second." To discover the truth of reality in the reproduction of reality—that's what excites me about film. I want to see images in which, at least for short instants, I can rediscover my own past, present, and future; images of people, their feelings and stories, which after a while I can feel in my head and in my belly. Not necessarily "bigger," but in any case "quicker than life."

From the German films of last year's season only a few images really stuck with me: the bitter face of Pepe, perhaps, as he's being beaten by his father (Reinhard Hauff's *Der Hauptdarsteller/The Main Actor*), the incorruptible child's gaze of the blond boy on the bicycle from Edgar Reitz's *Stunde Null (Zero Hour)*, Michael, how he falls flat on his face and stands in front of the brash Anschi, uncertain and embarrassed (Rüdiger Nüchtern's *Anschi und Michael*), or the exhausted, unshaven Maschkara, who stands before the mirror of a cigarette machine and lets out a primal scream even if he is no tough Tarzan (Uwe Brandner's *halbe-halbe/Fifty-Fifty*).

When I watch a film, I'm like a video camera that "engraves" images when its attention is focused too long on one and the same object, so that for a while all succeeding images coincide with the engraved one.

This is the way I like to walk out of the cinema onto the street again: with engraved images that get between me and reality or merge with it, which protect me against reality or make me more sensitive to it, in a way that imparts to my private way of seeing an additional depth of focus.

The majority of films here leave me with nothing like this. The images rush over the screen in lovely Kodachrome, and their truth, if they ever possessed any, dissolves in the space between the projector and the screen. Afterward I only have a couple of pounds of jelly beans in my belly and nothing else.

This cannot be my problem alone. There must be reasons for this. Why do I remain so unmoved in the cinema and why do I so often have the feeling that the camera resolutely overlooks those things which would EXCIIIITE my head and belly?

I'll make it easy for myself and blame our filmmakers, for not getting in touch with our reality, not giving it a chance, not analyzing it in a vital way (namely dissecting it in twenty-four frames a second); instead they paralyze the spectator about 144,000 times in 100 minutes of film. Granted: it's difficult here to perceive vitality in the everyday. It's concealed, held secret and in check; at times, it is forbidden, it's suspicious and dangerous. We don't find it in the street, but more often in the living room. But even if we don't have such a ready feel for it as people perhaps do in other countries, we should nonetheless remain all the more open to it. Assuming we believe in it. In vitality or in life itself—as you will. And I expect that of anyone who makes films. There is no other truth.

Costard says: "Something always compels us to spell out our own misfortune." It is this compulsion which I don't see in our films. Instead of accurately spelling out our collective fortune or misfortune and in that way producing a little bit of truth, many filmmakers would rather grab into the past with both hands and let, for instance, Eichendorff's Good-for-Nothing traipse across the screen as a vital and lusty German anomaly. The viewer is expected to find the present in the past, to undress the expensive images in his inner eye so that the truth might peer through for a moment.

I believe in the sincerity of most of our filmmakers who try to bring our reality onto the screen via clever historical detours, but I still think that these literary and high-culture diversion tactics are the worst way possible to do this. At best I can see truth in the work of set designers and makeup artists.

In the public sphere not too much is going on here—for that reason perhaps so much more happens in private, behind the scenes. To anticipate this backward motion on the screen and to go back even further is, to my way of thinking, irresponsible and also a bit cowardly. If there were at least an equally prominent countertrend, I could accept it as a form of celluloid pluralism.

For me Uwe Brandner is on the right path, for instance, when he says: "I want my films to become more private and personal, so radically personal that they will be of interest to a wider public!"

Only a minority tries to search for stories in a gray Germany. Some colleagues have recently started to dream intensely about the USA. It's clear, there reality hits you over the head, in a vital way. There you see things happening on the street, it's apparent that more is going on. Still others retreat bitterly to France and seek to punish the German critics who cannot and do not want to stomach their films. They take revenge on the crudeness of a few German cultural bigwigs and at the same time deny the German public a chance at last to see "the other cinema." (That their films in the end are not "other," are no real alternative, is another story altogether.)

These kinds of reactions to the wretched German film situation are for me ultimately intellectual "bullshit"; the filmmakers are not taking leave of the cultural ghetto, but rather slamming doors helplessly.

The dilemma is confusing: on the one hand, film here has never gained acceptance as a legitimate form of culture; on the other, exclusively middle-class culture standards are used to judge the quality of film productions. In the committees, be it in television stations, the Ministry of the Interior, or the Film Subsidy Board, one finds a majority of ossified drivelers from the culture scene and spineless vultures from the film industry. Anyone who wins one of their annual prizes is either on their side or a token black. A small clique of stern gentlemen determines which and how much truth flashes over the screen.

This situation is miserable, all the filmmakers agree. To produce films in an alternative manner and without these committees is almost impossible, because making films, plain and simple, costs a bundle of money. For private investors with bread, trafficking in celluloid is of no interest, because it is not even a risky business, but rather a sure-fire deficit enterprise.

Despite this seemingly hopeless situation, I still chide our filmmakers for their lackadaisical, opportunistic, and cowardly behavior. Real truth or true reality which might be put on the screen (that is, with a lot of effort and trouble) for 100,000 to 500,000 marks does not as a rule cut it in committees. Instead of standing steady, one speculates with expensive costume films, with acceptable, that is to say, culturally "qualitative," contents. As long as these kinds of projects are submitted to committees, we are going to find a sort of truth on our screens which represents a particular group and its particular interests. We have to ask ourselves if this is our truth.

German film has for a long time been a ware that is not dealt with according to demand, but rather is a state-supported spectacle, perspective, and point of view. And quite carefully one selects what the camera may and may not see. And in general it politely looks past the things I want to see.

In order to find a way out of this *misère*, all the filmmakers should energetically join together in a quest for truth. It's autumn again. They should together try to shed light on the fog, instead of holding a God- and committee-given filter in front of the camera lens. A utopia, perhaps . . . but it's my wish for next year's film season. There is a fluid space between the street and the cinema and vice versa. Only we don't (yet) know it.

Dörrie's critique above all addresses the wave of literary adaptations produced in West Germany during the so-called "Literaturverfilmungskrise," the literary adaptation crisis of 1976 and 1977 which brought forth such highly subsidized films as Bernhard Sinkel's Taugenichts *(Good-for-Nothing). Dörrie had started making films already in the midseventies while receiving her training at the HFF in Munich. She also wrote film criticism on the side for the Süd- deutsche Zeitung and played an active role as an organizer at the Hof Film Days. Her debut feature,* Mitten ins Herz *(Straight through the Heart, 1983), would be followed by* Im Innern des Wals *(Inside the Whale, 1984), her international success* Männer *(Men, 1985), and* Paradies *(Paradise, 1986).*

75. Rosa von Praunheim
With Fond Greetings to Champagne-Schroeter (1979)

The criticism of friends does not only show a lack of solidarity; it can, I think, be productive and stimulating. To go public with such criticism should help us to find a way out of this moribund and false cultural situation. Wolfgang Limmer took a first step in this direction with his devastating review in *Spiegel* of Edgar Reitz's film, *Der Schneider von Ulm (The Tailor from Ulm)*.

I would have expected a much better film from Edgar and I hope he won't despair about the review, but instead gather energy for new and better films, the kind of work he has done in the past. (I thought *Die Reise nach Wien* [*The Trip to Vienna*] was a great and sensual film about women.) I think it was justified that he got clobbered because the three million marks he threw away on this production could have financed a whole bunch of films by newcomers. Werner Schroeter and I usually only had no more than 50,000 to 80,000 for our films and some of these run over two hours.

How many young people in Germany would be more than pleased to have 100,000 marks to make their first feature film? (I don't mean the film academy students who often make things too easy for themselves.) How much energy and intensity they would invest in this first opportunity, in contrast to the old hands who have played themselves out? (Film history shows us how directors' first films are often their best ones.)

The *Kuratorium* and the Ministry of the Interior are not enough. They usually only support people one already knows, people who have established themselves in the cultural scene.

The newcomers have to get organized or we oldsters should encourage these young people and make them realize that the arrogant medium of film also belongs to them.

Two years ago we, that is, a producer friend of mine and his wife, had the idea to make ten films for 100,000 marks each. Entirely new people were to be given a chance to direct their first film, five men and five women. The directors' names were not to be given at the films' premieres, just the titles that were going to run—each film was to play for a week, every week a new premiere, and this in ten different German cities. The first film in Berlin was to be the second one in Hamburg, the third one in Cologne, etc.

We imagined that all of this would cause something of a sensation.

The producer wanted to get the necessary amount of a million marks in part from exhibitors (rental fees paid upfront) and from subsidies, etc.

We started writing people, encouraging them to write scripts from which we would choose. We wanted to be certain that the scripts would be close to reality and easy to understand, i.e., of use for the cinema. We wanted to form a group that would not leave the author alone, but would rather help him communicate his thoughts.

Work on this plan made the producer so sick that he has to this day not completely recovered.

This said in passing as an important impetus for the support of newcomers, which in my mind is more important than supporting a new film by Herzog or Fassbinder.

You have no idea how happy I was when I learned that Werner Schroeter had the money to make his first film in 35mm.

In the past he had fascinated us with his dreamlike beautiful world of images and music, which nonetheless was not understood by mass audiences. I hoped he could now put his talent to work to make a film that would not just please the culturally chic fringe.

While teaching with me in San Francisco during the summer of

1977, he finally showed me the script he had written together with Wolf Wondratschek, about whom he seemed to be ashamed.

He wanted to make the film in one of the largest slums in Europe, in Naples, a fortune teller predicted he would have a bad accident, he proceeded with work on the production bravely, nonetheless.

Then, once again, I was proud to hear about his great success in Cannes, about the grand prize in Taormina, the Silver Hugo in Chicago, etc. I could hardly wait and finally, two weeks ago, I saw the film *Die neapolitanischen Geschwister (Kingdom of Naples)* in a private screening. My joy quickly turned into pure horror and forces me now (as perhaps the only one amongst the joyous throng of Teutonic critics) to react negatively.

The film follows the history of Naples from the Second World War up to today concentrating on a pair of siblings. An Italian version of the Buchholz family, consciously trivial and kitschy. The pseudo-documentary commentary is irritating, it feigns a realism which the film as a whole lacks.

In contrast to other Schroeter films, this one is without humor, it takes itself dead seriously. It deals with suffering and death in Italian families, constantly we see the funeral hearse, one woman dies in the midst of opera arias, others are shot, one mother goes crazy. The whore dies in the end, her scream is Schroeter's great revelation. She is damned reminiscent of Fassbinder: everything is in vain, we're all done for.

This makes me really furious. I refuse to believe that we can't summon up energy and courage to resist those powers that oppress us. I find the sobbing throes of Fassbinder's transvestite in [*In einem Jahr mit*] *13 Monden (In a Year of 13 Moons)* every bit as nauseating and self-pitying as Schroeter's sentimental masochism. Especially the poorest of the poor constantly evince an energy and joy which I fail to see in the overweight and lethargic middle class. Naples is a particularly good example of this.

Didn't one quote Werner Schroeter in this regard in *Spiegel,* that he "so very much admired the courage and the energy of the poor brave people in Naples?"

What an outrageous thing to say. Champagne-Schroeter, who lies around after finishing his shooting with champagne and caviar, admires the courage of the poor people.

Especially the scenes with homosexuals in Schroeter's film made me angry. The Christian Democrat naturally has to be fat and disgusting. As evidence of his incredible decadence, he stands in front of an aquarium and, with trembling hands, tries to fondle a little boy. With cutaways, appropriately enough, to slithering slimy fish. Why didn't Herr Schroeter play this role himself as a demonstration of his homosexual self-hatred?

When I recently asked him to sign a coming-out statement by homosexuals for the magazine *Stern*, he turned me down with the smug reply that *Stern* wasn't serious enough for him. He much preferred the tidbits of gossip in the same periodical.

Another scene where an exploitative female director of a factory is the incarnation of calamity, with red hair and too much makeup. She talks with a young employee (Viktoria). The music suggests all the evil in the world as the director sets out to seduce the young innocent. Lesbian intentions become apparent. At the moment when the pure child is later just about to be seduced by a rich friend of the family, she flees; the director, her eyes rolling in front of a blazing fire in the fabric hall, reminds one of the evil Cruella in the Walt Disney film, *101 Dalmatians*. Herr Schroeter, with his decadent charm, would have been the appropriate person to play this role. Hasn't one learned in the meanwhile that it's not always the innocent children who get seduced but rather that usually just the opposite is the case?

Viktoria, one of the pale siblings with whom one cannnot identify, in a marvelous phrase, says to her mother: "You ruined my life with this Negro" (the mother had fixed her up with him).

When one of the mothers goes insane, we see her in an asylum that is so hackneyed that one looks in vain in world literature for something so stupid. Of course the crazy woman has to sing with little flowers between her legs. Some other inmates, looking as insane as possible, accompany the brother and sister to the door.

Herr Schroeter might perhaps have done some research before he made the film. He would have found out that Italy in fact has one of the most progressive policies toward psychological disorders. The insane asylums have been shut down and, instead, one gives patients a chance to live in open communes.

If I were insane I would feel discriminated against by this scene.

But it is the hooker who has the largest cross to bear; she is repeatedly given the opportunity to stick out a leg exotically behind a red curtain. For her remain only the night and death and old age and ugliness, as she is made to formulate it so idiotically.

Cliché after cliché, like everything else in this film, and that without any thought and with no intention to undermine stereotypes.

Doesn't one know that hookers in our society are often a much more vital (and in any case more honest) possibility than the dull likes of a totally administered uncreative job?

Schroeter has a hard time with matters of content; when he tries, he is all too banal. Those on the right are fat and gay and redheaded, the simple people on the other hand are brave communists, but the party lacks a sense of reality and can't help them either. All that remains is despair.

There is for instance not a single reference to the Mafia in his film. But he was only able to make the film because he had the support of the Mafia, and isn't the Mafia the most vital and important force in Italy?

Of course one is thankful that Schroeter is at least capable of telling a story (is it the stupid script that caused his failure?). But I would rather see him stick to his outstanding lyrical collages which made his old films so honest and fascinating. It makes me angry that the film dupes the spectator with its entertaining diversions and makes one overlook its many acts of discrimination. That is the only way I can explain its success.

Even the camera in his Naples film is impersonal, gray and blue. It passes on very little information and only helps the plot take its course (Thomas Mauch). The jubilation that Werner finally had enough money to put his camera on tracks led to one of the worst scenes in the film, the wedding scene. It is too arty and theatrical. In Schroeter's other films, where he did the camera work, he is a master of light and color and composition. He is personal, precise, and brilliant.

Even the music in his film is flat and used stupidly—and yet he has a reputation for being a master at finding just the right music.

One hears that Werner Schroeter plans to make an Italian trilogy. Italy has many more clichés just waiting for him.

The film demonstrates just how little personal contact he has with people living in Naples, even if the local color antics of certain actors often lead one to think differently. The acting is devoid of love and cold. The actors have no depth, neither formally nor in terms of content. Is this because the artist Werner Schroeter has become increasingly ego-centric and out of touch with others? Anyone who knows him realizes how hard a time he has understanding himself and others. He seems to be driven by hysteria and hecticness and aristocratic pretensions which are amusing when they parody themselves. His recent acclaim has paralyzed him. He takes himself seriously and unfortunately also the things that he used to quite rightfully make fun of.

He deserves fame and fortune, he earned them with more than twenty outstanding films. It's just a pity that critics only start to sing praises and award prizes at the point where his work is at its worst and most superficial, but that is of course nothing new in the culture scene.

Limmer's notice on Reitz's Der Schneider von Ulm *appeared as "Sturzflug"* in Der Spiegel, *18 December 1978, p. 177.*

76. Rainer Werner Fassbinder

Homage to Werner Schroeter* (1979)

Werner Schroeter was for over a decade—a long time, then, almost too long—the most important, the most exciting, the most influential as well as the most resolute director of an alternative film, a sort of film generally referred to as "underground" film, a well-meaning gesture that delimits, diminishes, and in the end suffocates this kind of film in a tender embrace.

In reality there is no such thing as an "underground" film. That only exists for those people who can neatly distinguish between an above, a below, and a place on high. In reality there are only films and they exist in the midst of a gray entirety. And there are also the people who make these films. And in the same way these people and their films differ from each other, so too of course do the reasons for making films. And many people simply cannot desist from making films until they finally have the one or the other silly credentials that prove they are professionals, these people with their devil-may-care attitude about making films, no matter if it's 35mm or 8mm.

The culture scene, however, in many regards perhaps more powerful here than in other countries, has simply divided filmmakers into those it calls "professionals" and those it calls "underground," and insists on strictly maintaining this clear-cut distinction. If a person has been dubbed an "underground" director, he should, for simplicity's sake, remain one, preferably forever. For that reason it is hardly ever the case in the FRG that a director can break out of the ghetto he has been stuck into and—this should not go unmentioned—one of course makes oneself more or less at home in such cubbyholes. And that makes a person quite easily become lazy or even cowardly, depending on your perspective. But the resistance to the move of a filmmaker from the "underground" to "mainstream cinema" in the German culture scene is strangely stubborn and unanimous, making many people discouraged and ruining for certain a great deal of talent.

Werner Schroeter, who will in years to come assume a place in film history similar to one I would describe in literature as somewhere between Novalis, Lautréamont, and Louis Ferdinand Céline, was for ten years an "underground" director, a role one did not want to let him slip out of. The great filmic vision of Werner Schroeter's world was constrained, repressed, and at the same time ruthlessly exploited. His films received the quite useful "underground" pedigree, which rendered them in a flash as beautiful, but nonetheless exotic plants, ones so far away which blossom in such a strange fashion that one in the end could not really deal with them. And ultimately, that goes without saying, also did not have to deal with them. And precisely that is just as simple as it is wrong and stupid. Because Werner Schroeter's films are not far away; even if they are beautiful, that still does not make them exotic. On the contrary.

The director Werner Schroeter, whom they tried to make into a miniature, whom they tried to imprison in tiny, foolish cubbyholes and to call his films, I'll say it again and again, "underground" films, the kind of things which exist somehow, but only in the lower reaches, and besides, these films are too cheap to be important, especially in the minds of those people unwilling to grant them more money—this Werner Schroeter, anyway, has been graced with a much clearer and more comprehensive gaze onto this globe that we call earth than anyone else who produces art, no matter what kind. And just a little bit, it seems to me, this fortunate and privileged soul has access to strange and marvelous secrets of the universe.

If it is not self-evident, let me say in passing that this fortune and this greatness I have been describing of course in no way mean that the person I have depicted in this manner stands above everything and is satisfied, as a living being, as a physical body. On the contrary. Outside of myself, I do not know anyone else who chases so desperately and persistently after a most probably infantile, idiotic utopian vision of something like love (these words, ladies and gentlemen, make things painfully clear, do they not?) and constantly stands helplessly before the small brutal experiences. But: experience makes you grow stupid. Both of us will probably carry on in this fashion.

Back to matters at hand. Werner Schroeter, this was our starting point, has managed to do something which hardly ever happens. What exactly? Ten years "underground," supported by the department "Camera Film" at ZDF for years as a dependable fool whose work, you could bet on it, consistently brought the department hymns of praise from domestic and foreign observers, something that no doubt raised the self-estimation of these would-be midwives, but at the same time allowed them to look on blindly as just about every film by Werner Schroeter ended up costing a lot more than Schroeter was paid to make it. But for a long time this situation did not move them to generous, fresh ideas, why bother, anyway, when someone is in debt, they have no choice, they're almost dependent, so let them carry on like this. For a pittance. And anyway. Werner Schroeter, longer than many others, was stuck in this vicious circle, of course harboring the whole while a strong, indestructible hope that he might break out of it some day. To make films for the cinema.

Films for people, the more the better. But nothing seemed to change, nothing at all.

In the meanwhile there were only a very few people who had chances to make films who didn't borrow from Schroeter. I learned decisively from his films, that must be said or written in all clarity. Daniel Schmid is unthinkable without Schroeter, as is Ulrike Ottinger; Walter Bockmayer was able to learn a lot from Schroeter's films. There are a large number of students at the Film Academy in Munich whose films are fundamentally experiments influenced by Schroeter, from Eberhard Schubert to Bernd Schwamm. There are young colleagues in France for whom Schroeter's films are at least as important as Sternberg's. With good reason ultimately.

And a quite resourceful Schroeter-imitator has come forward, who, while Schroeter was waiting helplessly, skillfully marketed what he had pilfered from Schroeter. In Paris people for a good while actually believed this trafficker in matters of plagiarism, Hans Jürgen Syberberg. It was pretty exhausting to tell people in France that it wasn't we who were the epigons of the more slippery Syberberg, but that we had been the victims of a brutal ripoff, in part of our most personal wares. But even Syberberg, independent of the great desire to be able finally to let things surface, represents the great opportunity to make "great films" with Werner Schroeter's own personal discoveries, an opportunity denied the original talent.

Then, at a time when many, even Schroeter's friends, had slowly but surely begun to resign themselves to the fact that Schroeter would most likely never make a great feature film, that now after all the years of shyness, hesitation, and lacking opportunities, he would not put it together, the kind of situation in which quite a few despaired or simply gave up and others, after an unsuccessful attempt, like for instance Rosa von Praunheim's *Berliner Bettwurst (Berlin Roly-Poly)*, became unjust and sad—now, in this situation, Werner Schroeter made the film *Die neapolitanischen Geschwister (Kingdom of Naples)*. A great, significant film. Incredible, after all these terrible years of waiting, always on the verge of simply drying up. A film that one can place without hesitation among films like Visconti's *Ossessione*, Fellini's *La Strada*, Pasolini's *Mamma Roma*, Visconti's *Rocco and His Brothers*, Chabrol's *Les Bonnes Femmes*, Bresson's *Le Diable probablement*, Buñuel's *The Exterminating Angel*, among others. Germany thus does not only have three or five or ten film directors to offer, Germany now has one as well who has certainly been absent. A great breath of fresh air. A great one, plain and simple.

Finally, because this culture page is surely being read by many people who also read *Filmkritik*, a periodical referred to here on occasion with a measure of enthusiasm, permit me to mention a repugnant and repulsive article that Rosa von Praunheim wrote there about Werner Schroeter's last film. One needs to air private matters to explain things here: Rosa von Praunheim and Werner Schroeter were very close a long time ago. While Rosa was already making films meant for a wider audience, Werner Schroeter began slowly to make films as well. But Schroeter made these early films for his friend, out of "love" for him. Rosa von Praunheim thanked him with mockery and derision. Played out precisely with the sorry superiority enjoyed by people who love less than their partners. Werner Schroeter's honesty and his unconditional objectivity toward Rosa von Praunheim sometimes had an almost debilitating effect.

Rosa von Praunheim, someone so progressive, whose mind is so much freer of our middle-class longings that he actually thinks he alone has the right, a monopoly of sorts, to use the medium film to reflect his own or whoever else's homosexuality: Werner Schroeter always obeyed this decree. Now, in *Kingdom of Naples*, Rosa von Praunheim thinks he has come across the one or the other supposed homosexual element. Reason enough, apparently, to disguise his own, God knows, justifiable despair at still never having made a great film or never having had a chance to do so, to disguise his despair, even in front of himself.

Things are that bad, the kinds of things filmmakers in the FRG suffer, and I say this completely free of irony, things are so bad, that in order to ward off this pain, this fear, and this sorrow, they betray perhaps the only friend they have.

For Fassbinder's homage to Bockmayer, see "Der deutsche Film wird reicher: Jane bleibt Jane von Walter Bockmayer," Die Zeit, 29 April 1977.—For another perspective on Schroeter's early films, see Wim Wenders, "Filme von Werner Schroeter," Filmkritik, May 1969, pp. 318–19.

77. Herbert Achternbusch
A Rose for Rainer Werner Fassbinder (1982)

A certain lack of success troubled and destroyed Fassbinder. His successes did not correspond to his hard work, the public didn't take him to heart enough. Any other recognition besides the public's is an insult. But this insult is nonetheless a lot, a lot more than nothing. I only saw Fassbinder three times, the last time at the *Viktualienmarkt*, which he entered walking quickly, as if he had to be seen and at the same time forgotten. He wore jeans and a small shirt, of course he was smoking. I

turned around and looked at him. I felt like a granddad piddling through
my daily routine. I would have liked to have a beer with him but it didn't
seem appropriate. He looked to me like someone you don't dare interrupt. Before that I saw him in Seefeld at the Castle Toerring. Night,
light, long traveling shot. Lili Marleen runs out, two takes, cut. I was
among the gapers and heard the others talk, unutterable nonsense, the
film's recreation of Nazi gestures was criticized. People suggested that
Fassbinder should have fought in the war instead of making such
ahistorical garbage. In the cinema I was surprised how little of the
production values were on the screen. I didn't like the film, only Fassbinder's appearance. From the large swastika banners only the old ones
were stolen. But for days now I see him running, in his white suit with
the long pants, tempo, tempo, if he takes a step back, I said to myself,
he's going to trip over his baggy pants and go flying. In bars I often
defended Fassbinder, not "his crap," because you couldn't explain his
work to people who were intellectually handicapped slaves, but rather the
energy that moved this man along, his ambitiousness, and his frantic
desire for pleasure, all of these were impressive. And they of course knew
me, what an idiot I am, because I'm sitting with them, and they can
mock me openly, very seldom even praise me, and now no one can hold a
candle to Fassbinder. Did he maybe die in the cold? The political things
that terrified him, they were too much. The political shit that has
happened is too much, it doesn't let a person with sensitive artistic
means, the sensibility of tongues, eyes, or other organs, react any longer
or defend himself, much less digest and eliminate these things. This
made him crazy. And an artist would rather be kaput than crazy. But let
us talk instead about the hot sultry weather that stifles everyone's heart—
and which crushed his. In my mind he died of a broken heart. The lover
of every artist, crude and raw reality, despised him. What he made, ha,
and what he got back. A person who can eat crap and shit gold, isn't that
a marvelous man? I couldn't stand this pain, this pain which now comes
down so hard together with his death. Yesterday I sneaked along a couple
of streets with my friend Gunter. We felt so rotten that we drank vinegar
water. We wanted to see one film or the other in the Türkendolch. This
cinema is such a long narrow tube that you squeeze into and await ecstasy
up in front. This eternal dog shit on the sidewalk made me want to puke!
And these boutiques! And things in general! In one of the windows in
front of the Türkendolch there are no stills, no poster. A small magazine
photograph of Fassbinder. And a long rose from a cup of yogurt reaches
toward this photograph on which Fassbinder points at his nose with a
finger. No, he wasn't my kind of guy, because no one is, but his little
boy's eyes in the Perlach graveyard are a goddamned shame, such a

goddamned shame. No, I didn't watch *Händler der vier Jahreszeiten (Merchant of the Four Seasons)* that night on television, no, I simply don't even want to think about the man who always listens to the same record and looks out the window. And the lover behind the gravestones, no, I don't want to think about all this. These are completely crapped-out times where bleeding emotions are the last ones to open up a bit of humanity. I would much rather say: Fassbinder was a man who produced no kind of dependency. No one noticed his death. Without doing anything he neither increased nor lessened the comforts of life. Oh damn! Oh damn!

The Viktualienmarkt *is a public market near the* Marienplatz *in Munich.—For another personal response to Fassbinder's death, see Hans Jürgen Syberberg, " 'Sie haben ihn zum lächerlichen Gartenzwerg ihres Selbstmitleids heroisiert': Zu Rainer Werner Fassbinder,"* Medium, August 1982, pp. 35–37.

78. Rosa von Praunheim
From Beast to Beast (1982)

They were chided as grave robbers, people devoid of shame and dignity, those who wanted to liberate themselves from Fassbinder by writing a book, and that as quickly as possible.

Fassbinder in my eyes was never a saint and it always made me angry how his wild, eccentric, neurotic, power-hungry life was played out in stiff and prudish middle-class dramas. He seemed to be ashamed of himself in his films and dreamed of naïve artificial worlds that made life more bearable or comprehensible for critics and viewers.

I never liked him and never concealed that. We were too much alike and one often tends to deal much more critically with what one knows well rather than what one does not. Both gay, we both started at the end of the sixties to make films, our own producers, working with amateurs, with types—and nonetheless we were total opposites. I'm more interested in life than art and for that reason also more interested in Fassbinder's life than his films.

The first biographies have something to say about his life. In the "Heyne Bibliothek," a pocket book by Bernd Eckhardt. You read it quickly and you forget it equally quickly.

Gerhard Zwerenz wrote about the *Slow Death of Rainer Werner Fassbinder* and, halfway through, I tossed it out: it's so self-important. Zwerenz talks more about himself than Fassbinder. One genius talks about another one and because Zwerenz is not honest, but rather false like most writers, and also not even literary in this book, he is boring. He talks about how much he loves Fassbinder, but apparently only because he once intended to make a film of the Zwerenz novel *Die Erde ist unbewohnbar wie der Mond* (*The Earth is as Uninhabitable as the Moon*) and occasionally gave him a small role.

The third book is one of the most incredible ones I've read in a long time and makes me like Fassbinder for the first time. Over 360 pages Kurt Raab describes *The Yearning of Rainer Werner Fassbinder* and compares it to his own. Raab is a beast, he is envious, jealous, competitive and he writes in such a marvelously bitchy and shrill way about Fassbinder and all the people around him that it takes your breath away. It feels like one is in the world of Greek myths where Zeus punishes others, carries on intrigues, deceives, and tricks people in the most imaginative fashion.

The book's first pages describe Fassbinder's funeral, in an incredible manner devoid of dignity and respect: the battle about the body, who indeed is the widow, whose mourning is real, where are the king's assailants? Even the *Bild-Zeitung* had trouble topping this gossip. It reminded me strongly of scenes from Genet's play *The Walls* in which the hired female mourners fight among each other. Who else allows us such intimate access to the life and death of a great and powerful man?

Kurt Raab was one of Fassbinder's closest friends; he loved and hated him, was totally dependent on him, psychically and materially; he watched how Fassbinder shut people out, wrecked their lives and was responsible for their deaths. I can identify with him very well. Everyone who has power and money and success knows about these dangers.

Throughout Kurt Raab's book Fassbinder becomes human in his complexes and neuroses, his passion and his inability to love. His co-workers had to become slaves, his actors often mere marionettes, and it's remarkable how many of them accepted these roles with gratitude, how many people yearn (not only in Germany) for a strong hand, for a genius who frees them of all responsibility for their decisions. Not only the sadist is the guilty party, often the masochist is more subtle in his yen to be tormented: the seemingly oppressed soul becomes a vampire who wears out the stronger party and sucks him bone-dry. Fassbinder never let things go so far. His regime was protected from the press and cultural supporters. He became untouchable.

Kurt Raab compares his own childhood with Fassbinder's. Raab came from a proletarian family and had the desire to be middle class. The upper-middle-class Fassbinder was ashamed of his background and tried to be proletarian, grimy, and obscene. Only rarely did he allow himself to be nice, sensitive, and weak. Throughout his entire life he tried to punish his mother rather than free himself from her.

He sought recognition and warmth and could only respond with humiliation and coldness. Irm Hermann, who idolized him, was tormented and tortured by him for over a decade. Irm confesses to Kurt in an interview how grateful she is to Fassbinder nonetheless: he made her aware of all this. Ursula Strätz takes refuge in alcohol in order to forget Fassbinder. His lovers of many years, El Hadi Ben Salem and Arnim Meier, commit suicide. Fassbinder dedicates films to them. Art excuses everything. But didn't it always, from Gründgens and Brecht to Elvis?

Even if everything in Raab's book is a lie—one reads it with a great amount of interest and emotion. Compared to us everything about Fassbinder is larger, more powerful, and more kaput. (One automatically is reminded of Dallas and J.R., who, no matter how evil he is, never ceases to fascinate us.) With this book Kurt Raab tries to free himself from Fassbinder; his death was the best thing that could have happened. One only wonders, though, whether for the sake of art, it would have been better if Raab had died. And one wonders whether it is possible for someone else to die in place of another, whether it wouldn't have been better if the critic Wolfram Schütte of the Frankfurter Rundschau, who loved Fassbinder so tenderly, might have sacrificed himself. Or Hans-Christoph Blumenberg. Here I would rather not think about Wolf Donner.

Excuse me for being cynical, Fassbinder always was himself, you can read about that in detail in Raab's book. I know I'm being provocative, but Fassbinder was, his whole life long, in his person and in his films. Only the blend of extreme devotion and repulsion made him and his work so interesting.

The book ends with an incredible scene in which Fassbinder's mother, who doesn't want to divide the estate with the father, calls on Juliane Lorenz to substantiate her putative marriage to Fassbinder. The document still is in Florida, claims Juliane, who then goes on in court to admit with a shamed face that she is single.

Fassbinder will live on, and out of the German culture scene new energetic personalities will emerge about whom one can gossip. Because what is more wonderful than gossip and intrigues and corruption and baseness? Otherwise we wouldn't any longer know what to make films about.

Von Praunheim discusses the following books: Bernd Eckhardt, Rainer Werner Fassbinder (Munich: Heyne, 1982); Gerhard Zwerenz, Der langsame Tod des Rainer Werner Fassbinder (Munich: Schneekluth, 1982); and Kurt Raab and Karsten Peters, Die Sehnsucht des Rainer Werner Fassbinder (Munich: Bertelsmann, 1982). A translated passage from the Raab book appeared in English as "My Life with Rainer," Village Voice, 3 May 1983, pp. 43–45. A fourth book is Harry Baer's Das atemlose Leben des Rainer Werner Fassbinder (Cologne: Kiepenheuer & Witsch, 1982). Ronald Hayman, in his monograph, Fassbinder: Filmmaker (London: Weidenfeld and Nicolson, 1984), has recycled these German accounts, making certain to include the most grisly and scandalous passages. For another critical review of Fassbinder biographies, see Karsten Witte, "Nachruf, Nachrede und kein Widerwort: Die Biographen des Rainer Werner Fassbinder," Frankfurter Rundschau, 19 April 1983.—Wolf Donner is a film critic and, for three years during the second half of the seventies, was the Director of the Berlin Film Festival.

X

Taking Stock

The Oberhausen Manifesto was the first taking of stock (albeit with a negative balance) in what would be a series of such acts during the next two decades and a half. West German filmmakers have always manifested a particular insistence on documenting their activity and recording the process behind their endeavors, one reason perhaps why so many productions have given rise to both a film and a book about that film. From the start Young German Film maintained an auto-reflexive penchant, a highly self-conscious sense of its constituting a countertradition, a desire to break with a certain fatal legacy in German cinema, and a will to reconstitute a viable film culture that once existed. This tendency became apparent in works that commented on the state of affairs in West German film culture, comparing utopian designs with the actual operating realities. This virtual subgenre of metafilms stretches from Spieker's *Wilder Reiter GmbH* (*Wild Rider, Inc.*) to Fassbinder's *Warnung vor einer heiligen Nutte* (*Beware of a Holy Whore*), Schilling's *Die Vertreibung aus dem Paradies* (*The Expulsion from Paradise*), and more recently, Wenders's *Der Stand der Dinge* (*The State of Things*), Münster's *Dorado* (*One Way*), Achternbusch's *Wanderkrebs* (*Wandering Cancer*), and the final portion of Kluge's *Der Angriff der Gegenwart auf die übrige Zeit* (*The Blind Director*). Kluge's volume of 1983, *Bestandsaufnahme: Utopie Film*, does more than answer the question whether there is life after Fassbinder (and Zimmermann and the new media). Like the continuous endeavors of himself and other colleagues over the years, this taking of stock addresses itself to an atmosphere of continuing turmoil and is couched in an oppositional endeavor and unrelenting obstinacy. A national cinema, in its many voices and with its many visions, has searched over the last twenty-five years for a more encompassing sense of the other. West German filmmakers have cherished, obscured or marginalized chunks of reality in

eccentric collections, viewing their cultural mission as that of preserving
historical experience and capturing haptic immediacy, casting themselves in the role of an ongoing vehicle of national identity—recognizing
fully, however, the forces seeking to undermine, resist, and eliminate
these ambitions, not to mention the persistent power of such forces in
German history.

79. Edgar Reitz
Love of Cinema (1962)

The challenges waiting for us recently became clear to me when an
older German film producer suggested that we should try out our film
experiments in television, because television is well-supported and could
cope well with such endeavors. This producer belongs to the generation
of filmmakers who suffer from the competition of television.

We have to ask ourselves today if this competition from television
really is a factor. When we examine a TV show we quickly see that it
exists almost exclusively in terms of traditions and experiences we know
from film and only rarely does it demonstrate an artistic or a formal
innovation. The necessity of finding new forms of expression is—strictly
speaking—much greater for television than for film. Television will come
to recognize this some day. It will distance itself from film and cease
trying to replace it or to serve it up in living rooms in a diminished form.
We cannot learn from television what films should look like.

In the meanwhile the German film is in a crisis. The producers of
the crisis curse television, cast furtive glances in the direction of state
subsidies, and play the cultural bigwigs. One thinks imprecisely. The
cause of the crisis is well-known: the German film finds no popular
response. This does not only mean that the box office returns were bad.
It also means that the movies were not attractive enough. The "sure-fire"
recipes for scripts, production numbers, stars, and sets amounted to
misinterpretations of previous successes. If our generation today seeks a
new approach, then we dare not begin by taking on the problems of our
elders and posing new solutions to them. We have come to realize that
their problems quite simply were false ones.

We don't believe in the "new film" but rather in the "new cinema."
The cinema is the place where "film" happens. The dark room, the
mystery that constitutes the "audience," a glowing screen, music, voices
and sounds that fill the room, an event, a fluidity that sweeps up the
audience, which needs it as an integral part of cinema . . . that's

"cinema." Cinema is not the same as "film." "Cinema" is a third component, it is the synthesis of film and spectator.

A film cast along these lines cannot be directed against the audience, because such a film needs it, because such a film demands it, because only with it does film become a reality in the cinema.

It is absurd to judge the audience, to classify it. The Joe-Blow mentality exists only in the arrogant vocabulary of the older generation. The experience of cinema as a rule knows no special conditions. Every spectator can be engaged and be emotionally addressed.

The cinema is an imaginary space where things take place which can only happen there.

The spectator is a witness.

The crisis of the German film is a crisis in the relationship between filmmakers and their audience. If we want to be successful, then we can become so only out of a love of cinema.

The competition of television is a bogus problem, the crisis of the film industry a symptom.

80. Volker Schlöndorff
A Dream (1966)

In the midst of the tiny difficulties that had taken on nightmarish proportions during the making of my film, I recently had a utopian vision: in Germany there was a flourishing film industry with centers in Berlin, Hamburg, and Munich, which, in a tough competitive battle, each outdoing the other qualitywise, were fighting for giant foreign markets. All of these people were proud that they were filmmakers. They loved their profession and expected more of the films they made than of the ones they saw. Every film was for them a single product which they oversaw with love and expertise, from the script conception through showings in the provinces. The opportunists who had in the past only taken on a new film project so that they could pay back the debts incurred by their last one now resorted to such measures for ambitious projects they could not have financed in any other way.

My dream also led me to a shooting site. The first thing that struck me was the quiet. The acoustic and the moral quiet. Resourceful production assistants had provided for the former because they were almost exclusively filming using original sound. Every single worker emanated this moral quiet. Everyone was well prepared, for weeks now they had considered the possible difficulties, and did not rely in the last minute on makeshift improvisations. They acted with the earnestness of craftsmen who have learned their trade and are proud of it. They thought about how what they were making would later look on the screen. They knew that the result depended on the participation of each and every person involved. I didn't hear them say: "It doesn't matter at all anyway . . ." and I didn't see any propman or set designer showing up with sheet metal objects, claiming they would look like copper on the screen. They had the same expectations of themselves as they would of a doctor or a car mechanic. They all had the feeling that they were working in a vanguard branch of industry and technology. Stagehands experimented with new dollies and cranes instead of schlepping around monstrosities made before the war. Lighters knew on which cable a good lamp was connected; production assistants provided for good warm meals that kept everyone in a good mood. Actors knew their lines and tried to forget their acquired stage voices for the sake of a natural language. Each film had a specialist who oversaw and determined the technical quality of the daily rushes. Sound engineers had access to directional microphones from German firms, ones developed following American prototypes. Projectionists were sober and awake. Critics encouraged instead of asphyxiating. The audience listened without signs of boredom. Authors didn't deem making entertainment films below their dignity. There were stars, starlets, directors, cameramen, and what all.

The more intelligent producers suddenly realized that making films could be more than just a way to keep themselves above water. Films that had only been conceived for the home market because people had not had the courage to think beyond national borders, and which, therefore were from the start doomed to be financial losses, were noticed abroad and made money. Producers came out of their mouseholes to which they had retreated in embarrassment and they started to plug into the international market. They made money and financed films that at first looked like risks, but which seldom enough turned out to be ones. Newcomers stopped drinking coffee, talking, passing out manifestos and banners, and stationed themselves behind cameras.

An industry once again took shape, one that no longer consisted of supplicants, assistants, careerists, and artsy pretenders, and which no longer was looked at askance and smirked about.

In short, it was a dream, a utopia, one I don't want to hear about anymore, because it makes reality even more painful for me than it already is.

The film Schlöndorff was working on is Der junge Törless (Young Törless).

81. Herbert Achternbusch
Amerika: Report to the Goethe Institute (1979)

Thanks to Heiner Müller I enjoyed a three-week stay in America (financed by the Goethe Institute), in the California cities of Holy Francisco and Last Angeles. He recommended me to Tom Luddy. Tom Luddy is the boss at the Pacific Film Archive in Birkli, and I owe it to him that I finally received a professional evaluation of two of my films. He recognized, namely, that they are great films because they consistently expand from an obscure beginning to a logical end. He said that under the friendly California sun which laughed in a friendly way as only poached trout do in Germany. He wore a small yellow feather, a canary yellow feather, on his grey Hammett hat. His facial features are enigmatic, his mouth not talkative. His mind likes to emit the name Wim. Whenever I was with Tom I knew exactly where Wim was: writing his script, and what he planned for the next few days: scriptwriting. When I planned to meet him at Coopla's house, Wim called a half hour before midnight to say that he would meet me somewhere at half past. It was Friday and he didn't have time because he had to finish his Hammett script by Monday. On Monday I met him at Coopla's office, in the hallway, more grown-up than ever, and he had no time because he had to finish his script by Friday. Which he has been writing now for over two years. I had the impression that Coopla keeps his eye on him. Tom said that Wim will become an American, that he knows his way around America better than Tom himself, but it was said with an undertone that suggested no American in America wants to know his way around like a German. Damn it, I was standing too close to this lowerlip Coopla, I offered him a punch (sic) of snuff and already he was talking about his Octoberfest visit when he ate snuff in the pissoir. I recommended my Octoberfest film to him because he seems to know all too well how it runs. His old house was nice and green, and there was a restaurant below called Wim and there was a Wimburger which I downed (downed because it was too huge), and I swear that I ate no other burger during my visit because I too thought I was stricken with Wimeritis. How can a man who radiates such seriousnesss produce so much trivia? Herzog had tattooed on his shoulder a skull which stuck out its fleshy tongue, and he had trouble with Fox. Brandner followed an actor with a dark look. I didn't belong here, I listened to the noises, let myself be driven over the Golden Gate Bridge, enjoyed Frisco as it awaited its decline, huddled together. The Bay is said to be clean once again and stocked with fish. At this crossing the Mafia caused a car accident, and Kurosawa has already chucked two stars from his new film, and I also had time to myself. Yes! Yes! No! No! The Director of the Goethe Institute showed us the redwoods, those mammoth trees that just stand there and let people look under their skirts and are shamelessly tall. And then, for the second time, I met a Negro painted white; he was from Iran, he was from France, he was from Germany, where he almost has a harder time than I do raising money for his films, for his austere films, films so beautiful that other films look like frivolous underwear. How is it possible that such frivolous films are made in Germany? Because it is possible, I said. The only right answer. In LA, too, a good-for-nothing from the Film Subsidy Board was prowling around, I don't remember the name, Today or Yesterday. I called these little films Filmburgers, which amused the Yankees. For no matter how glued on their smile is—glued on to be pulled off—they let themselves be carried away and laugh. Even in my films they laughed at scenes and at sentences where the German audience pretended to think. But to get back to this Iranian director who makes the best German films, he suddenly appeared and everything got easier for me. Because he didn't like America, it was easier for me to find something to like. (In Germany we don't have even one postage stamp that says writing is the source of democracy.) I liked the elephantitis of young American women. LA's diffuseness was nice. The mocking emptiness of Universal, however, was not. (I thought to myself, though, that I want to see the Fox Studios again.) Asked by the wife of the Goethe Institute director, this filmmaker said that *Knife in the Ass* is an anarchic animated film. At a public discussion we said nothing because once someone talked about the absent Hauffs and Bohms, and, as Herzog rightly pointed out, these Americans couldn't comprehend that there isn't only *one* German cinema. Therefore, the Goethe Institute should be thankful that this Bavarian and this Iranian didn't sing but drank whiskey. Moreover, this discussion took place before our films were shown, and you have to be a real driveler just to be able to talk about films, and if I have to talk with someone after seeing my film, then he is also a real driveler. Of course we were supposed to be representatives: the film festival of the reserve troops, as the third squadron we were supposed to mark off the terrain for the heroes, to demonstrate the unlimited possibilities in German film, we two nihilists who always escape the tentacles of positive ass-licking by means of horror, these know-it-alls without spark. What could you talk about if it wasn't even certain that the films would arrive from one day to the next. Ron Holloway tried hard to get the prints, the Goethe Institute let him use their telephone so that he could shake the Export Union out of their coma, and the secretary Erika paraded in front of him so that his gaze didn't freeze with his waiting ear. He accompanies a package of German films with charming patience through various American cities, building up an organization in Minneapolis which—instead of a distributor—is supposed to help place the films of progressive filmmakers directly with the cinema owners. The traditional wheeler-dealers say it will never work. With his wife Dorothea, Holloway prepared a brochure for which he was author, editor, and manager. Only after it was finished did the FFA graciously provide the printing costs. FFA is in fact the abbreviation for Film Fetus Board because it acts more as an abortion clinic than a funding board. Who is the scriptwriter Peter Steinbach, Herzog asked quite rightfully. He is pictured in the brochure sitting over a cup of coffee, looking glumly at a self-made film. The Bavarian and the Iranian were carried away by the excellent projection of their films at the Castro in San Francisco. The theater has stood there proudly since 1913 with its 1,500 seats. That was something else compared to the dingy or luxurious mini-theaters in Munich. The name of the Iranian director, who makes the best German films, is Sohrab Shahid Saless. Is he the first that would support me for Chekhov? At the Vox (sic) Venice cinema I saw his documentary film, *Die langen Ferien der Lotte H. Eisner* (*The Long Vacation of Lotte H. Eisner*, 1979). Watch out for creativity, I heard her say again and again. The Nazis sent her to Paris on vacation, but she never wanted to return to her fatherland. She is poor, but rich in spirit, which the FRG today still doesn't know how to use. Sohrab told her about me, my films. ". . . And I have the feeling I would like them. I'd like to show them all at the Cinémathèque Française. How is it that your films aren't distributed in Paris like those of Werner Herzog, Wim Wenders, and Fassbinder?" Her letter is postmarked with a Swiss stamp on which Thomas Mann looks back severely at Germany. Yes, how is it? It looks as if the German cultural institutes will not have enough money to provide French titles for my films. Yes, we come from the land of culture. (And the Goethe Institute is more an artists-in-residence enterprise than a cultural institution.) Don't forget, it is embarrassing enough to appear in foreign countries, because I am not at the beginning only H.A. but also the representative of a culture. I come from a seven-hundred-year-old family which has always produced oppositional peasants and only two bootlickers, a bishop and a high-level administrator in the seventeenth century. And now here I am, feeling all too strongly the impropriety of public life. I quickly got the Yankees on my side with my clownery. Or I sent them packing with questions about Germany. (And America? If America is a dog, I said, then we have the dog shit.) I do not feel responsible for Germany. I do not care how many states this monster had in the past or has in the present. The potential injustice in any state cannot be so great that the people do not identify with it. The German people have only really accepted one form of state, dictatorship. I tried to relax in California, which I was able to do for hours while watching the Pacific. If you asked the girls whether the sun was always so delightful here, they were happy. My room was robbed once. And I got to know a cowboy with whom I drank a bottle of Tequila-Tokillyou. Even Wolfgang Ebert appeared, who didn't want to be a car in San Francisco. And I stayed away from drugs and laughed uncontrollably anyway when Sohrab had his calf humped by a dog named Badweiser, even though he tried to be friendly toward the little bitch. The best American beer is also called Badweiser. I told jokes and made faces and represented German culture. I had my newest play in my pocket, GUST, a thirty-four page monologue by an old man who summarizes his life while his wife goes through her silent struggle with death. He was fit for life, a spendthrift, and saved the above-mentioned 700-year-old family. I wrote the play in Austria, it was too loud here, too inhuman and ugly. Sentences I have been storing up for thirty-five years. And whenever I found someone who was culture-starved in America, I spoke these sentences about the play. And if someone was cunning, he recognized my own situation. (Electric power line = Germany/ the leather cap = my artistic creativity). Gust once went to his cousin Otto's, a farmer in Nattenberg. There were clouds on the horizon, and it rained. It got BLACK, they had to hurry, they had to get to work so that he could still see something while disconnecting the electric power. He has to remove roof tiles because he has to climb up the roof pole, except that he can crawl and slide over the tiles. But of course he didn't consider that the barn is much higher than the pole, and as he crawls out, he is standing with his leather cap touching the line. Jesus, he thinks to himself as he turns a bit. Christ Almighty, he thinks to himself as he touches his ear. Those damn wasps, he thought to himself. There must be a wasps' nest there, he thought to himself. Stung me all-right! His ear was electrified just as if a wasp stung him. And as he makes a cut, he sees that he is pressing on a wire with his cap. Then he meekly retreats, then he carefully disconnects the wire with a laugh. What would have happened without the cap! That bit of insulation. What would have happened if he had touched it with his bare head? Man alive. He could have been dead. And he thought it had felt like a wasp sting. I even cried out. Jesus, he had said, there's gotta be a wasps' nest there. And I was touching the power line. Wasps, huh!

November 23, 1979

Names which I misspelled in the rush: Coppola/Berkeley/Goethe/ Schürmann/Budweiser

Achternbusch's "Octoberfest film" is Bierkampf *(Beer Battle, 1977).—Uwe Brandner is a writer and filmmaker, director of, among other films,* Ich liebe dich, ich töte dich *(I Love You, I Kill You, 1971) and* halbe-halbe *(Fifty-Fifty, 1977).—The director of the San Francisco branch of the Goethe Institute at that time was Ernst Schürmann, an individual highly regarded for his creative cultural programming, especially in matters of film.—The Film Subsidy Board official Achternbusch speaks of is Robert Backheuer, playing on his name with the words "heuer" and "gestern" in the German original.— Knife in the Ass is Achternbusch's title for Reinhard Hauff's* Messer im Kopf *(Knife in the Head).—Ron Holloway at the time was a foreign correspondent for* Variety, *operating out of West Berlin. He and his wife, Dorothea Moritz, publish the quarterly journal,* Kino: German film. *(The FFA would later cease all support for the magazine in the wake of an article critical of the film subsidy system in West Germany.) Holloway was responsible for a "German Film Tour" that traveled through the U.S. Cf. his essay reflecting on this experience and several other commentaries: "Neuer deutscher Film in USA,"* Medium, *March 1980, pp. 31–35.—Regarding Lotte Eisner and Achternbusch, see her tribute to the director, "Herbert Achternbusch," in* Herbert Achternbusch, *ed. Jörg Drews (Frankfurt am Main: Suhrkamp, 1982), pp. 143–45.*

82. Rudolf Thome
Thoughts about Filmmaking in the FRG (1980)

How Everything Started

After having written several film reviews for the Bonn daily newspaper, *Der Generalanzeiger,* in February 1962, I wrote the journal *Filmkritik* and asked if I could write reviews for them too. They sent me a friendly answer and said "yes." On the envelope of this response was a green sticker with the text: *"Papa's Cinema is dead."* I was impressed because I had just read the manifesto of the Oberhausen rebels in the newspaper (give us five million and we'll make ten films) and my wife and I (we had just gotten married) moved from Bonn to Munich.

Several months later someone at the university stuck a leaflet in my hand. It was an invitation to a free screening of short films by the same directors who had signed the Oberhausen Manifesto. There were films by Kluge, Reitz, Peter Schamoni, Senft, Houwer, and Strobel-Tichawsky. I was curious and went that afternoon to the Arri-Kino. Most of the films had been shot beautifully and that impressed me already at the time no small bit.

Then, six months later, I met Eckhart Schmidt. I had just bought an 8mm camera in order to film my wife and my son Harald, who had just been born. I spoke with Schmidt about the kind of short films one should be making right now at this moment. We looked for stories that could express our present feeling. We agreed that they would have to be very simple, everyday stories. We both wrote reviews for the *Süddeutsche Zeitung* and for the periodical *Film*, which had been established early in 1963, and through the films of Godard and *Cahiers du Cinéma*, we discovered American cinema. We shocked our colleagues when we gave films like Preminger's *The Cardinal* four stars. Max Zihlmann, also a critic for *Film*, joined up with us. And in the summer of '64 we then started shooting the short film *Die Versöhnung (The Reconciliation)* in 8mm, based on my screenplay.

All in all the shooting for the film lasted four months. I had disagreements with Eckhart Schmidt. We had a falling out. Klaus Lemke, who had worked as an assistant director in the theater and in fact already made a short film (Zihlmann and I had seen it, a sort of fairy tale about a girl who runs through the city with a crown), filled Schmidt's place. He suggested that we redo the entire film. In 16mm. I grabbed my heart and sacrificed all of the money left over from what I had inherited from my mother: 5,000 marks. We completely rewrote the screenplay several times, recast the leading roles and finally just about completed the film so that it would be ready for Oberhausen in the winter.

Before Oberhausen, Michel Delahaye from the *Cahiers du Cinéma*, whom we had sought out in a screening of a short film by Roland Klick, and Jean-Marie Straub saw our film. We were terriby anxious about Delahaye's reaction. But he didn't say anything after the screening. But Straub did: "*C'est un film très bon.*" At the time we didn't realize what a compliment that was. But from then on Straub was our friend and advisor for every critical situation that would come along. The film was turned down by the Oberhausen selection jury and even Atlas-Film, which had wanted to buy the film, suddenly said that it would only buy it if we redubbed it. We (supported by Straub) said no. For all that Atlas ultimately paid to have the film blown up to 35mm.

In Oberhausen a friend of Straub's, [Peter] Nestler, joined us and so that our film might at least get a midnight showing, we formulated a joint leaflet, a sort of new Oberhausen Manifesto. This of course was directed against the established Oberhausen signatories, against their demand for a socially relevant film, which for us was just a trendy rehash of the old German problem films of the fifties. We wanted a cinema that looked like the films of Hawks and Godard. A cinema that was fun. A cinema that was simple and radical. We finally got our screening and also the judgment of the Oberhausen critics. In their eyes our films were nothing more than dilettantish and banal. Enno Patalas of *Filmkritik* was the only one who started to like them.

Lemke, Zihlmann, and I established in 1965 a small film production company, which, because Max Zihlmann was in love with Alexandra Steward, we called "Alexandra-Film." We made the first short film by Max Zihlmann, *Frühstück in Rom (Breakfast in Rome)* (Zihlmann got the money from his parents), and we looked for a producer to do the first short film by Klaus Lemke, *Kleine Front (Small Front)*. We found Franz Seitz. We were so involved with these short films, with living and going to the movies, that we didn't know anything about the bundles of money which our colleagues in the meanwhile had gained access to.

In 1966, Franz Seitz financed my second short film, *Stella,* as a reward for my having sold Lemke's *Small Front* to Atlas. A very free version of Goethe's *Stella.* Seitz wanted to redub it after I had finished the film. But Straub, also present at the final screening, told Seitz that precisely what he didn't like (the original sound) was in fact good. The FSK actually wanted to ban the film. Only through the intercession of a university professor was I able to release the film. The FSK claimed that the film was a challenge to civilized society. Straub said he had tears in his eyes when he first saw the film.

I broke off my studies and worked in a bank as a credit manager. Early in 1967 I had convinced Rob Houwer to finance my next short film, *Galaxis.* He wanted the men in this film (which was set in the year 2000) to wear miniskirts. That was in at the time. I told him that if he insisted on this, I wouldn't make the film. Fortunately Houwer didn't insist. The film did not receive a predicate from the FBW, which meant that no one would buy it. Volker Schlöndorff liked it so much (?) that he wanted to use it as a short before screenings of his *Mord und Totschlag (A Degree of Murder).* But nothing came of it. For all that, Klaus Lemke, who played one of the male leads in the film, at least got to know Dieter Geissler and Monika Zinnenberg in the process. This was the basis of the team for Lemke's first feature film, *48 Stunden bis Acapulco (48 Hours to Acapulco).* Lemke wanted me to be production manager and I was eager to use this chance to go to Acapulco and I said yes. I came up with a shooting schedule and a budget. But three days before shooting started, Lemke decided that I was much too interested in Christiane Krüger (with whom I had chatted perhaps a bit too long about the shooting of Howard Hawks's *Hatari!*) and he fired me. Nonetheless I had learned how easy it is to make a real feature film and, without a break, I starting working on one. Together with Max Zihlmann I wrote the script of *Supergirl.* I found a distributor right away (the same one Lemke had) and this distributor had already rented the film to about two hundred cinemas before the script was finished. That's the way things were at the time. Unfortunately the distributor didn't like the final script. They thought the story was much too normal. If only Supergirl, the girl from another planet, at least had had fins between her toes or something weird like that!

I bought a very used Ford 17 M-Cabriolet and became an assistant director for Elfi Petramer's *Fensterl zum Hof* (*Little Window onto the Courtyard*). In my free time, I wrote a new script for a short film, *Jane erschiesst John, weil er sie mit Ann betrügt* (*Jane Shoots John, Because He's Having an Affair with Ann*). A woman wanted to give me 3,000 marks to help finance the film. But at the point she was supposed to give me the money (or a part of it), she told me that her small daughter had fallen down and cracked her front teeth and that she needed all the money now to repair her daughter's teeth. I was pretty desperate because I had already put together a crew. I heard that Lemke would be arriving back from Nice (in the meanwhile he had finished shooting his second feature film *Negresco* there) and I decided to pick him up at the airport. This made Lemke happy and I asked him whether he could give me the unused leftover negatives from *Acapulco* for my short film. I drove home with Lemke and took the film rolls with me. Later Straub gave me the remainders from his Bach film. At least I now had enough negative material. I made the short film finally in December '67, without a single penny, in cinemascope. The money you see in the film was lent to me each time by Max Zihlmann. The money I really had to spend, e.g., for gas, I had to borrow, five marks at a time, from friends.

After shooting was over, Arri suddenly said that they would not hand over the master copy until I paid them. I signed two promissory notes and got the master copy. Together with Danièle Huillet (she is a wonderful editor) I was able to cut the film. By mid-January 1968, the film was finished and at the same time the first note was due. Straub gave me the thousand marks Truffaut had given to him and I was able to pay the note. At the same time there was a private screening of his Bach film in the *Theatinerkino*. Straub really wanted to show my short film before his own. I told him that the two films—just listen to their different music—would not work well together. Straub said both films had something in common (at least they had in part the same negative material) and I agreed. All three distributors present at the screening wanted afterward to buy the short film. I needed money right away and sold it to Constantin-Film.

Two months later I received the predicate "particularly noteworthy" which meant an automatic 30,000 marks from the FFA. All of my friends expected me to make my first feature film soon.

Enno Patalas, Marquard Bohm, and I traveled by car to Oberhausen. Enno Patalas told me during the trip about Petra Nettelbeck who had just inherited money from her father and financed a short film by Hellmuth Costard. In Oberhausen I met Petra Nettelbeck and asked her whether she could give me 30,000 marks for a feature film. With that much money in hand I would be able to bring off an inexpensive, small film in black and white. She believed me. I sent her the exposé Max Zihlmann had written and three weeks later I drove to Luhmühlen and signed a contract with her. I promised to start making the film on 7 June 1968 and Max Zihlmann began to write the screenplay. I found a team and a crew and on the seventh of June we got started. I soon realized that the money would not come close to covering costs and I looked all over the place for additional sources of money, not wanting to make Petra Nettelbeck even poorer. On the day that the first check I had given to Kodak bounced, and I knew I could carry on for at best one or two days, I called up Carol Hellman, a real old-school producer, and asked him for an appointment. Hellman, speaking through Franz Seitz, had earlier offered to assume financing if I agreed to start over and remake the film in color and change its title to *The Go-Go-Girl from Blowup*. Hellman had a contract with Columbia to make a film like this. I had declined. Nonetheless he was still friendly enough to sit down and talk. I explained my situation to him, exactly how things were. He told me that he liked my candor and that he probably could help me. He asked for twenty-four hours to think things over. Just as the Pope has his advisors, so too did he have his. I was excited. And twenty-four hours later, during a lunch break from shooting, I learned from his production manager that I could stop by and pick up the first check. That's how I had always imagined working in Hollywood would be.

When I finished shooting *Detektive (Detective)*, I promised Hellman that I would complete the initial editing in two weeks. I hired two cutters, rented two editing rooms, and did two people's work. After two weeks the first cut was finished and the film was about 150 minutes long. Hellman saw it and thought that the film was a catastrophe. He demanded that I agree (I had a clause in the contract granting me the sole right to make artistic decisions) to postdubbing (it had been made with original sound), that it be shortened to ninety minutes, and that I add three sex scenes at points in the film where this was possible. For two months we didn't speak and finally when I realized that the film would not be released unless I gave in, I said I would accept point one and point two of his conditions. So that the postdubbing would not be a catastro-

phe, Hellman hired Alfred Weidenmann to assist me. I must confess to
the credit of Alfred Weidenmann that he behaved very honorably in this
complex situation and really did help me as well.

Later, after the film had received a predicate from the FBW, Carol
Hellman watched *Detective* all alone in his private screening room. He
must have been very moved by it. Because, as his projectionist later told
me, after the film was over, he sat in the room for a long while. No
wonder, the film is about two young men (Ulli Lommel, Marquard
Bohm) who try to steal money from an old man (Walter Rilla).

On an extremely beautiful Pentecost weekend, *Detective* finally
opened in Munich, in the Lehnbachkino, where most of the Young
German films played. Several girls and I distributed leaflets to the sun-
bathers lying on the shores of the Isar, and so it happened that the
evening performances were not as poorly attended as I had feared. One
person who attended was another film producer, Heinz Angermeyer. He
liked the film so much that he was willing to finance my next film, *Rote
Sonne (Red Sun)*. Not with money from the FFA or from the Ministry of
the Interior, but plain and simple out of his own pocket! That was ten
years ago! To be sure, he did so under the condition that Marquard Bohm
and Uschi Obermeier star in the film. After *Detective* I never wanted to
work with Marquard again, and Uschi lived with [the student activist]
Rainer Langhans in Commune 1 in Berlin. Engaging her turned out to be
extraordinarily difficult, because Rainer Langhans was afraid he would
lose her if she made the film. At the Berlin Film Festival in '69, Uschi
ultimately signed the extremely complex contract which granted her
three days off after every four days of shooting (during this period she and
Langhans flew back to Berlin and the flight came out of the production
budget) and the (for the time) substantial salary of 20,000 marks.

After the film was completed, it went on 14 November 1969—on
my thirtieth birthday (I was certain this was going to be my lucky day)—
to the FSK and the FBW. The Chair of the FSK came to me after the
screening and congratulated me on my "work" and told me that the film
reminded him of a Greek tragedy and gave me considerable reason to
believe that the predicate "particularly noteworthy" was in the offing.
Because I was not allowed to attend the meeting of the FBW, I left in a
good mood to go have something to eat and drink. When I inquired as to
the outcome two hours later, Dr. Hebeisen told me that, unfortunately, I
had not received a predicate. I didn't understand the world anymore,
took my print, and rode the train back to Munich, because on the way to
Wiesbaden, shortly before Nuremberg, the engine of my beautiful
Porsche Carrera had broken down.

The seventies didn't start well for me. Although the January issue of

Filmkritik contained three positive articles about *Red Sun:* by Wim Wenders, Klaus Bädekerl, and Enno Patalas. I was hatching plans to make a film about a large commune in an uninhabited gigantic out-of-the-way building—behind the house with the apartment where the girls in *Red Sun* dwell. The film would have been about drugs (hash, LSD), mysticism, and astrology. My producer, Heinz Angermeyer, was interested, because he was almost one-hundred-percent certain that *Red Sun* would receive a Federal Film subsidy bonus of 200,000 marks. We didn't receive it. He was so bitter about this that he stopped making films completely for several years. Later he learned that the jury hadn't even looked at the film. That meant an end to the commune project.

During this period I met Karin Brandner. She asked me to check over her initial budget for Uwe Brandner's *Ich liebe dich, ich töte dich (I Love You, I Kill You)*. Watching *Red Sun* at a private screening, she had tears in her eyes when the film was over. We fell in love. In the midst of location shooting for Uwe Brandner's film in a small village north of Ingolstadt, I suddenly got a telephone call from WDR. They were interested in making a film with me. If possible based on a script by Zihlmann. Under the condition that the film had to be finished by 31 December 1970. Another project had fallen through and they absolutely had to spend the money by the end of the year. *Supergirl* came to mind. A week after I went to [the WDR offices in] Cologne I had the go-ahead from the Administrative Council *(Verwaltungsrat)* for the project. But I now came to the sorry realization that I would only get money if it was secured by a bank. And because a bank won't secure anything unless one has money (or a house or bonds or gold or something like that), I was in a jam. Distressed, I sought out Fassbinder, who just had received the Federal Film Prize in Gold and 650,000 marks for his second feature film, *Katzelmacher*. I asked everyone I knew. Finally Karin found a rich private source in Hamburg who was willing to lend us part of the money (125,000 marks). We went on to make *Supergirl* with this money. The production was a technical *tour de force*. But on the day before Christmas Eve Karin and I sat in the train to Cologne with the copy that would be shown on TV. The final version was accepted and I'm not exaggerating when I say that the TV editors were excited. The film was aired in March and I received numerous crank calls from people who threatened all kinds of things. They thought I was putting them on. They thought that I wasn't serious about the story of Supergirl, this girl from another planet.

When Erich Müller of Columbia saw *Supergirl*, he told me that it was high time that Columbia made a film with me. Together with Siegfried Schober, I came up with the story of two friends who take off for Venezuela one day to hunt in the jungle for diamonds. That was right

at the time when Herzog was making *Aguirre* and Antonioni was working
on a film about the half-overgrown Amazon city, Manaos, which around
1900 had had one of the largest opera houses in the world. Unfortunately
only Werner finished his film. I never forgave him for not showing the
jungle as I imagined life in the jungle. The script was finished by the
summer of 1971, but the Columbia people in London in the end said
"No." I still owed 50,000 marks from *Supergirl* and had also already stuck
a bunch of money into the pre-production of "Rio Guaniamo" and
thought that the only way to get out of this situation was to make a black-
and-white film, a real B movie, as quickly and cheaply as possible. I ran
all over Germany while Zihlmann wrote the script and got cinemas to
agree that they would play the film—its title was *Fremde Stadt* (*Strange
City*)—once it was finished. I was certain this would work. Even Arri
believed it would, because they were willing to loan me 50,000 marks.

But it didn't work. The advertising costs for each play date were
almost always more than the box-office take. I was completely broke and
constantly occupied with fending off my creditors. I submitted "Rio
Guaniamo" to the Ministry of the Interior in hopes of receiving a script
subsidy. I wrote a new screenplay—this time without Zihlmann, who
didn't want to work with me anymore: "Die Geschichte der Billie" ("The
Story of Billie"), the tragic story of a junkie, and also submitted this
script to the BMI. Unsuccessfully.

I started writing film reviews for the *Süddeutsche Zeitung* again, and
in the summer of 1973, I finally left Munich and moved to Berlin.

The Straub film mentioned is, of course, Chronik der Anna Magdalena
Bach (Chronicle of Anna Magdalena Bach).—*Petra Nettelbeck
coproduced Costard's infamous* Besonders wertvoll (Particularly Noteworthy).—*Alfred Weidenmann is a director clearly identified with the old guard, a
filmmaker who got his start in the Third Reich and worked steadily and
frequently throughout the next decades in a number of popular veins.*—Thome
continued his account in a second installment which appeared in Filme, *no. 2*
(1980): 44–47.

83. Helma Sanders-Brahms

"New German Cinema, *jeune cinéma allemand*, Good Night": A Day in Oberhausen, 1982 (1982)

I came from the funeral for a friend to Oberhausen—a funeral after a
terrible accident on the freeway between Berlin and Hannover, in mid-

spring, three people seriously injured, one dead, one not injured at all. I had forced myself, despite everything, to go to Oberhausen, because I thought I owed this city a lot, this beginning of the German film, because one had told me that I would meet old friends there, Hilmar Hoffmann, Alexander Kluge, whom I would have liked to see there again, especially on this day. Twenty years of Oberhausen. Birthday. I felt like an old circus horse as I trotted into the hall, still the same old tickets, everything like it always was, and also in front the buffet, where you could get the eternally same potato salad with a cold cutlet or sausage, was still there and now with a somewhat larger selection. Everything was like a dream. I couldn't sob after what I had been through, I was completely paralyzed inside, and I just wanted not to collapse and to make good on my promise to be there, to take a seat at the podium in the center auditorium. And so I went into the center auditorium where cold cutlets were forever—and still now—being eaten, where cigarette smoke and the smell of beer and various other smells hung in the air, everything you would expect of the coal industry setting. I had to go up to the podium, there was still a seat for me on the side. Next to me sat Herr Bieberstein from the Federal Ministry of Economy, Peter B. Schumann was there with whom about a year ago I had collected money in a film reel can for Latin American filmmakers, he seemed to be in charge of everything, and further on down sat Clara Burckner, the present distributor of my films, and next to her, Manfred Hohnstock from the Federal Ministry of the Interior, and an old resident of Oberhausen was there as well, but we hadn't met. Otherwise I recognized few familiar faces when I looked around in the hall, Wolfgang Ruf, yes, and a tan and much trimmer Hans C. Blumenberg. Rosa von Praunheim giggled in a corner with Joachim von Mengershausen, they looked as if they had somehow found just the person they had been looking for. Fee Vaillant was also there and I think I also caught a brief glimpse of Ulrich Gregor, yes, and Helmut Herbst, who also was there back in the days of my hand-made films, and fortunately still remains today a little bit like he was then, with this genuine fire, this unconditional enthusiasm about a kind of film we used to envision: the other, the better cinema, different from the endless commercial repetitions, an inventive, original, imaginative, a political cinema, with new ways of writing, new ideas, new images, new sounds, a cinema against the flabbiness that produces money and desire for even more money, a cinema for the street—peace to the cottages, war on the palaces.

Yes, the cottages. There still was really no one there from the Oberhausen cottages, even from those behind the so-called smelting works, outside of the obligatory union bigwig and sundry bureaucratic small fries, and, perhaps in the audience a few disaffected young people, unemployed children whose fathers have dust in their lungs, the people who were originally supposed to benefit culturally from this festival. This festival which then brought about the Young German Film. *Le jeune cinéma allemand.* New German Cinema. All over the world, while the young lads from the mines and smelting works and their girl friends for whom this was actually, actually intended, sat in front of their TV sets and swarmed in droves to German soccer games, or who knows where, anywhere but the nearby Municipal Auditorium where these weird young filmmakers sat around, in those days still accompanied by the token worker they had flown in from Berlin, in front of the cameras of the TV show *Aspekte*, Walter Schmieding, who still was alive then, talking about film, about their own films, it goes without saying, even at that time this fanatic egocentric behavior, this navel-picking of one's own work, whose significance would be then pulled out of the navel, cleverly and with bravado by Kluge, less cleverly by others, that's right, but one still talked about the workers. Really. Everyone was speaking out for the workers, everyone thought about the workers, there was this euphoria of '68, everything one did had to be socially relevant, many films (even one of mine) ended with the prospect of a general strike or some other kind of incredible event that would immediately bring an end to the old social order—and we were in favor of the new order, we and these workers who would of course join us, these workers whose consciousness we so brashly thought we could raise, we, we of all people, who couldn't even listen to each other, we were adamantly convinced that each and every worker would have to listen to us, would have to be overcome by us, would have to be altered and revolutionized—if only we had read our Marx, our Hegel, our Engels, our Wilhelm Reich, our Rosa Luxemburg, our Stalin, our Mao; one had to read, read, read, the way to the cinema was paved with books, making films meant for a while making "films for special audiences," and the first question one was always asked when one showed up with one's handmade film was: "For what special audience is the film intended, anyway?" and pity the soul whose answer did not come shooting back like a bullet.

Apropos of shooting. One makes films—one can also say: one shoots them. It follows, one said at the time, that the film camera is a weapon. In class struggle. "When the oppressors have finished speaking, then the oppressed will speak," we knew this from Brecht, and we thought that the oppressors had spoken much too long and because we now wanted to have our say, it was logical that we identified with the oppressed whose turn it was now to speak. Shooting. Shooting films.

Sitting on stage in the center auditorium this year in Oberhausen I did not speak. Not a word. I felt like a fool sitting up there, almost like one of the oppressors who have been talking forever and still can't keep their mouths shut while the oppressed down below meanwhile want to say something but don't get a chance to do so. The people sitting down below didn't want to talk about oppression anyway. Not at all. Besides the discussion revolved entirely around bread, not the kind one eats in the cottages, but rather the kind of bread one buys a 16mm negative with, with which one pays the laboratory and rents a camera and a Nagra and a cutting table, the bread without which nothing happens in this job, one to which I have devoted myself since those early days. I couldn't take part in this discussion because this bread everyone was talking about is still a problem for me just as much as it is for the growing generation of newcomers out in the central auditorium, and because I don't have any bread myself, I hardly could help them to get some of their own, I too would like to know how I'm supposed to launch my next film, but in the face of their difficulties I didn't feel like bothering them with my own. Besides that, apart from financial questions quite crucial for the production of a film, no further questions were under discussion. It somehow seemed to be a foregone conclusion that if one had successfully taken care of the financing of a project everything else would fall into place, substance, form, audience, nothing to worry about, the main thing was to get the dough. I knew this kind of argumentation, even if from another direction, from many years before, from "Papa's Cinema," from Gyula Trebitsch and the kind of people who said you have to have money, money, who cares about content, who cares about form, as long as people line up at the box office. Those were the days of the German entertainment film with large audiences, now we were talking about the subsidized German film and who was going to get a piece of the pie, me, me, me. H.C.B. then asked very timidly what kind of words and images would be included in these forthcoming projects, and Helmut Herbst, well, he was the only one left from the old days, he repeated the same question, this time with more verve, with more fighting spirit and more disappointment in his voice. Short applause, then the next person asked for the microphone and once he had it, he asked for money for yet another new work.

Silently the old warriors spooned their potato salad, silently I finished my glass of mineral water which the festival organizers always provided for those sitting at the podium, meanwhile, a disaffected youth, who was not to be subdued and who had found the Mosel wine sold at the Oberhausen cold-cut buffet much to his liking, got hold of the microphone, again and again, and babbling on and on, demanded money, for super-eight I think, pouring more and more wine down his throat, gazing from eyes lined with shadows which were becoming increasingly glassy, his hair increasingly ruffled, I think quite justifiably so—no one was listening to him any more, he was not even listening to himself, and at one point toward the end of this babbling that went on and on, Peter Schumann brought things to a conclusion, and that was the conclusion of the birthday party for Oberhausen, for the Young German Film, New German Cinema, *jeune cinéma allemand,* good night.

I couldn't contain myself any longer and I decided to wet my whistle. I climbed down from the microphone and headed for the buffet straight to the Mosel wine. I had said nothing, nothing, absolutely nothing.

That was not to remain the case for long, though, because afterwards the TV station WDR III had invited people to gab about twenty years since Oberhausen, the uncontrollable youngsters weren't going to be there, just the controlled oldsters, among whose number, whether he liked it or not, Rosa von Praunheim also had to figure, and I think he did so gladly. I was in a much better mood after three quick glasses of Mosel, what I had experienced during the afternoon became a haze, "clearer and nonetheless mild," like the sailor Kuttel Daddeldu, I saw colleagues like Hansjürgen Pohland and Heidi Genée chatting with Hans-Christoph Blumenberg, I heard Rosa say something nasty without giving it a second thought, or rather, I think in fact I said, "Rosa, you're as nasty as a pink rat!" but that didn't appear on the tape and Rosa took revenge quickly, but more friendly than ever—in the breaks, the great works of the absent supermen of New German Cinema were played in excerpts, Herzog, Fassbinder, Syberberg, and H.C.B. was sweating; and charitably, because the colleague from makeup couldn't be everywhere at once, I dabbed away the drops of sweat from his face with a handy powder puff, and when the breaks were over, the leftovers still there had a chance to speak, to pick their navels, to celebrate themselves, as is customary in German territory. Me too. Me too, me too.

Then that was over as well and in search of something else to drink, the remaining few of the leftovers combed the Municipal Hall and were even permitted to spend another hour in the dining hall downstairs, where so many careers were launched over dinners with backers and, in the process, people made their first steps toward takeoff. The young New Wavers and Super-eighters weren't here either. This sixties elegance with wool and linen coverings and rectangular tables decked in white with an offering of diverse kinds of sandwiches is not exactly their style and, besides that, they weren't invited anyway. But I still had to deal with my depression, that is to say, not my personal one which had floated away with the Mosel and hadn't resurfaced since, but rather with my depression about Germany which was considerable—you know what I mean. This melancholy that surfaces in the face of melancholy. This continued around the rectangular table covered in white. Fee Vaillant was there and smiled gently at me while I stood there drunk as a skunk, H.C.B. melted from enthusiasm because I hadn't gone off to bed yet (later the traitor cut out every halfway sensible thing I said during the discussion and only kept the incoherent nonsense, which, given the three glasses of Mosel in my brain, was unfortunately not very well formulated, oh shame, oh disgrace!) and Clara, I'm happy to say, was even more gone than I was, which gave me cause to order another Mosel and charge it to my distributor.

After drinking that one I didn't feel very well at all and the nightmarish trek through Oberhausen that followed in search of the reserved, but I guess unreserved (do you understand the secrets of the WDR computer?) hotel room suffered additionally from these mental disturbances. In the end Heidi Genée came to my rescue and found a place for me, in a gigantic room with two beds, cold, without a shower, but with a wash basin and a very thin blanket. Yes, that was Oberhausen, and the next morning the good Ruhr-pot coffee with Clara, who bears hangovers with the same Prussian discipline as I do, yes indeed, that was Oberhausen for me this year, and actually I didn't want to talk about it at all, but maybe we all should laugh a bit about the old ugly love that nonetheless manages to overcome one at the old train station. . . . It was like being at funerals and they are also always a bit funny even if one feels more like a good long cry.

Hilmar Hoffmann, Cultural Head of the City of Frankfurt, was for a number of years the Director of the Oberhausen Film Festival.—Sanders-Brahms's filmic reflection about the student movement is Unter dem Pflaster ist der Strand *(The Beach under the Sidewalk, 1974).—Gyula Trebitsch is a well-known producer who was quite active during the fifties; he is one of the figures commonly associated with* Opas Kino.*—Kuttel Daddeldu is a figure in the poetry of Joachim Ringelnatz,* Kuttel Daddeldu *(1920).—For a more recent self-portrait, see* "Ich drehe," Augen-Blick *(Marburg), no. 1/2 (December 1985): 52–58.*

84. Helmut Herbst

New German Cinema, 1962–83: A View from Hamburg (1983)

Dear Friends,

When I received your invitation a while ago to prepare an introductory address for the conference on "Style and Ideology in New German

Cinema," I asked myself why I should be here relating to you my own very personal view of New German Cinema. I think it is because I can offer a somewhat distanced, and therefore unconventional, perspective. It is a view from Hamburg, not from the film capital, Munich, and, for this reason, does not call for a film critical balancing act, or a special, intimate knowledge of film political relationships. It is the perspective of someone who has been making films since 1960, who started making animated films, who created special effects for his own films and for others, who made films about film and art historical topics, and who, finally, in 1981, directed his own feature-length dramatic film. In addition, starting in 1964, I also became a kind of producer for independent filmmakers in Hamburg, an advisor on special effects cinematography, and in the same vein, an instructor at the Berlin Film and Television Academy from 1969 to 1979. One way or other, I've had a hand in quite a few films produced in Hamburg and Berlin. I still run a small studio in Hamburg, which is equipped with an optical printer, and where people like Hellmuth Costard, Heinz Emigholz, Werner Nekes, Klaus Wyborny, and others, come to work—all names connected with the Hamburg group of filmmakers which dominated the realm of avant-garde film in the 1960s and into the 1970s.

The fact that my own range of activities is so varied and my filmic output not easy to classify made me feel from the start that I was always straddling two chairs. But since then, I've come to appreciate my peculiar position—it turns out to be a rather advantageous vantage point for an overview of the so-called "New German Cinema."

I came to the decision to become a filmmaker while I was a "habitué" of the Cinémathèque Française in Paris at the end of the 1950s. I went there on a scholarship as a young art student, but soon I began neglecting painting to go to the Cinémathèque, which, at the time, was just a few steps away from where I lived, in the Rue d'Ulm. It was there that I discovered German films of the pre-1933 period. I saw Das Cabinet des Dr. Caligari (The Cabinet of Dr. Caligari) for the first time and the films of Fritz Lang, was deeply impressed by the early films of Luis Buñuel (L'Age d'Or, Un Chien Andalou, Las Hurdes) and the films of the French avant-garde, and decided to make films myself—personal films, the kind I had seen for the first time on the screen at the Cinémathèque. When I went back to art school in Hamburg with this idea of filmmaking, I found myself totally alone. No art school at the time had any such thing as a film department—no cameras or film screenings, no books about or any interest in film. My fellow students proudly carried around their color-smeared paint kits and looked at me like some kind of oddball. At the time, West Germany had no film schools, just film clubs at the universities, like the one at the University of Hamburg attended by Hellmuth Costard and Klaus Wyborny.

The film industry at that time was a "closed shop," firmly controlled by the old Ufa generation. There never was a cultural rebirth of the West German film industry after the war. After a while, the one-time Ufa collaborators began again to make films in just about the same way as before, as reflected in the films' aesthetic qualities; and since the Cold War prevailed at the time, very soon the old political viewpoints emerged as well. The only exception was Wolfgang Staudte, who came to West Germany after directing *Rotation* (1949) and *Die Mörder sind unter uns* (*The Murderers Are among Us,* 1946) for DEFA in East Berlin. The German industrial and public relations film which flourished during these years found itself firmly in the hands of the one-time cronies from the propaganda companies which, among other things, produced the Nazi newsreels. They had taken their Arriflex cameras home with them after the war and received lucrative assignments from their old comrades now in the P.R. departments of industry. Those were the famous gold-rush days of the industrial film. Their official representative was the German Culture Film Producers Association (*Deutscher Kulturfilm-Produzentenverband*), one of whose functionaries in Hamburg, a certain Herr Obscherningkat, had signed "certificates of approval" as a member of the Nazi Ministry of Film.

I decided to seek out my friends and confederates among the television people. My friend, documentary filmmaker Klaus Wildenhahn, who at the time was starting his career at NDR, North German Broadcasting, the Hamburg television station, introduced me to Gert von Paczensky. Paczensky gave me the chance to make short animated sequences and also to draw animated political cartoons for the new television magazine show *Panorama*—such things were possible in those pioneer days. I rented an old Ernemann wooden camera from the twenties that had a silent film aperture—without registration pins, and consequently, very poor frame registration. After a while I was able to replace it with an Askania camera.

I made short satirical films for the satirical magazine show, *Hallo Nachbarn* (*Hello Neighbors*). That's how I came to make my film *Schwarz-Weiss-Rot* (*Black-White-Red,* 1963), for instance. But by 1965, that was all over. Paczensky had to leave the station—his flippant style of commenting on official Bonn politics was considered much too "biased." And shortly thereafter, *Hello Neighbors* was simply canceled just prior to broadcast, another sacrifice to the television ideal of political "impartiality." I haven't done any political commentary in animated film form for German television since then. This brings to mind a few other general observations. The kind of political cartoons found in every average newspaper does not seem to be translatable into animated political cartoons for television. Even the hidden caricatures of Hoyer in the top-rated pop music broadcasts were quickly discovered and taken off the air as a bad influence. The intolerant attitude of the television stations (and this is not only in the Federal Republic) toward critical political caricatures can be simply explained. It was felt that they would bring about the collapse of the whole balancing act of quasi-objective impartiality in the way they clarify political situations in unexpected ways and make fun of the establishment.

There arose a very impressive group of new filmmakers of short films—among them Alexander Kluge, Hans Rolf Strobel, Heinrich Tichawsky, and the Schamoni brothers, Peter, Thomas, and Ulrich, who, in 1962, in the so-called Oberhausen Manifesto, declared their intention to create a new German dramatic film. They looked to the French New Wave and adopted the battle cry, "Papa's cinema is dead!" By that time, Dr. Alexander Kluge was already something of a control center for a new film politics, and he was its incredibly active architect, functioning with equal success both in front of and behind the scenes.

New filmmakers also arose in Hamburg; Franz Winzentsen, today the most renowned creator of animated films, worked with me for eight years at my Cinegrafik Studio. He, Hellmuth Costard, Tom Struck, Klaus Wyborny, and others came out of the Film Workshop (*Arbeitskreis Film*) at the University. Right from the start, the Hamburg filmmakers' attitude toward filmmaking differed from that of their Munich colleagues, who had called for the take-over of feature film production. In Hamburg, there was a distinction from the outset between "*Kino*" and "*Film*"—the way one differentiates between the publishing business and literature. While the Munich group eventually took over the German film industry, this movement to revive the feature film bypassed Hamburg. The film of personal expression, the short film, the experimental film, and radical political and aesthetic expression are hard to realize in feature film—and there was neither money nor sponsors for feature-length films in Hamburg. Thus, Hamburg became, by the end of the 1960s, the continental center of avant-garde or "underground" films, as they were called at the time.

Nineteen sixty-seven was a significant year. Dore O. and Werner Nekes came to Hamburg and encountered the Hamburg group, which at the time published its own film newspaper, *Filmartikel*. P. Adams Sitney presented a major show of "New American Cinema," and, for the first time, we saw the films of Stan Brakhage, Andy Warhol, Robert Nelson, Gregory Markopoulos, Jonas Mekas, etc. We were inspired, felt validated, and founded our own Hamburg Filmmakers Cooperative that same year to distribute our films and those of our American and English friends. The New Year, 1968, saw a whole surge of new German independent filmmakers at the Film Festival in Knokke.

Then in February, we had our own festival of independent films in Hamburg—the first "Hamburg Filmschau." The films and the "happenings" of the Vienna Action group made the public's head spin. Hellmuth Costard and Tom Struck received first prize for their film, *Der warme Punkt (The Hot Dot)*.

That same year, we targeted the Oberhausen Short Film Festival for a decisive confrontation with the dominant film culture. We were convinced that we were now in a position to bring about that break with the cinema of the past which did not occur in 1945. We managed to raise havoc at the Festival with a successful boycott. Until then, Oberhausen had been a festival of established 35mm short film production. Now, in flowed a new wave of politically and aesthetically radical 16mm films by previously unknown filmmakers. We used Costard's film, *Besonders wertvoll (Particularly Noteworthy, 1968)* as the battering ram with which to open the floodgates. We said, "You have to swallow this film"—which, given the prevailing attitudes at the time was highly shocking, even pornographic—"or risk a boycott." The boycott was successful and Oberhausen became a different festival. This moment was the high point of the Filmmakers Cooperative's film political effectiveness. Rosa von Praunheim, Wim Wenders, Werner Schroeter, and many others joined in.

In the third issue of *Filmartikel*, I attempted to define this new cinema as consisting of five categories, under the heading of "Das andere Kino" (The Other Cinema):

1. Films with a large measure of innovation which do not accommodate the traditional viewing habits of the film consumer.
2. Political films, which, because of their critical stance toward the establishment heretofore had no chance.
3. Films indifferent to so-called middle-class morality.
4. Films that have previously been classed within the realm of the visual arts.
5. Films that, because of their unusual technical characteristics (for instance, 8mm films, multi-screen projection, multimedia, etc.) require a new marketing set-up.

With a beautiful, naïve gesture of overestimation, we actually believed for a moment that we would be able to strip away the old film culture from the Federal Republic like an old skin. I still did not see myself as an avant-garde or experimental filmmaker—basically, as always, I was straddling two chairs, since, for many of the newcomers, I was too commercial.

The Cooperative soon came up against the limits of its commercial viability—it was never given so much as a penny of support from the government or municipal offices for its distribution work. In any case, this union of politically and aesthetically radical films was not to prevail in the long run. Soon, the "Socialist Filmmakers Cooperative" broke off from us. In 1975, the Hamburg Filmmakers Cooperative was officially laid to rest, and its films were entrusted to the care of the Berlin *Freunde der Deutschen Kinemathek.*

In 1969, I made a film about Dadaism in Germany in the 1920s and learned in doing so that things happened in much the same way with the Dadaists. It occurred to me that there was some law of culture that runs through history: in a time of cultural and political upheaval, radical political and aesthetic activity go hand-in-hand for a while, as they did in 1918 and 1968; people work together because they hope for something new and great to come out of it. That's how it was for Arp and Huelsenbeck, Grosz, and Heartfield, who worked together during the famous first Dada period. Then—one goes off and joins the Communist party, and the others go into the artistic cloister.

The magic word that set us soaring at that time was *Veränderung* (change)—changing the way of seeing, changing society. That's why Werner Nekes picked up a 16mm projector in his hands and projected his flicker film *Schnitte für ABABA* (*Cuts for ABABA*, 1967) directly into the audience—to "open up their eyes." We wanted to change society through some kind of cultural revolution, to have new sensations for the eye and for the mind. All that ended when the Socialist Film Co-op broke away. I remember how it happened, in a restaurant on the *Autobahn* on our way to the festival in Mannheim where Werner Nekes and I met Alfred Hilsberg, who managed the Co-op at that time.

At the same time, the Munich filmmakers got their impetus from the Film Co-op. The cultural climate had decisively altered, but none of us from the Hamburg group really "profited" from this. In Munich, Wim Wenders followed his 16mm experimental films with larger projects. I remember one afternoon when I visited him in the cutting room at the Bavaria Studio, where he was working on his feature film, *Der scharlachrote Buchstabe* (*The Scarlet Letter*, 1972). He was having a bit of a hard time and said he was going to go back to the Co-op method of making "dirty 16mm films." It is surely no loss that he didn't do that.

The fact that the New German feature cinema did not emerge in

Hamburg is certainly not only due to the fact that the producers and the money weren't available here. There was also a very basic kind of opposition in Hamburg to the story-telling methods that had evolved in American movies. Klaus Wyborny, the avant-garde filmmaker and film instructor, provided a brilliant analysis of these American movies, films with which he, like so many others, was involved in a kind of love-hate relationship.

In 1969, I went to work as an instructor at the German Film and Television Academy in Berlin and stayed until 1979—ten years, during which I only sporadically worked on my own films. Berlin is the third center of the New German Cinema, and just as different from Munich as Hamburg. The so-called Berlin *Arbeiterfilme* (worker films) of Marianne Lüdcke, Ingo Kratisch, Christian Ziewer, and Max Willutzki were conceived from the perspective of the outraged, not of the establishment. They wanted to show the working world that heretofore had been neglected in postwar German film, so they filmed in factories and the grim concrete suburb, the *Märkische Viertel*. The image sticks in my mind of a certain bright, overstated carpet in all the workers' apartments, an image that perhaps relates to my impression that the claims these films made were also a bit overstated.

The Berlin Film Academy began its work in 1966, and in 1968 was so shaken to its foundation by a "palace revolt" of students that it threw its rigid structure overboard and opened up to student co-governorship. Eighteen student activists who had been expelled soon formed the core of the new Berlin filmmakers. Klaus Wildenhahn, who got me my job on Paczensky's *Panorama*, also brought me to Berlin in 1969. I was the first instructor appointed with the students' participation. The students had only a one-third voice in the appointment of instructors and the admission of new students. Yet, the utopian ideal of a free, independent academy, out of which, in one great common effort, a new aesthetically and politically radical German film would arise, evaporated very quickly in petty infighting among dogmatic political factions. Thus, one came to terms by choosing new students according to an "average" sampling, measured by Socialist Worker standards: of course, no one was admitted who was not highly talented, but also excluded were those obsessed with film—the "colorful birds," as they were called. This is why, for example, neither R. W. Fassbinder nor Helma Sanders-Brahms were accepted by the Film Academy. I had already made a whole series of political films and found myself at the Academy in the position of defender of the personal filmmakers, the more or less "crazy" and film-possessed. For ten years I tried to negotiate an integration of radical politics and radical aesthetics in filmmaking, but I have to admit that I lost that struggle.

In 1969, I started teaching special effects and animation; film history and basic film technology were added later. I utilized the wonderful film collection of the *Deutsche Kinemathek*, which was housed in the same building with its library and collection of early film apparatus, to get to know the early history of German cinema as a function of the contradictory interdependence of technical and aesthetic invention. At that time, we didn't have much in common with the films of the Ufa period, and if we were rejecting our fathers, we at least wanted to know as much as possible about how our grandfathers made films. Behind all this for me was the issue of a new definition of professionalism in filmmaking. A model for this was the famous cameraman of the earliest silent film period, Guido Seeber, who had made films since 1896 and died in 1940 while head of the special effects department of Ufa in Berlin. He was not only the highly regarded cameraman of Asta Nielsen films and of *Der Student von Prag* (*The Student of Prague*, 1913), and *Die freudlose Gasse* (*The Joyless Street*, 1925), but during his whole life he remained the film pioneer he was in those early years: technician, inventor, special effects specialist, filmmaker—all in one person. In addition, he became the first to formulate a history of film technology in his books and approximately one thousand articles, and with his "Kipho-Film," he became one of the first German avant-garde filmmakers. I owe Guido Seeber a great deal. The *Kinemathek* organized an exhibition for his one-hundredth birthday in 1979 and published a book about him. I have made a film about him, called *Synthetischer Film oder wie das Monster King Kong von Fantasie und Präzision gezeugt wurde* (*Synthetic Film, or How the Monster King Kong Was Born of Fantasy and Precision*, 1975). My second feature film, which I have planned for 1985, also owes something to my research about him.

I made my way back to Hamburg in 1979 in order to get back to making more films. Something new was happening in Hamburg at this time—a fresh upsurge of independent filmmaking. The makers of New German films gathered at the Hamburg Film Festival, an independent film festival sponsored by the City of Hamburg and its Mayor Klose. Under the coordination of Alexander Kluge, they composed a manifesto which said:

We will not allow ourselves to be divided
—the feature film from the documentary film,
—experienced filmmakers from newcomers,
—films that reflect on the medium (in a practical way as experiments) from the narrative and commercial film.

This manifesto was signed by nearly every well-known German filmmaker, Fassbinder, Herzog, and Hauff among others, and it marked

the beginning of a new form of film subsidy controlled by the filmmakers
themselves—the so-called Hamburg plan. According to this plan, the
City of Hamburg places three million marks on a yearly basis at the
disposal of the Hamburg Film Bureau. We converted an old three-story
screw factory into a film center with offices, cutting rooms, and meeting
rooms, installed the most essential sound and special effects equipment,
and a restaurant as a gathering place for the filmmakers. In the meantime, a second self-sufficient film center has been established in the state
of North Rhine–Westphalia in the Federal Republic, and other regional
film subsidy systems are in preparation. Filmmaking activity in the
Federal Republic of Germany since the end of the 1960s would have been
limited to a few major productions if it had not been for government
support. In the course of a year, and not without the efforts of Alexander
Kluge and the *Verband Neuer Deutscher Spielfilmproduzenten* (Association
of New German Feature Film Producers), a rather intricate system of
various funding committees was established, to be fed with government
money, money to be raised at the box office, and money from the
television networks. Then came other regional film industry–oriented
subsidies from the cities of Munich and Berlin. However, in the course of
that year, these committees also gave rise to a new power elite: film critics
and cultural office functionaries, who traveled through the country with
their little black attaché cases and their judgments, which we felt did not
take into account the real potential and needs of the filmmaker and the
public. The resources at the disposal of the Hamburg Film Bureau make
up only about 4 percent of the entire film subsidy budget, but we believe
that, with our films and our film political work, we have an important
function. This is especially true now because in this year, 1983, the
opportunities available from the government committees have been reduced even further since the new CSU Minister of the Interior Friedrich
Zimmermann in Bonn has come down with a hard line against undesira-
ble filmmakers. The case of Herbert Achternbusch is probably familiar to
you. After the sweeping measures applied by the Minister to the film
subsidy system, which is under his jurisdiction, Achternbusch's film
Wanderkrebs (*Wandering Cancer*, 1983) could only be produced with the
help of Hamburg film subsidy money. We are afraid that the *Autorenfilm*,
films by "troublesome" filmmakers like Achternbusch, Schroeter, Elfi
Mikesch, and others, will disappear for the sake of international
coproductions and Zimmermann's "good entertainment film."

Jack Lang, France's Minister of Culture, who is said to be very much
interested in New German Cinema, is anticipating future competition for
a share of the international media market. He has a plan for encouraging
creative endeavor in France, and for expanding support for film culture,
including conventional film distribution, in order to secure a future for

the *Autorenfilm* in the forthcoming competition with major American companies. He believes that this is the only way to ensure the survival of European film culture. And I agree with him.

This is an expanded version of Herbst's keynote address held at the conference, "Style and Ideology in New German Cinema, 1962–83," on 7 December 1983 at the CUNY Graduate Center.—For an account of more recent work from Hamburg, see Joyce Rheuban's report, "Secret Life: New Films by Hamburg Filmmakers," Millennium Film Journal, no. 13 (Fall/Winter 1983–84): 46–61.

85. Alexander Kluge
Pact with a Dead Man (1984)

There at the podium of the CSU hearing on film policy stands Minister of the Interior Friedrich Zimmermann and tells stories for an hour: the German film in the throes of its deepest decline. This is true because it is in the New Year's issue of *Stern*. The Minister has to intervene. One reason for the decline, the German film's loss of popularity, is the "self-realization" that is tantamount to "self-gratification." This is harmful. Van Gogh, for example, who needed only a brush and a piece of canvas for his "self-realization," needed to sell but one oil painting during his lifetime. For the German film, the Minister informs his audience, it is different, because every can of film costs a substantial amount. That is the industrial side of film which rules out the obsessive quality characteristic of works of art and witches.

The Minister's presentation is defensive, energetic. The sentences are clipped, the tone authoritarian. As you learn in speech class: each sentence contains *one* thought. Then a pause. Then one more sentence, with great decisiveness. Each of the sentences is, taken by itself, something to which the uninitiated listener would nod his head. This rhetorical technique corresponds to nearly complete ignorance. Nothing the Minister says during this hour has a thing to do with anything I am familiar with in German film production. I found nothing factual in the insipid New Year's article in *Stern* about why German culture, and film especially, is in bad shape in 1983. I might be more tolerant if I had not been hearing the same kind of nonsense about the *difference* between *economics* and *ability* for twenty years now.

My impression: we are not there for the Minister to practice on us. One will have noticed that neither I nor my colleagues (neither Fassbinder, for example, nor Costard, neither Helke Sander nor Margarethe von Trotta, and so on) fall back on culture or artistic quality in an affirmative sense. There is one thing that triggers our attack: negative culture politics. Whoever (with 1 percent chance in the marketplace against 99 percent impossibility that on the free market ability can win out over money) uses political financial support measures to distort competition against this 1 percent—they can be sure that we will take countermeasures.

The Minister also has a retinue. Eighty percent of what he asserted as fact regarding film stems from the whispered promptings of this retinue. Now, for example, the President of the Head Organization of the Film Industry (*Spitzenorganisation der Filmwirtschaft*), which represents the American films. He exaggerates mightily: it is the very "pinnacle of liberality" that the Minister himself is here to listen to discussion of his decree. Next is the representative from the Conference of Bishops: what a liberal Minister this is, how profound to hear his cultural word. . .

More energetic is the President of the Film Theater Guild (*Hauptverband der Filmtheater*). He is not content to watch the Minister convert the last little bit of cultural support into economic support. According to the film theaters, the Ministry of the Interior is responsible for the New German Film. These German films ought to be cleared out of the movie market and out of the economic support clause of the Film Subsidy Law. In this regard, says the President, a "hard-nosed economic law" is the order of the day. Hans Jürgen Syberberg answers: the German film theaters are a sham facade for the idea of cinema. Film history does not take place in these viewing rooms. There is no room for it in these minitheaters divided up into their A, B, C, D, E, F, and G stink-hovels. Syberberg: the motion picture theaters' absolute indifference toward film and toward an audience interested in film history guarantees the continued sorry state of German cinema. Following that: angry shouting among the panel.

Meetings like these hold us back. In the future, we directors will refuse to take part in these discussions (they have been going on uninterrupted for twenty years; newcomer Zimmermann only joined in 1983) because of their falseness. We advise our colleagues in the press to search their consciences. It is impossible to demand that in every concrete situation we repeat like prayer wheels every standpoint. There are such public spheres comprised of communiqués; that is not our kind of public sphere.

Whether a film is good or bad cannot be discerned based on the number of tickets sold. Murnau's *Sunrise* was a so-called box office failure. But this film was re-released in 1984. In that sense, it has been seen by substantially more viewers over the years than the most popular film of 1929. Two more points here: I for one would not like to be a part of a film history that has no *Sunrise*. And I never assume my audiences have lesser wishes than I do. As Brecht says: "There are effective films that have an impact on people who see them as kitsch, but there are no effective films made by people who see them as kitsch."

This attitude, which at least the author-filmmakers among us maintain *under all circumstances,* and which therefore cannot be suppressed by any Minister of the Interior nor by the renewal of the legal weepy cartel planned by the Minister's film industry retinue, this attitude has been lustily denounced for the past twenty years, as long as it has been among us, denounced as misanthropic, hostile to the audience. In fact just the opposite is true: we say: "The film takes on its existence in the spectator's head"; "Spectators are the producers of their own experience." In every spectator there lies ability. So it is misanthropic in reverse if we do not expect anything of them. It is misanthropic to speculate with spectators *à la baisse.*

Hans Richter, *Der Kampf um den Film* (*The Battle over Film,* 1929): "The inferiority of most films is explained by pointing out that the audience *wants* bad films, the producers would go bankrupt if they did not obey the dictates of the public, etc. It is undeniable that the public at large finds much pleasure in bad films. But, fortunately, such a sweeping analysis of the audience is inaccurate. Because, on the one hand, the audience is just as diverse as our society itself and contains positive and negative forces, constructive and destructive ones, those that seek truth and those that do not want to see the truth, progressive and reactionary ones. On the other hand: *everyone constantly takes in stimuli—on the street, in the office, in the subway—and he constantly processes those stimuli. This ability to process things receives no meaningful challenges in the cinema.*"

The main point of contention for our opponents in 1983 was: the share of German films in the total revenue of movie theaters has dropped to 5 percent. How one distorts and distracts can be illustrated by this one example. That argument has no factual basis. Had it been a matter of fact, the conclusions that our opponents draw from it would still be false. (When I say *we,* I mean Hans Richter, Fassbinder, film history, others who have passed away, my colleagues, the spectators, hence: all the good guys, et al.).

The box office figures, disseminated since the summer of 1983 by the Press Secretary of the Ministry of the Interior, did not originate at the Ministry. They were passed along covertly by the Head Organization of the Film Industry. They also put the 3,000 film theater owners in a rebellious mood. It is an argument quite in keeping with the new political climate. All journalists, including radio and TV (most recently the evening news program, *Tagesthemen*, on January 28, 1984), accept this obscure 5 percent as fact. A lack of curiosity. A lack of professionalism. . .

When people started talking about this 5 percent in March 1983, it caught my attention. It was the same *key* (I have stopped listening to the content of our opponents' speeches, I just listen for the variations between C minor and A-flat major, listen in other words for the degree of hysteria, and that tells me for what the bells toll) as when the Film Subsidy Law was renewed in 1979. In the second half of the year, ticket sales for *Die flambierte Frau* (*Woman in Flames*), *Die Supernasen* (*The Super Noses*), and *Kehraus* (*Clean Sweep*) increased sharply. But there was no change in the bureaucrats' tears of woe: German films down to 5 percent share of the market. In October a professional checked the figures for us. Every journalist has access to these figures since they appear in the magazine *Filmecho*. According to those figures, the market share of German films in October was 24.5 percent. The average for the year was 11 percent.

Assuming it were not a falsehood but a fact: then a decline in the German film's share of the market to 5 or even 1 percent would mean that one would have to come up with something to raise the percentage. It must never be taken to mean: now we should clear away the remains of German-language film and replace them with American bookings.

Film history is ninety years old. During this entire period there have been repeated crises where film audiences dried up because filmmakers produced monocultures that drove away *those* spectators who had *other* interests. So, for example, *Jaws*, when it is the only film in town, drives away all interested spectators who are not interested in sharks, while it fills the house with people who are interested in pleasurable anxiety.

But the most frequent reason why people stop going to the cinema is not a matter of film production but rather the consequence of *cinemas* that develop a monoculture. It is easy to show that our country has a stable, interested audience, but that at the moment this audience does not comprise a majority in our cinemas. The same films that only reach the art houses reach viewers two years later when they are shown on television, not to mention the screenings in communal cinemas, non-commercial sites, and so on. In this regard: the majority of New German films continue to be seen by a majority audience. Interestingly, this is particularly true of films that are daring, banned, and—in matters of film language—risqué.

In the U.S.A. there is a much larger gap between film language and audience tastes. It was not clearly predictable that Fassbinder's *Berlin*

Alexanderplatz would be chosen film of the year at the end of 1983 (by *Time*). After all: it is fifteen hours long; it was considered a failure among viewers, too dark—as the Springer press wanted us to believe. But something does not become film of the year without the viewers having a say. (In the future I will never repeat this defensive line of argument: "Look to New York." It is a wretched state of affairs that we have to explain and justify, again and again, in semiannual rhythm, why we exist.)

There is a *genuine* crisis in the cinemas and thus for film production. I can only discuss this in the terms Oskar Negt and I use, since there has been no public discussion of this on a practical level. The crisis does not just concern film. Nor just the media. If we look at the hierarchy of the buildings in the city centers, shopping mall–oriented pedestrian zones—in the completed construction which our cities will take on in the twenty-first century—then we come closer to the heart of the matter.

A crushing majority of people—city dwellers, country folk, working population, private persons—are losing their status as producers. That part of human qualities which becomes consumer categories, making the person a retiree, so to speak, by age six, getting the majority of people's internal votes. I am not just talking about the loss of workplaces in the business world but the loss of one's social workplace, occupied by what classical usage refers to as the subjective identity (also known as soul). The crisis, then, lies in the *production of experience*. Without looking closely one can therefore safely predict: this will always become a crisis in *the production of public sphere*: loss of public sphere.

At this point the imagination becomes on the one hand terroristic, on the other defensive. As a "terrorist of my experience," I want to retain the whole world of affects and effects. *Carmen*, love with knife thrusts, refunctionalization of opera, political theater, taking office and leaving it again. I am the *terroristic consumer*. I hope I do not have to explain to anyone why this is an unpractical mixture: it explodes or implodes. When it implodes, it *seems* as if nothing were happening. This is the defensive, passivistic side of the crisis. When all media users, consumers of their experience, are certain to remain passive, any of society's gangs of bandits can take over.

"The danger is not that people run wild, the danger is that they become stultified."

The way people are pre-programmed to be inactive is the basis for an aggressive society. This multipolarity: it looks innocuous, passive, magnetizes itself into an aggressive whole, corresponds to the tendency toward *replacing* the classical, critical public sphere (more or less an idea, but occasionally something real) with advertising and media corporations. The public sphere is expropriated. As in the Middle Ages, when the shared communal plot must be taken from the peasants first, and then the lords can take over the peasant's fields as well. This sort of expropriation, but now applied to the internal ecologies of the human consciousness. Until now one found there a threefold organization: (1) what I myself feel, but cannot explain to anyone else; (2) what authorities, parents, law, and war demand of me; (3) what I understand of all this and am able to discuss with others (= "public sphere").

In the process of this expropriation the most powerful group in society consists of: the *incompetence* already built into the institutions of the public sphere: the public institutions do not really know how to deal with images, shaping their programs along "broadcasting" lines instead, and this is intensified when the Ludwigshafen consortium lets loose the MBA's from the companies and the word-moderators from the news-papers 1:1 upon the new (visual) media. In this way incompetence is piled upon incompetence. And nowhere is there even a little time for learning processes, for development, and so on. It never really comes to life. Like something dead with an effect on people, it will inflict vio-lence. Then people will say that the living being defending itself is the source of the violence. This process of distorted argumentation is not new to us either.

This is the context surrounding the housecleaning measures meant to eliminate the New German Film. It is not that we (i.e., Hans Richter, Fassbinder, others who have passed away, and so on) are afraid of Interior Minister Zimmermann in any way worth mentioning. He does not know us at all, holds the purse strings for five million marks (and that only as long as he is able to maintain a majority coalition in the *Bundestag* which will support an objectively reactionary film policy) and finally: in the course of an average day he has so much to do with police, border patrol, the constitution, undercover operations, sports, etc., that he does not have the time for really intensive combat. The danger comes rather from those he raises his trumpet to please. The same people, who, under the safety of his shadow, really assert the combative measures. They are bureaucrats, lawyers with lots of time, lots of combative interest, because they are paid for it; but also with lots of impartiality, because they make no films.

What the Minister introduced into the public discussion, through his Press Speaker or in person, are in fact plain lies. Since the Minister and his office barely know the New German Film, these are not even *his* lies. The situation is clear and can lead to no agreement whatsoever between the directors and the Minister. His attacks against the films *Das Gespenst (The Ghost)* and *Wanderkrebs (Wandering Cancer)*, both by

Herbert Achternbusch; *Verführung: Die grausame Frau (Seduction: The Cruel Woman)*, by Elfi Mikesch; and *Vietnamkinder (Vietnam Children)*, by Karin Braun; the preliminary guidelines; and (predictably) the jury for the West German Film Prize, all move in *one* direction: exclusion of critical, political films, exclusion of erotic experience, coordination of censorial bans to the last iota, the suppression of independent cinema.

At the same time a significant portion of the public sphere treats the standoff between the Minister and the directors as a sort of game of nerves. Professional journalists set the tone against German productions. Other journalists now step in line with the political change. In the shadow of all this, the film theaters make their move. Justified fears regarding the new media circulate among these ranks. The pecking order and hierarchy between the various theaters reinforce this sense of crisis. What ensues is an *export of problems:* the sole culprit for the crises in the cinemas is German film output, which certainly does not extend as far as the inner sanctum of these theaters!

We have seen that our arguments can clearly win over individual exhibitors without changing the group dynamics in the theater arena. So, after thorough discussion, we filmmakers arrive at the conclusion in all three regards—our dispute with the Minister, the dispute within the constraints of public opinion, and the dispute within the film branch—that objective reasoning, which we have tried in each case, has no effect whatsoever. We can no longer penetrate a thicket of lies and group dynamics: except by way of our films.

The campaigns against the New German Film have remained the same for twenty years: the audience does not want to see it, it is arrogant, elitist, ideological, laden with problems, protestant, gothic, lacking in wit, fit for the blind, incomprehensible, etc. This campaign continues regardless whether a given year produces films that prove just the opposite. In one year or another, something like all this supposedly was the case.

The evolution of New German Film took place in spite of government support, not because of it. One of the most blatant lies of the current campaign is the insinuation that government support was set up at the request of New German filmmakers or that support was being administered in their interest. The opposite is true.

Meanwhile, German-language films are being produced today only along the lines of the New German Film, since the few productions of the old film industry have started to operate in exactly the same way. What is on the march against German film production: (1) the system of dumping mothballed films via Beta-Film and PKS-Film in the new media; (2) the group dynamics of the film theaters that want to squeeze 60 percent of the German film production out of the film market and out of government support programs; (3) the lawyers and bureaucrats from the Film Subsidy Board and the church, who wish to see their conception of order maintained; here, in this context, is where we must see Minister Zimmermann with his conceptions of order and censorship.

In the confused situation described here, we have no suggestions to make. The act that is now beginning belongs to our adversaries. They must play it out. We lay claim to the intermission that will follow and the final act. We would be insane to let ourselves become participants or clowns in a further battle of words as long as we have the capacity to express ourselves in our films; if need be in collective productions. Now that the public sphere grows accustomed to hearing from us occasionally, we are concerned that we make our future plans clear: pay attention to the films, pay attention to what happens in the film market, pay attention to which lies are being disseminated. *Do not expect us to repeat yet again everything we have already said.*

Every public discussion comes to a conclusion. It is about that conclusion I made a pact with R. W. Fassbinder. Pacts made with the dead are particularly binding.

Kluge's concern about the transformation of public space and the city is the subject of his film Der Angriff der Gegenwart auf die übrige Zeit (*the English title is* The Blind Director).—*The wave of Carmen films, by Jean-Luc Godard, Francesco Rosi, and Carlos Saura, stimulated a debate between Kluge and Jutta Brückner about its socio-sexual significance. See* Ästhetik und Kommunikation, *nos. 53/54 (1984): Brückner's essay, "Carmen und die Macht der Gefühle," pp. 227–32; and Kluge's response, "Anmerkungen zu Jutta Brückner," 233–34.*

Sources

1. Released originally as the "Oberhausener Manifest."
2. Released originally as the "Mannheimer Erklärung."
3. Released originally as the "Hamburger Erklärung." The complete version of the document appears in *Filmfaust*, no. 16 (December 1979): 43–44.
4. Released originally as "Manifest der Filmarbeiterinnen."
5. Released originally as the "Protesterklärung der Filmemacher" at the Munich Film Festival.
6. "Was wollen die Oberhausener?", *Kirche und Film*, November 1962, pp. 2–4.
7. "Wir haben zu arbeiten," *Film*, January 1965, p. 21.
8. Excerpted from Vlado Kristl, *Sekundenfilme*, ed. Wolf Wondratschek (Frankfurt am Main: Suhrkamp, 1971), pp. 11–17.
9. "Brief an die Export-Union vom 28. Juli 1975," *Filmkritik*, September 1975, p. 432.
10. Issued as an open letter entitled "Wir leben in einem toten Land." Abridged version translated by Barrie Ellis-Jones as "We live in a dead land," *Framework*, no. 6 (Autumn 1977): 12–13.
11. "Abhängiges Arbeiten: Über Regie und Produktion," in *Jahrbuch Film 79/80*, ed. Hans Günther Pflaum (Munich: Hanser, 1979). Slightly abridged.
12. "Etwas über Natur und Zensur," *tip*, 26 October 1979, p. 39.
13. Recorded comments of Helke Sander published as "die herren machen das selber, daß ihnen die arme frau feind wird: ablehnungsgeschichten," *Frauen und Film*, no. 23 (April 1980): 14–18. Slightly abridged.
14. "Thesen III," in *Bestandsaufnahme: Utopie Film*, ed. Alexander Kluge (Frankfurt am Main: Zweitausendeins, 1983), pp. 540–41.
15. "Zimmermanns Hinrichtungslinien: Ein Protestbrief von Volker Schlöndorff, der zur Zeit an seinem Proust-Film *Eine Liebe von Swann* arbeitet," *Die Zeit*, 16 December 1983.
16. "Ich klage an," *berlinaletip*, no. 2 (21 February 1985): 3.
17. "'. . . lieber nackte Mädchen': Eckhart Schmidt über seinen ersten Spielfilm *Jet Generation*," *Film*, January 1968, pp. 32–33.
18. "Emotion Pictures (Slowly Rockin' On)," *Filmkritik*, May 1970, pp. 254–57.
19. Reprinted from the press booklet materials to *Liebe Mutter, mir geht es gut* (Basis-Film) as "The Origins of *Liebe Mutter, mir geht es gut*," trans. Scilla Alvarado, in Richard Collins and Vincent Porter, *WDR and the Arbeiterfilm: Fassbinder, Ziewer and others* (London: British Film Institute, 1981), pp. 154–56.
20. Filmmaker's statement on *Das andere Lächeln*, reprinted in *Kino 78*, ed. Robert Fischer and Doris Dörrie (Munich: Nüchtern, 1978), pp. 21–22.

21. "Entfernung aus der Sicherheit esoterischer Asthetik: Perspektiven für das kommende Filmjahr," in *Jahrbuch Film 77/78*, ed. Hans Günther Pflaum (Munich: Hanser, 1977), pp. 54–55.
22. Filmmaker's statement on *Die Vertreibung aus dem Paradies*, reprinted in *Kino 78*, ed. Robert Fischer and Doris Dörrie (Munich: Nüchtern, 1978), pp. 169–70.
23. "Nachruf: Peter komm zurück!," *berlinaletip*, 24 February 1978, p. 5.
24. "Das ist eine Utopie: Das Kino, von dem ich träume," in *Jahrbuch Film 79/80*, ed. Hans Günther Pflaum (Munich: Hanser, 1979), pp. 76–79. Slightly abridged.
25. "Die Utopie Film," in *Die Patriotin* (Frankfurt am Main: Zweitausendeins, 1979), pp. 294–95. Translated by Thomas Y. Levin and Miriam B. Hansen, in *New German Critique*, nos. 24–25 (Fall/Winter 1981–82): 209.
26. "Michael Curtiz—Anarchist in Hollywood? Ungeordnete Gedanken zu einer scheinbar paradoxen Idee," in *Filme befreien den Kopf*, ed. Michael Töteberg (Frankfurt am Main: Fischer, 1984), pp. 94–96.
27. "Kultur als harte Währung oder: Hollywood in Germany," *Medium*, February/March 1983, p. 55.
28. "Vom alten Zopf befreien," *Film*, February 1965, p. 18.
29. "Kelek," *Filmkritik*, February 1969, pp. 113–14. English translation by Sheila Johnston appeared in her monograph *Wim Wenders* (London: British Film Institute, 1981), pp. 42–43.
30. Published as "Die Liebe zum Land. Love of the Country," in Eva Orbanz, *Der Dokumentarfilmer Klaus Wildenhahn/The Documentary Film Maker* (Munich: Goethe-Institut, 1980), pp. 18–21.
31. "Whatever happens between the pictures," edited and introduced by David S. Lenfest, *Afterimage*, November 1977, pp. 7–13. Abridged.
32. "Nach dem Schwulenfilm," in *Sex und Karriere* (Reinbek bei Hamburg: Rowohlt, 1978), pp. 10–11.
33. "Nicht geordnete Notizen zum konventionellen narrativen Film," appeared originally in *Boa Vista* (Hamburg), no. 3 (1976); reprinted in *Filmkritik*, October 1979, pp. 447–63. Excerpt cotranslated by David Caldwell.
34. "feminismus und film: 'i like chaos, but i don't know, whether chaos likes me,'" *Frauen und Film*, no. 15 (February 1978): 5–10. Translated by Ramona Curry, in *Jump Cut*, no. 27 (1982): 49–50.
35. From *Die Patriotin* (Frankfurt am Main: Zweitausendeins, 1979), pp. 300–301. Translated by Thomas Y. Levin and Miriam B. Hansen, in *New German Critique*, nos. 24–25 (Fall/Winter 1981–82): 210–11.
36. "Some thoughts about our filmwork," reprinted in *The German Experimental Film of the Seventies*, ed. Ulrich Gregor (Munich: Goethe-Institut, 1980), unpaged. Slight editorial corrections.
37. "Filme von Frauen sind Spurensuche," *Kirche und Film*, April 1981, pp. 9–11. Translated by Antje Masten.
38. Diary entry dated May 1982, published in *Heller Wahn: Ein Film von Margarethe von Trotta*, ed. Hans Jürgen Weber (Frankfurt am Main: Fischer, 1983), pp. 103–104.
39. "Der Zwang zum Genrekino: Von der Gefährdung des Autorenkinos," *Courage*, April 1983, pp. 18–21.
40. "Nachträgliche Wortmeldung: Alfred Behrens verlangt den Europäischen Film urban," *Frankfurter Rundschau*, 15 July 1986. Abridged.
41. "Die andere Tradition: Volker Schlöndorffs *Der plötzliche Reichtum der armen Leute von Kombach* im Münchner Theatiner," *Süddeutsche Zeitung*, 8 February 1971.
42. "Sein [sic] Tod ist keine Lösung: Der deutsche Filmregisseur Fritz Lang," in *Jahrbuch*

Film 77/78, ed. Hans Günther Pflaum (Munich: Hanser, 1977), pp. 161–65. English translation by Sheila Johnston appeared in her monograph, *Wim Wenders* (London: British Film Institute, 1981), pp. 58–61.

43. "Der Wille zur Unterwerfung: Siegfried Kracauers epochale Untersuchung *Von Caligari zu Hitler* neu gelesen," *Frankfurter Rundschau*, 16 February 1980. Translated by Antje Masten.

44. From a discussion entitled "Arbeit in Ulm," in Klaus Eder and Alexander Kluge, *Ulmer Dramaturgien: Reibungsverluste* (Munich: Hanser, 1980), pp. 31–32.

45. "Aus dem Produktionstagebuch," entry dated 14 January 1982, in *Liebe zum Kino: Utopien und Gedanken zum Autorenfilm 1962–1983* (Cologne: KÖLN 78, 1984), pp. 178–81.

46. "Die Eisnerin, wer ist das?" published in *Film-Korrespondenz*, 30 March 1982, pp. I–II.

47. "Eingedenken," *epd Film*, February 1984, pp. 3–4.

48. "Wie ein Klassiker zum Video-Clip getrimmt wird," *Der Spiegel*, 25 February 1985, pp. 192–95.

49. "That's Entertainment: Hitler," *Die Zeit*, 5 August 1977. Abridged.

50. "*Deutschland im Herbst*: Worin liegt die Parteilichkeit des Films?" as reprinted in *Ästhetik und Kommunikation*, no. 32 (June 1978): 124.

51. "Der deutsche Film und die Wirklichkeit" is the first half of Fassbinder's essay "*Die dritte Generation*," *Frankfurter Rundschau*, 2 December 1978.

52. "Die Kamera ist keine Uhr: Erfahrung beim Erzählen von Geschichten aus der Geschichte," *Medium*, December 1979, pp. 30–31.

53. "Mein Führer—Our Hitler. Über die Bedeutung kleiner Worte," in *Die freudlose Gesellschaft: Notizen aus den letzten Jahren* (Frankfurt am Main/Berlin/Vienna: Ullstein, 1981), p. 109.

54. "Erlebte Geschichte," in *ARD-Fernsehspiel Juli August September 1984*, p. 120, 123. Translated by Antje Masten. Slightly abridged.

55. As rendered in *Sight & Sound*, Spring 1985, p. 125.

56. As rendered in *On Film*, no. 14 (Spring 1985): 37.

57. Filmmaker's statement to his film *Der wilde Clown*, in *internationale hofer filmtage 22.–26. oktober 1986* (festival brochure), pp. 186–88. Slightly abridged.

58. Basis-Film Verleih press booklet for *Zischke*, entry entitled "Oktober 1986," pp. 7–8. Slightly abridged.

59. "*Nashville*: Ein Film, bei dem man Hören und Sehen lernen kann," *Die Zeit*, 21 May 1976. Excerpt.

60. "Stellungnahme zu *Der Müll, die Stadt und der Tod*," *Frankfurter Rundschau*, 31 March 1976.

61. "An Wolfram Schütte," in *Es ist ein leichtes beim Gehen den Boden zu berühren* (Frankfurt am Main: Suhrkamp, 1980), p. 135.

62. "Meine Kritiker, meine Filme und ich," *Kirche und Film*, September 1980, pp. 9–13.

63. From *Die freudlose Gesellschaft: Notizen aus den letzten Jahren* (Frankfurt am Main/Berlin/Vienna: Ullstein, 1981), pp. 278–79.

64. "Antwort auf H. C. Blumenberg," *tip*, 9 September 1983, p. 11.

65. "Ein Unterdrückungsgespräch: Vorgeführt am Beispiel einer Diskussion zwischen Margit Carstensen und Rainer Werner Fassbinder," *Fernsehspiele Westdeutscher Rundfunk January–June 1974*, pp. 76–82.

66. "Einiges über Ernst," *ARD-Fernsehspiel Oktober November Dezember 1977*, pp. 160–64.

67. From "*Die Blechtrommel*": *Tagebuch einer Verfilmung* (Darmstadt/Neuwied:

Luchterhand, 1979), pp. 94–95.

68. Diary entry dated 10 April 1979, in *"Schwestern oder Die Balance des Glücks": Ein Film von Margarethe von Trotta*, ed. Willi Bär and Hans Jürgen Weber (Frankfurt am Main: Fischer, 1979), pp. 138–41.

69. "Die Erika aus Würzburg: Ein Porträt der Schauspielerin Magdalena Montezuma," *tip*, 6 November 1981, p. 43.

70. From *Wind* (Frankfurt am Main: Zweitausendeins, 1984), p. 41.

71. "Feuer," *epd Film*, February 1986, p. 21.

72. "Aufruf zur Revolte: Über *Besonders wertvoll* und *Chronik der Anna Magdalena Bach*," *Film*, April 1968, p. 1.

73. "*Red Sun*: Baby, you can drive my car, and maybe I'll love you," *Filmkritik*, January 1970, p. 9.

74. "Kino 78," in *Kino 78*, ed. Doris Dörrie and Robert Fischer (Munich: Nüchtern, 1978), pp. 9–11.

75. "Mit herzlichem Gruss an Champagne-Schroeter," *Filmkritik*, January 1979, pp. 2–5.

76. "Klimmzug, Handstand, Salto mortale—sicher gestanden. *Neapolitanische Geschwister* von Werner Schroeter," *Frankfurter Rundschau*, 24 February 1979.

77. "Eine Rose für Rainer Werner Fassbinder," *Süddeutsche Zeitung*, 10 December 1982. The text also appears as a prologue to Achternbusch's film, *Der Depp* (*The Fool*, 1982).

78. "Von Biest zu Biest: Rosa von Praunheim über neue Fassbinder-Bücher," *Der Spiegel*, 11 October 1982, pp. 244–48.

79. "Liebe zum Kino," in *Liebe zum Kino: Utopien und Gedanken zum Autorenfilm 1962–1983* (Cologne: KÖLN 78, 1984), pp. 7–8.

80. "Ein Traum," *Film*, January 1966, p. 37.

81. "Amerika: Bericht ans Goethe-Institut," in *Es ist ein leichtes beim Gehen den Boden zu berühren* (Frankfurt am Main: Suhrkamp, 1980), pp. 143–49. Translated as "America" by Marc Silberman in *semiotexte*, no. 11 (1982): 8–15.

82. "Gedanken zum Filmemachen in der Bundesrepublik Deutschland," *Filme*, no. 1 (1980): 20–23.

83. " 'New German Cinema, jeune cinéma allemand, gute Nacht'/Ein Tag in Oberhausen, 1982," *Kirche und Film*, December 1982, pp. 1–4.

84. "New German Cinema, 1962–83: A View from Hamburg," trans. Joyce Rheuban, *Persistence of Vision*, no. 2 (1985): 69–75.

85. "Verabredung mit einem Toten," *Konkret*, March 1984, pp. 82–87. Translated by David Ward.

Selected Further Readings

The following inventory provides additional approaches to topics broached in the various sections of this volume. Any attempt at a comprehensive listing of the publications of West German filmmakers since the early sixties would be a herculean task, demanding a bibliography of many more pages than the present context permits. The selections mean to stimulate discussion, to foster further explorations, and, above all, to suggest other important voices of West German film culture which considerations of space did not allow me to include.

I. MANIFESTOS AND DECLARATIONS

Koch, Krischan. *Die Bedeutung des "Oberhausener Manifestes" für die Filmentwicklung in der BRD*. Frankfurt am Main: Lang, 1985.

Lewandowski, Rainer. *Die Oberhausener: Rekonstruktion einer Gruppe 1962–1982*. Diekholzen: Regie, 1982.

II. THE PRICE OF SURVIVAL: INSTITUTIONAL CHALLENGES

Buschmann, Christel. "Das Kino wird im Keim erstickt: Stoffe, Drehbücher, Drehbuchautoren." *Jahrbuch Film 78/79*, ed. Hans Günther Pflaum, pp. 111–19. Munich: Hanser, 1978.

Costard, Hellmuth. "Sehr geehrte Herren." *Filmartikel*, no. 2 (December 1967): 6–8.

Ehmck, Gustav. "Ketzerisch-kritische Anmerkungen zum Gremienfilm." *Filmfaust*, no. 24 (October/November 1981): 58–59.

Erler, Rainer. "Autor-Regisseur-Produzent." *ARD-Fernsehspiel April Mai Juni 1979*, pp. 53–57.

Farocki, Harun. "Filmarbeit in der Provinz: Filmklassen an Kunsthochschulen." *Filmkritik*, February 1972, pp. 64–66.

Fassbinder, Rainer Werner. "Die traurigen Augen von Cannes." In *Filme befreien den Kopf*, ed. Michael Töteberg, pp. 119–20. Frankfurt am Main: Fischer, 1984.

Glowna, Vadim. *Desperado City. Wie ein Film entsteht*. Munich: Hanser, 1981.

Kluge, Alexander. "Ungeduld hilft nicht, aber Geduld auch nicht." *Film*, March 1967, p. 7; continued in *Film*, April 1967, p. 7.

————. "1980: Auf Lorbeeren kann man schlecht sitzen." In *Deutscher Filmpreis 1951–1980*, ed. Manfred Hohnstock and Alfons Bettermann, pp. 75–86. Bonn: Bundesminister des Innern, 1980.

Krieg, Peter. "Die entscheidende Instanz ist das Publikum. Zur Praxis der Filmförderung: Kritik und Veränderungsvorschläge." *Medium*, January–March 1986, pp. 7–11.

Kückelmann, Norbert. "Filmkunstförderung unter sozialstaatlichem Aspekt." *UFITA. Archiv für Urheber-Film-Funk und Theaterrecht.* Vol. 59 (1971), 115–51.

Lemke, Klaus. "Hoffen auf das Kuratorium: Auf die Regisseure kommt es an." *Film*, August 1965, p. 33.

Minow, Hans-Rüdiger. "Ideologisch entblösst. Über das Ende der Unschuld bei ARD und ZDF." *Medium*, September 1984, pp. 11–12.

Sanders-Brahms, Helma. "Kino als Industrie." *tip*, 12 August 1983, p. 9.

Senft, Haro. "'Ich emigriere nicht': Über Filmen und Filmpolitik in der Bundesrepublik." *Film*, February 1968, pp. 1, 6–7.

Tremper, Will. "Die Blütenträume welken." *Film*, February 1967, p. 7.

————. "Abschied vom jungen Film." *Film*, September 1967, p. 7.

III. POPULAR APPROACHES: GENERIC MODELS AND UTOPIAN DESIGNS

Achternbusch, Herbert. "Der Tag wird kommen. Eine Erzählung." *Süddeutsche Zeitung*, 28 April 1973. (On American westerns)

————. "Das Mumienherz. Über den japanischen Filmregisseur Akira Kurosawa oder: Wir müssen aufschreien, sonst finden wir uns morgen begraben." *Die Zeit*, 30 July 1976.

Bohm, Hark. "Arbeit, Männergruppen und Frauen: Zu den Filmen von Howard Hawks." *Jahrbuch Film 79/80*, ed. Hans Günther Pflaum, pp. 27–37. Munich: Hanser, 1979.

Brustellin, Alf. "Das Singen im Regen. Über die seltsamen Wirklichkeiten im amerikanischen Film-Musical." *Film*, December 1969, pp. 10–20.

Fassbinder, Rainer Werner. "Imitation of Life. Über Douglas Sirk." *Fernsehen und Film*, February 1971, pp. 8–13. English version trans. Thomas Elsaesser. "Fassbinder on Sirk." *Film Comment*, November/December 1975, pp. 22–24.

Geissendörfer, Hans W. "Brief an die Redaktion." *Fernsehspiele Westdeutscher Rundfunk Juli–Dezember 1971*, pp. 98–100. (On the making of the western *Carlos*)

Hauff, Reinhard. "Kommentar zu *Desaster*." *Fernsehspiele Westdeutscher Rundfunk Juli–Dezember 1973*, p. 49.

Herzog, Werner. "Faszination über ein Sterben. Australische Ureinwohner im Film." *Süddeutsche Zeitung*, 1 April 1978. (On the films *Floating* and *Lalai Dreamtime*)

————. "Vom Ende des Analphabetismus: Paolo und Vittorio Tavianis grosser Film *Padre Padrone*." *Die Zeit*, 24 November 1978.

Klick, Roland. "Die Selbstanzeige der jungen Filmemacher (3): Roland Klick." *Film*, April 1966, p. 33.

Noever, Hans. "*Der Preis fürs Überleben*: In Amerika einen Film machen—Ein Bericht aus der Erinnerung." *Jahrbuch Film 80/81*, ed. Hans Günther Pflaum, pp. 153–60. Munich: Hanser, 1980.

Pohland, Hansjürgen. "Moderne Unterhaltungsfilme." *Film*, February 1965, p. 17.

Schilling, Niklaus. "Von Düsseldorf bis Basel: Drehbuchschreiben in einem Zug: *Rheingold*." *Jahrbuch Film 77/78*, ed. Hans Günther Pflaum, pp. 55–60. Munich: Hanser, 1977.

Schlöndorff, Volker. "Mein erster Lehrer." In *Jean-Pierre Melville*, ed. Peter W. Jansen and Wolfram Schütte, pp. 7–14. Munich: Hanser, 1982. Trans. Robin Sanders and Günther Krumminga as "A Parisian-American in Paris." *Village Voice*, 6 July 1982, pp. 44–45.

Thome, Rudolf. "Surrealistische Komik." *Film*, June/July 1963, pp. 46–47. (Review of Frank Tashlin's *It's Only Money* and comments on film comedy in general)

Wenders, Wim. "Ein Genre, das es nicht gibt." *Filmkritik*, September 1970, pp. 489–91. Trans. Carla Wartenberg as "Pop/Rock Festival." In *Wim Wenders*, ed. Jan Dawson, pp. 30–31. Toronto: Festival of Festivals, 1976.

———. "Im Fernsehen: *Furchtlose Flieger.*" *Filmkritik*, June 1971, pp. 320–22. (On Veith von Fürstenberg and Martin Müller's 1971 film and Howard Hawks's *Only Angels Have Wings*)

IV. DIFFERENT WAYS OF SEEING

von Alemann, Claudia. "Das Dunkel am Ende der Treppe." *Frauen und Film*, no. 16 (June 1978): 5–9.

Bitomsky, Hartmut. *Die Röte des Rots von Technicolor*. Neuwied: Luchterhand, 1972.

Engstfeld, Axel. "Andere Filme entstehen lassen—Filmbüro NRW." In *Filmförderung—Entwicklungen/Modelle/Materialien*, p. 105. Munich: HFFM, 1985.

Engström, Ingemo. "Etwas über Schlussbilder und meine Liebe zum Kontinent." *Filmkritik*, March 1976, pp. 128–41.

Fechner, Eberhard. "Über das 'Dokumentarische' in Fernseh-Spielfilmen." *Akzente*, August 1973, pp. 310–20.

———. ". . . den kulturellen Auftrag nicht preisgeben!" *Medium*, June 1985, pp. 7–9.

Hübner, Christoph. "Das Dokumentarische als Haltung: Notizen zu einer Erneuerung des Films." *Medium*, August 1983, pp. 37–39.

Hübner-Voss, Gabriele. "Die Öffentlichkeit zu Gast: Überlegungen zu einer Erweiterung des dokumentarischen Blicks." In *Bilder aus der Wirklichkeit: Aufsätze zum dokumentarischen Film und Dokumentation*, ed. Werner Biederman and Angela Haardt, pp. 91–96. Duisberg: Stadt Duisburg/Filmforum der Volkshochschule, 1981.

Huillet, Danièle. "Appunti sul giornale di lavorazioni di Gregory." *Filmkritik*, September 1975, pp. 398–419. Rendered into English as "Notes on Gregory's Work Journal." *Enthusiasm*, December 1975, pp. 32–55. (On the making of *Moses und Aron*)

Krieg, Peter. "Fragen an meine Kollegen und mich selbst." *Medium*, December 1981, pp. 37–39.

———. "Ende oder Anfang? Thesen zum Dokumentarfilm." *epd Film*, October 1986, pp. 8–9.

Minow, Hans-Rüdiger. "Zur Organisierung des Films in der oppositionellen und revolutionären Arbeit." *Film*, March 1969, pp. 42–46.

Nestler, Peter. "Zusammenhänge." *Filmkritik*, May 1974, pp. 228–35. (On a film about Chile and its subsequent censoring in TV)

Sander, Helke. *DER SUBJEKTIVE FAKTOR, vertrackt*. West Berlin: Basis-Film, 1981. (On the reception of *The Subjective Factor*)

Schübel, Rolf. "Was mir so zu meinen Erfahrungen mit dem deutschen Fernsehen und dem Dokumentarfilm einfällt." *Rundfunk und Fernsehen*, no. 3 (1976): 272–78.

Senft, Haro. " 'Erziehung ist eine Tat der Liebe.' " *Jahrbuch Film 82/83*, ed. Hans Günther Pflaum, pp. 128–35. Munich: Hanser, 1982. (On films for children)

Stöckl, Ula. "Noch ein Super-8-Pamphlet." *Filmkritik*, December 1970, pp. 642–44.

———. "Von 'Markenzeichen' und anderen unklaren Begriffen: Filmemacherinnen re-
ferierten und diskutierten ihre Arbeit." *Film-Korrespondenz,* 21 May 1985, pp. 6–8.
Theuring, Gerhard. "Schnitt im Schnitt." *Filmkritik,* September 1972, pp. 454–74.
Wember, Bernward. *Objektiver Dokumentarfilm?* West Berlin: Colloquium, 1972.

V. DISCOVERING AND PRESERVING GERMAN FILM HISTORY

Achternbusch, Herbert. "Neues von Ambach. Anstelle eines Berichts über eine Retro-
spektive mit Karl-Valentin-Filmen im Münchner Stadtmuseum." *Süddeutsche Zeitung,*
24 July 1976.
Bitomsky, Hartmut. *"Der Geist des Films."* *Filmkritik,* October 1972, pp. 536–39. (On
Béla Balázs)
———. *"Lola Montez:* Die bezeichnende Lust und der bezeichnete Schmerz." *Filmkritik,*
June 1974, pp. 259–78.
Brustellin, Alf. "Kanon, ungeschützt." In *Bestandsaufnahme: Utopie Film,* ed. Alexander
Kluge, pp. 517–19. Frankfurt am Main: Zweitausendeins, 1983.
Herbst, Helmut. "Neugier." In *Das wandernde Bild: Der Filmpionier Guido Seeber,* ed.
Stiftung Deutsche Kinemathek, p. 6. West Berlin: Elefanten Press, 1979.
Kristl, Vlado. "Die Art des Sagens (über Karl Valentin)." *Kirche und Film,* January/
February 1983, p. 1.
———. " 'Für ein Festival der genialen Werke.' " *epd Film,* August 1984, p. 35.
von Praunheim, Rosa. *"Das Weib des Pharao* (1921)." In *Lubitsch,* ed. Hans Helmut
Prinzler and Enno Patalas, pp. 143–45. Munich/Lucerne: Bucher, 1984.
Sanders-Brahms, Helma. "Zarah." *Jahrbuch Film 81/82,* ed. Hans Günther Pflaum,
pp. 165–72. Munich: Hanser, 1981. (Tribute to Zarah Leander)
———. "Ein kleiner Mann: Anmerkungen zu einem deutschen Publikumsliebling."
Jahrbuch Film 82/83. Ed. Hans Günther Pflaum, pp. 52–60. Munich: Hanser, 1982.
(On Heinz Rühmann)
———. *"Madame Dubarry* (1919)." In *Lubitsch,* ed. Hans Helmut Prinzler and Enno
Patalas, pp. 132–36. Munich/Lucerne: Bucher, 1984.
Schroeter, Werner. *"Carmen* (1918)." Ed. Hans Helmut Prinzler and Enno Patalas,
pp. 129–31. Munich/Lucerne: Bucher, 1984.
Stöckl, Ula. "Appell an Wünsche und Traumbilder." In *Wir tanzen um die Welt: Deutsche
Revuefilme 1933–1945,* ed. Helga Belach, pp. 94–118. Munich: Hanser, 1979.
Straub, Jean-Marie and Danièle Huillet. "Straub and Huillet on Filmmakers They Like
and Related Matters." In *The Cinema of Jean-Marie Straub and Danièle Huillet,* ed.
Jonathan Rosenbaum, pp. 5–8. New York: Public Theater, 1982.
Thome, Rudolf. *"Sunrise."* *epd Film,* January 1984, p. 34.

VI. COLLECTIVE MEMORY AND NATIONAL IDENTITY

von Alemann, Claudia (with Dominique Jallamion and Bettina Schäfer), ed. *"Das
nächste Jahrhundert wird uns gehören."* *Frauen und Utopie 1830–1848.* Frankfurt am
Main: Fischer, 1984.
Behrens, Alfred (with Volker Noth). *Berliner Stadtbahnbilder.* 3d ed. Frankfurt am Main/
Berlin/Vienna: Ullstein, 1984.
Bitomsky, Hartmut. "Der Kotflügel eines Mercedes-Benz: Nazikulturfilme, Teil I: Filme

von 1933 bis 1938." *Filmkritik*, October 1983, pp. 443–73. "Teil II: Filme von 1939 bis 1945." *Filmkritik*, December 1983, pp. 543–81.

Brückner, Jutta. "Vom Erinnern, Vergessen, dem Leib und der Wut. Ein Kultur-Film-Projekt." *Frauen und Film*, no. 35 (October 1983): 29, 47.

Engström, Ingemo, and Gerhard Theuring. "Fluchtweg nach Marseille." *Filmkritik*, February 1978, pp. 66–97. Trans. Barry Ellis-Jones with introduction by Steve Neale and Paul Willemen as "Dossier: *Escape Route to Marseilles*." *Framework*, no. 18 (1982): 22–29, and no. 19 (1982): 40–45.

Farocki, Harun. "Zwischen zwei Kriegen." *Filmkritik*, November 1978, pp. 562–606.

Fleischmann, Peter. "Not a Film." Trans. Charlotte Vokes-Dudgeon. *Framework*, no. 12 (1980): 15. (On *Holocaust*)

Herzog, Werner. "Neun Tage eines Jahres." *Filmstudio*, no. 44 (September 1964): 19–21. (On Michail Romm's Soviet film)

Kluge, Alexander (with Oskar Negt). "Entwurf." In *Die Patriotin*, pp. 26–37. Frankfurt am Main: Zweitausendeins, 1979. (On the historical importance of the events surrounding the "German autumn" of 1977)

Kotulla, Theodor. "Sich erinnern und durcharbeiten: Einige Notizen zu *Aus einem deutschen Leben*." *Jahrbuch Film 78/79*, ed. Hans Günther Pflaum, pp. 85–94. Munich: Hanser, 1978.

Reitz, Edgar. "Statt *Holocaust*: Erinnerungen aufarbeiten!" *Medium*, May 1979, pp. 20–22.

Sanders-Brahms, Helma. "Exposé mit Vorrede. Geschrieben im Sommer 1976." In *Deutschland, bleiche Mutter*, pp. 9–11. Reinbek bei Hamburg: Rowohlt, 1980.

———. "Der Himmel war blau wie nie, als der Krieg zu Ende ging." In *Trümmer, Träume, Truman. Die Welt 1945–49*, pp. 9–12. West Berlin: Elefanten Press, 1985.

Schubert, Eberhard. "Naziblond—Oder: Das merkwürdige Eigenleben von Klischees, angetroffen bei der Arbeit an einem Film über Deutschland im Jahr 1932." *ARD-Fernsehspiel April Mai Juni 1979*, pp. 217–24. (On his film *Flamme empor*)

Syberberg, Hans Jürgen. "Die Kunst als Rettung aus der deutschen Misere: Ein Essay." In *Hitler, ein Film aus Deutschland*, pp. 7–60. Reinbek bei Hamburg: Rowohlt, 1978. Abridged translation by Joachim Neugroschel appeared in *Hitler, a Film from Germany*, pp. 3–22. New York: Farrar, Straus and Giroux, 1982.

———. "*Holocaust*: Indiz der grössten Krise unserer intellektuellen Existenz." *Medium*, April 1979, pp. 15–18. Translation by Barrie Ellis-Jones as "*Holocaust*, A Symptom of the Biggest Crisis in Our Intellectual Life," *Framework*, no. 12 (1980): 11–15.

VII. FILMMAKERS AND CRITICS

Brückner, Jutta. "Fördert Filmliteratur! Fördert Filmliteratur! Fördert Filmliteratur!" *epd Film*, September 1984, pp. 11–12.

Farocki, Harun. "Kreimeier lesen." *Filmkritik*, March 1974, pp. 103–8. (Regarding Klaus Kreimeier's book on postwar German film)

———. "Progreß und Prozeß." *Filmkritik*, November 1979, pp. 527–35. (Talk held before a meeting of film journalists)

Fassbinder, Rainer Werner. "Schütte: Von der Dialektik des Bürgers im Paradies der lähmenden Ordnung." In *Filme befreien den Kopf*, ed. Michael Töteberg, pp. 129–30. Frankfurt am Main: Fischer, 1984. (On the Frankfurt film critic, Wolfram Schütte)

Schlöndorff, Volker. "Bescheiden vor der Realität." *Der Spiegel*, 27 June 1966, pp. 97–98. (Review of Ulrich Gregor's *Wie sie filmen*)

Straub, Jean-Marie. "*Filmcritica*, Eisenstein, Brecht." *Filmkritik*, July 1973, pp. 300–303.

Syberberg, Hans Jürgen. "Film-Alltag." In *Syberbergs Filmbuch*. Munich: Nymphen-
burger, 1976, pp. 95–142.
———. *Die freudlose Gesellschaft: Notizen aus den letzten Jahren*. Munich: Hanser, 1981.
(See paragraphs 301 and 302 for Syberberg's thoughts about Susan Sontag)

VIII. DIRECTORS AND PLAYERS

Achternbusch, Herbert. "Zu Chaplin. Weg mit den Feuilletonstränen." *Frankfurter
Rundschau*, 25 February 1978. Trans. Ronald Holloway as "Achternbusch on Chaplin:
The Throne is Vacant." *Kino: German Film*, no. 1 (October 1979): 21–23.
Blumenberg, Hans-Christoph. "Der Mann im Bunker. Letzte Lieder der ersten Stunde—
Ein imaginäres Video zu Marius Müller-Westernhagens *Lausige Zeiten*." *Hallo!* (Ham-
burg), 4 March 1986, pp. 8–9.
Bühler, Wolf-Eckart. "Sterling Hayden. 26.3.1916–23.5.1986." *epd Film*, July 1986, pp.
8–9.
Fassbinder, Rainer Werner. "Hanna Schygulla. Kein Star, nur ein schwacher Mensch wie
wir alle." In *Hanna Schygulla. Bilder aus Filmen von Rainer Werner Fassbinder*, pp. 169–
87. Munich: Schirmer/Mosel, 1981.
Geissendörfer, Hans W. "Über Heinz Bennent." *Das Fernsehspiel im ZDF*, no. 4 (1974):
31.
——— and Angela Winkler. "Erinnerungen—ein Tagebuch zum Film." In *Ediths
Tagebuch. Erinnerungen, Essays, Personenbeschreibungen*, pp. 5–97. Munich: Nüchtern,
1983.
von Praunheim, Rosa. "Weibchen, Mutter und sympathische Schlange. Die skandalöse
Lebensgeschichte der Evelyn Künneke." *Mühldorfer Anzeiger*, 3 April 1975.
Reitz, Edgar. "20. April 1981." In *Liebe zum Kino: Utopien und Gedanken zum Autorenfilm
1962–1983*, pp. 152–57. Cologne: KÖLN 78, 1984. (On working with the actors of
Heimat)
Sanders-Brahms, Helma. "Hilde." *epd Film*, April 1985, pp. 7–8. (On working with
Hildegard Knef)
Syberberg, Hans Jürgen. "Warum Ufa-Stars? Anlässlich der Karl-May-Premiere (1974)."
In *Syberbergs Filmbuch*, pp. 224–25. Munich: Nymphenburger, 1976.
———. *Der Wald steht schwarz und schweiget. Neue Notizen aus Deutschland*, pp. 205–6.
Zürich: Diogenes, 1984. (On Edith Clever)
von Trotta, Margarethe, ed. *Wir—die Schauspieler*. Munich: Desch, 1969.
Wenders, Wim. "Alte Narben, neuer Hut: Eddie Constantine." *TWEN*, no. 10 (October
1970). Trans. Carla Wartenberg as "Eddie Constantine." In *Wim Wenders*, ed. Jan
Dawson, pp. 28–30. Toronto: Festival of Festivals, 1976.

IX. FILMMAKERS AND COLLEAGUES

Achternbusch, Herbert. "An die deutschen Filmbrüder." *Die Zeit*, 20 October 1978.
———. "Kluger Kluge." In *Wellen*, pp. 15–18, Frankfurt am Main: Suhrkamp, 1983.
von Alemann, Claudia. "Maulwurf, Löwenzahn und Pusteblume. Einige unzusam-
menhängende Gedanken zum Begriff 'Kollektiv.'" *Frauen und Film*, no. 8 (June 1976):
4–6.
Bitomsky, Hartmut. "Aufzeichnungen." *Filmkritik*, November 1979, pp. 522–25. (On
Alexander Kluge)
Brustellin, Alf. "Kino, nichts als Kino." *Film*, March 1968, pp. 28–29. (On Klaus
Lemke's *Negresco* ****-*Eine tödliche Affäre*)

————. "Bloss nicht schlafen." *Film*, April 1968, pp. 38, 41. (On George Moorse's *Der Griller*)

————. "Das Kino, ein Leben." *Film*, April 1969, p. 32. (On Rudolf Thome's *Detektive*).

Costard, Hellmuth. "Die unschuldige Frau." *Der Spiegel*, 21 November 1977. (On Peter Handke's *Die linkshändige Frau*)

Farocki, Harun. "*Schneeglöckchen blühn im September.*" *Filmkritik*, March 1975, pp. 138–39. (On Christian Ziewer and the *Arbeiterfilm*)

————. "Guten Tag, Herr Rossmann. Langsame Annäherungen an Haltungen und Sprache." *Die Zeit*, 1 July 1983. (On Straub/Huillet's *Klassenverhältnisse*)

Fassbinder, Rainer Werner. "Alexander Kluge soll Geburtstag gehabt haben." *tip*, 17 February 1982.

Keller, Roland. " 'More dirty little pictures . . .' " *Kino* (Hamburg), no. 2 (February 1980): pp. 62–65. (On low-budget films by newcomers)

Kluge, Alexander. "Das ganze Maul voll Film." *Frankfurter Rundschau*, 21 November 1974. (On Edgar Reitz)

————. "Vier Geschichten für Herbert Achternbusch." In *Herbert Achternbusch*, ed. Jörg Drews, pp. 224–30. Frankfurt am Main: Suhrkamp, 1982.

Lambert, Lothar. "Vergleichende Analyse der Filme *Abschied von gestern* (Alexander Kluge) und *Mahlzeiten* (Edgar Reitz)." M.A. thesis, Free University of Berlin, 1968.

von Praunheim, Rosa. "So schlagen uns die Etablierten tot. Fassbinder, Herzog und andere: Polemische Bemerkungen eines deutschen Filmemachers." *Die Zeit*, 13 May 1977.

————. "Schöne Sucht nach neuen Bildern." *tip*, 24 October 1980, pp. 30–35. (On Elfi Mikesch)

Sander, Helke. "zu kluges *gelegenheitsarbeit einer sklavin.*" *Frauen und Film*, no. 3 (1974): 16–22.

Straub, Jean-Marie. "Peter Nestler." *Filmkritik*, October 1968, p. 694.

Theuring, Gerhard. "Filme von Wim Wenders." *Filmkritik*, May 1969, pp. 315–317.

Thome, Rudolf. "*Harlis.*" *Filmkritik*, May/June 1973, pp. 274–75. (On Robert Van Ackeren)

————. "*Der Beginn aller Schrecken ist Liebe* (I)." *epd Film*, May/June 1984, pp. 23–25. (On Helke Sander)

Wenders, Wim. "*Katzelmacher.*" *Filmkritik*, December 1969, pp. 751–52. (On Rainer Werner Fassbinder)

X. TAKING STOCK

Adlon, Percy. "Wolfschlucht—Gedanken beim Gehen im Gebirge nach siebenunddreissigstem Drehtag." In *Die Schaukel. Ein Film nach dem Roman von Annette Kolb*, pp. 145–60. Frankfurt am Main: Fischer, 1983.

Bohm, Hark. "Der Regisseur vor dem Drehbuch." In *Hamburger Autorenseminar über die Erstellung von Drehbüchern: Dokumentation*, ed. Gyula Trebitsch, pp. 181–91. Hamburg: Studio Hamburg, 1979.

Herbst, Helmut. "Ein Filmmacher zwischen den Generationen." *Hamburger Filmgespräche* IV (1972): 132–34.

Herzog, Werner. "Mit den Wölfen heulen." *Filmkritik*, July 1968, pp. 460–61.

————. "Warum traut sich keiner mehr vorwärts? Ein Traum und Gedanken an den deutschen Film." *Jahrbuch Film 77/78*, ed. Hans Günther Pflaum, pp. 109–12. Munich: Hanser, 1977.

Kluge, Alexander, ed. *Bestandsaufnahme: Utopie Film.* Frankfurt am Main: Zweitausendeins, 1983.

Reitz, Edgar. "Das Kino der Autoren lebt! Gegen die Verkäufer, Rezeptebäcker und Profiteure." *Medium,* May 1980, pp. 32–34.

Sander, Helke. " 'Der Seele ist das Gemeinsame eigen, das sich mehrt.' " *Frauen und Film,* no. 8 (June 1976): 10–12.

Schilling, Niklaus. "Ist das Kino tot?" *Die Zeit,* 17 February 1984.

Stöckl, Ula. "The Medea Myth in Contemporary Cinema." *Film Criticism,* Fall 1985, pp. 47–51.

Strobel, Hans Rolf. "Der junge Film und die Zeitkritik." *Hamburger Filmgespräche II* (1965): 32–34.

Syberberg, Hans Jürgen. "Die Zukunft des Kinofilms aus deutscher Sicht. Umfrage des *Playboys.*" In *Syberbergs Filmbuch,* pp. 226–28. Munich: Nymphenburger, 1976.

Wenders, Wim. "Verachten, was verkauft wird." *Süddeutsche Zeitung,* 16 December 1969.

———. "Hat das Kino noch eine Zukunft? Wim Wenders befragte seine Kollegen." *Süddeutsche Zeitung,* 15 January 1983. (Selections from his film, *Chambre 666*)

———. "Unmögliche Geschichten." *tageszeitung* (West Berlin/Frankfurt am Main), 24 October 1986.

Wicki, Bernhard. "Das Drehbuch als Arbeitsgrundlage des Regisseurs." In *Hamburger Autorenseminar über die Erstellung von Drehbüchern: Dokumentation,* ed. Gyula Trebitsch, pp. 37–43. Hamburg: Studio Hamburg, 1979.

Index of Names and Films